THE HANGED MAN

THE HANGED MAN

Psychotherapy and the Forces of Darkness

SHELDON KOPP

Science and Behavior Books, Inc.
701 Welch Road
Palo Alto, California, 94306

Library of Congress Catalog Card Number: 74-79081

ISBN 0-8314-0036-6

To my sons, whom I'll miss so very much
   Jon, the wandering poet
   David, the tough-minded romantic
   Nick, the lovable athlete

LIST OF ILLUSTRATIONS

TABLE OF CONTENTS

Chapter One

THE MYTH IS EVERYONE'S STORY

Sometimes I feel as though I am four hundred years old, heavy with wisdom, knowing too much and burdened with the pain of it. I miss the wonder and the hopefulness that I experienced when I was young, though now I can hardly recall how it once felt. I've seen too much that made no sense, witnessed too much pain about which I could do nothing.

What sort of a world is this? Not much of a world. A lunatic life filled with suffering, void of meaning. Yet it is all the world there is. One can only choose life, or choose death. Having chosen life, I must live it as it is. Complaining about it is part of living this life. But one must complain without hope of life being improved in response to the complaints. No one is listening who can do anything about it. The only ones who will hear my complaints are the other complainers who are also trapped in this hollow space, this one and only available life.

This, then, is to be my message to myself: I can only become who I am. And I can only live this particular life that I have been given. The only meaning here for me is to go on, feeling it all, discovering as much of it as I can take in, seeking not improvement or even change, but only the courage to see it all, every last detail, without hope of it becoming any different.

Why bother to write about it at all? What for? It won't get any better. I am reminded here of the old Jewish legend of the Lamed-Vov, those thirty-six hidden Just Men whose mission it was to roam the earth caring about human suffering, knowing they could not relieve it. Traditionally it was believed that so long as the heart-breaking depth of their caring went on, then only that long would God allow the world of ordinary men to continue to exist.

Now, I am no Lamed-Vov; no hidden saint. My anguish is more for my own place in this world than for mankind's lot. I can identify best with that Just Man who went to Sodom, hoping to save its people from sin and punishment.[1] He cried out to them, preaching in the streets, urging them to change their ways. No one listened, and no one responded, and yet he went on shouting his message of warning, his promise of redemption. Then one day a child stopped him, asking why he went on crying out when there was no hope of being heard. And the Just Man answered: "When I first came I shouted my message, hoping to change these men. Now I know that I am helpless to change them. If I continue to cry out today, it is only in the hope that I can prevent them from changing me." And so it is with me as well. I do psychotherapy not to rescue others from their craziness, but to preserve what is left of my own sanity. Not to cure others, but to heal myself.

I have said that my problem is that I am too old, too burdened by experience. But that is a lie. My trouble really is that I am too young, chronically a naive child of wonder, a primitive lacking in understanding, blind, helpless, forever newborn. I look at the world with wide, uncomprehending eyes, neither trying to classify its contents intellectually, nor to achieve technical mastery for some practical purpose. I feel a sympathy for all that is, without understanding my own place in the time and space in which I live. I have the savage's dread of unseen foes. And like the primitive who stands for the first time before a giant Sequoia or at the ocean's edge, I am again and again filled with awe by experiences of a world which my mind cannot encompass.

I am bewildered even by the experience of my own hand. It is outside of the phenomenal "me" (located somewhere in my head and chest) and yet it is part of me. It follows my intuitive command (most of the time), yet it seems to have a life partly its own. And should I lose it, I would still be me. *Or would I?*

I am continually amazed that other people have selves of their own, not quite just like mine. It is so hard to believe that they are wholly other, that they are *not* me. Bad enough (and good enough) to realize that each tree is separate from me, yet without having to therefore encounter it, understand it, somehow deal with it. But the cursed/blessed existence of other people, what am I to make of all of that? Sometimes I think that if any of us could for just one moment see the world through the eyes of another person, look out from inside *his* skull, have a chance to contrast *his* experience with our own, surely at the moment we would go mad.

And as though it were not more than enough to have to deal with another human being who is not me, there is further the lovely, lunatic, frightening, unresolvable otherness of the Woman. Her presence challenges, delights, undoes, and completes my maleness. It is more than I can bear to experience for more than moments at a time.

Sometimes just being alive feels like having no skin, just raw flesh...vulnerable, responsive, irritable, in constant danger. Those are the times when I need most to sense my place among other people, to hear their tale and know that it is mine as well. I need so badly to be sure that someone can hear me, to receive his answering cry, to respond in kind.

At such times, my dreams seem more reliable than my waking experiences. I have long trusted my dreams as prophetic visions. I do not mean that they foretell the future, only that they illuminate the present when my eyes are closed enough so that I may see clearly. Unhampered by reason, far from the distraction of conventional wisdom, free of the distortingly protective rituals of social interactions, in my dreams I can see most vividly who and where I am. That is why I so often prefer to trust my nocturnal judgment, and make decisions on the basis of the morning's recollections. It seems to me that Jung is correct when he says that our dreams are "nothing else than a message from the all-uniting dark soul."[2] Openness to my own dreams puts me in touch with the oldest, most human aspects of who I am, helps me to find my place in the community of man.

Just as *dreams* are the inner voice of humanity's most basic struggles, joys, ambiguities, so *myths* are its outer expression. The recurrent motifs of legend and fairy-tale offer concentrated images of perennial human concerns, perceptible patterns of universally human modes of behavior. So it is that, like my dreams, these old tales carry me beyond the limits of my personal history, back into the transpersonal stream of mankind. They retain their powerful mystery and compelling wisdom even now that we have become too enlightened to any longer "believe" them. If we are not too sophisticated, too civilized, too scientific to be open to their messages, we may still be instructed by them. To the extent that each of us is open to his own unconscious, he will be moved by the mythic legends of long ago people who did not know any better than to believe that the world is controlled by dark forces and hidden powers. It is in this folk wisdom of the world that we can come to understand the patterns which reveal our common humanity.

So it is with the story of Pandora, Greek mythology's tale of the first mortal woman on earth. Angry at man because Prometheus had stolen the Olympian fire, Zeus had Pandora created as an instrument of vengeance, an evil being whom all men would desire. Pandora's very name means "bearer of every gift." Athena gave her knowledge of the arts, while Aphrodite made her beautiful. Armed with the cunning and flattery of Hermes, and elegantly adorned by the Graces, she was truly irresistible. So it was that Epimetheus (brother of Prometheus) was smitten and adoringly welcomed her to the world of mortals.

With her, Pandora brought a box which Zeus had warned her never, never to open, and not to peek into even for a moment. At last, her curiosity became more than she could any longer resist. She lifted the lid of the box, just for one quick look at the secrets it held. But in that unguarded moment when Pandora opened the box, all the miseries of man flew out. Into the world swarmed Greed, Vanity, Slander, Envy and all the other deadly vices. Horrified, she slammed the lid of the box closed once more. In so doing, she retained for man what was left in the box, his most basic virtue: Hope.

Had the miseries not been unleashed, surely Hope would have remained trapped beneath them. Although the evils had been unknown to mankind before Pandora's curiosity set them free, so too had man's spirited willingness to live with his imperfections. Suffering makes us neither good nor bad. It is only necessary that in our wish to avoid pain and evil, we do not turn away from the growing edge to which our curiosity leads.

How are we to understand this vortex of primitive instruction? How is it that the wisdom of the ages comes in the form of seemingly senseless nocturnal visions and in the ageless entertainments of the oral traditions of folk tales? How can it be that the intuitive grasp of those experiences which are most human occur in the solitude of dreams which so often seem irrational, and in the fragments of legends and early dramas which civilized man would like to see himself as having outgrown?

Jung's concept of the archetypes offers a bridge between the recurrent themes in world literature and mythology on the one hand, and those of contemporary man's dreams and fantasies on the other. However, there are distorting factors which obscure the timeless and universal meanings of the archetypal themes. Their primordial power is circumscribed by the cultural context in which they arise, bound by historical conventions of the time, and reduced by concrete ties to a particular individual's life experiences.

In hopes of transcending these distortions and restrictions, an attempt was made to represent the archetypes of psychic transformation in the form of unelucidated visual images. In this way, their primitive messages might be responded to directly, without the transfiguring media of language, literary devices, and historical contextual restrictions. Personal response might then be less cluttered and more intuitively full and vivid when evoked by pictorial images which "show ... the steps that must be taken, the many phases of the inner work, (which) ... ensure ... a universality that transcends cultural and linguistic conventions. This is *Tarot*."[3]

The earliest known date of the Tarot Cards is 1390 A.D., but the picture cards of the Major Arcana (which appear as illustrations throughout this book) are said to be derived from ancient Egyptian sacred writings. Some Tarot scholars insist that their origins are Chinese, while others maintain that they were transported from India by the Gypsies. Whichever hypothesis is correct, or even if the cards turn out to be directly related to Jewish Cabalistic sources (as some claim), they are surely very old, perennially enthralling, and rich in mystic symbols.

There are 78 Tarot cards to a pack. The Minor Arcana include 56 cards divided into four suits and numbered in a way which serves as the forerunner of modern-day playing cards. Together with the 22 cards of the Major Arcana (with which we shall be concerned), they form a fortune-telling pack with which many have claimed to be able to read the past, the present and the future.

I myself do *not* concede the alleged fortune-telling power of the Tarot. Like the I Ching, the Holy Bible, or gurus and therapists (past and present), the Tarot is a poor oracle. Yet each may serve as a source of universal wisdom by providing an immersion in timeless human concerns and symbol-heavy imagery in a "dreamlike atmosphere . . . (in which the subject or patient) has nothing to rely upon except . . . (his) own so fallible subjective judgment."[4]

In this way even ordinary men can open themselves to the timeless wisdom usually thought to be restricted to the enlightened few. So it is that the Tarot symbols may serve as a guide to archetypal revelations from the transpersonal or collective Unconscious. These images awaken deep echoes of the psyche, putting men in touch with forgotten wisdom and untried personal powers.

The reading of the Tarot pack, along with alchemy, astrology, numerology and witchcraft, has traditionally been associated with the black arts. And "the driving force behind black magic is hunger for power."[5] But the power I seek is not that of spells and hexes, nor of diabolical mumbo-jumbo. Instead I would turn myself and my patients toward those hidden unconscious recesses of ourselves, which science, civilization, and conventional wisdom have obscured.

The serpent in the Garden of Eden told Adam and Eve that if they ate of the fruit of the Tree of Knowledge: "Ye shall not surely die: for God doth know that in the day ye eat thereof, then your eyes shall be opened and *ye shall be as gods,* knowing good and evil." [6] For me, *to be as gods,* means finding within ourselves those qualities most profoundly human. These oldest of human concerns are fascinatingly depicted among the pictorial symbols of the Tarot's Major Arcana. First there is *The Fool,* the joker of the deck. This naive youth with eyes fixed on the distant horizon is pictured as about to step off the edge of a precipice. The abyss holds no terror for him. He is about to pass through the gates of experience as he begins the supreme adventure of seeking cosmic wisdom. The white rose he holds, the dog at his feet, the serpent crawling away in the dust, the wallet of unused knowledge which he carries--all of these are heavy with symbolic meanings. In the upright position, this card bespeaks of creative spiritual choices in life, choices which must be made with great care. Reversed, viewed upside down, The Fool warns of faults and failures and of the ways in which life sometimes makes fools of us all. But for the mystic fool, the pursuit of youthful folly can bring wisdom. To be simple-minded enough to ask "Who am I?" is to begin to become wise.

Another symbolically moving figure in the Major Arcana of the Tarot is that of *The Magician.* It is he who has fulfilled all that The Fool has only promised. With one hand he raises his wand toward the Heavens, while the finger of his other hand points toward the earth. He draws his spiritual power from above, but manifests it in the direct experience of his daily life. The horizontal 8 above his head and the snake devouring itself which forms the belt of his toga are symbols of Eternity. At his command on the table before him are the natural elements of life: air, fire, water and earth, represented respectively by the suit symbols of the Minor Arcana playing cards. There are the Swords (spades) of Strife and Misfortune, the Wands (clubs) of Enterprise and Glory, the Cups (hearts) of Love and Happiness, and the Pentacles (diamonds) of Money and Interest. This magician's state of

attaining the Higher Self when it comes across in the upright position suggests the union of personal will with divine meaning, the accomplishment of mastery, skill and power. Reversed, this Tarot card implies the destructive use of power, or its immobilization in weakness and indecision.

I will describe just one more card at this point, to complete the Tarot triad which most drew me toward my hidden self. As I first spread the pack, knowing nothing of the ascribed meanings traditionally associated with each image, I felt compelled to gather up *The Fool, The Magician* and *The Hanged Man.*

The last of these figures hangs suspended upside down from a cross of living wood. Arms folded behind his back, forming a living cross with his unfettered leg, his head hangs down in a bright cloud of deep entrancement, He is in a position of reversal of mind, paying off old debts as he surrenders to the redemption of absorption in matters both spiritual and occult. This card in the upright position suggests the reversal of a man's way of life. It is during this prophetic pause, that he suspends decisions, as he verges on yielding completely to personal consciousness. Reversed, the card implies false prophecy, arrogance and resistance to spiritual influences.

As I gathered up the three cards, I could not decide which way to hold The Hanged Man. Pondering the meaning of these three images which so enthralled me, I realized that I am indeed at a Crossroads in my life. As a grown man, a teacher, and a therapist I have attained much of The Magician's mastery, his skill, and his power. But becoming the potent Guru has cost me much of The Fool's innocence, idealism, and curiosity. Along with my wisdom has come a world-weary cynicism, which has left me jaded and ritually stylized.

Through the monumental blow of a brain tumor, life made a fool of me. When this fell upon my head, without warning or justification, my magical powers seemed empty of meaning, and I retained too little of youth's spontaneity to find my way again. And so, at this point I am back in therapy as a patient once more, paying off old debts, seeking redemption, pausing once more to find my way. Spiritual absorption and surrender to occult/unconscious concerns have led me to write this book, seeking knowledge of the patterns and powers that shape our lives. Risking that my Hanged Man will come up in reversed position, I will struggle with my arrogant temptation to false prophecy. Only in this way may I learn whether I am headed for Redemption or just "hung up."

In the early history of man, and remaining still in those cultures which are primitive, dreams and myths are seen as religious realities. They constitute an unquestioned culture-determining aspect of life. As cultures "advance," the meaning and profundity of these stories and experiences are diluted by science and reason. However, science has just *not* done the job. And so, more recently, man has become aware of some loss. Explanations do not satisfy. Knowing that this or that is *nothing but* a myth or a dream leaves us lost and wandering, with a deep sense of alienation, lost meaning, and emptiness. And so in our century, technology, once the promise of happiness, has now become the threat not only to our way of life, but perhaps to its very continuance. Poets, thinkers, and social scientists are open to restoring the larger significance of myths and dreams. They experience new hope in the possibility of our recapturing the wisdom of childhood, the power of innocence, the sophistication of the primitive. As a result, the new approach to myths and dreams has been used as a means of regaining access to lost existential truths. Symbolism and an intuitive approach to meaning reopen the possibility of contact with the transpersonal substance of being human. Reducing myths and dreams to simple things that we can explain, and thus come to feel that we can understand more completely, drains the cultures which such myths and dreams once supported and to which they once provided substance. Perhaps what we are learning is to recognize that, as the poet Archibald MacLeish wrote, "*a world ends when its metaphor has died.*"[7]

It is instructive to understand just how these powerful metaphors have been drained of their meaning by hyperrational attempts at explaining them away. The unquestioned tale from which primitives drew their strength, and around which they shaped the meanings of their lives, came to be seen by scholars as *nothing more than* stories about Gods, not much different from those sagas in which people are the active characters. Anthropologists with views distorted both by the Enlightenment and by the residue of self-righteous Western Christian perspectives, were quick to see primitive myth as somehow *less than* religious. Not only did they denigrate the remnants of mythic images from early societies, but somehow they also came to feel that even contemporary African groups, for instance, had little more than childish tribal mumbo-jumbo to guide them. These primitives had not even recognized that there is only one God, and their symbolic cannibalistic rites could in no way be seen as equivalent to the practices of those contemporary Americans (anthropologists included) who weekly dined on the body and the blood of a dead God.

Myths separated from legitimate contemporary involvement in spiritual life, seen as something less than religious, or pre-religious, resulted in their being reduced to *nothing more than* the naive primitive's attempt to explain something in nature which he was really too ignorant to understand. The mythic attempts to explain how the universe came into existence, the creation myths which exist in every society, came to be seen in the same light as the preschool child's questions about where things come from, born out of ignorance and curiosity. No longer could they be understood as arising out of the appreciation of man's perennial lostness in the universe filled with powers and having origins which man can in no way finally tie down and of which he can never be sure.

It is only in recent decades that we have all become aware that science will *not* save us, that reason is whore who misleads us, that disillusion is the keynote. Men have once again begun to take seriously their myths and dreams as expressions of man's striving for a total world view, for an interpretation of what is meaningful in his life, as serious attempts to integrate experience and reality.

Existentialism arose in Europe when men's hopes and dreams had been shattered by yet a second world war, one which involved genocidal barbarism, too grotesque to be finally comprehended. It was then that Kierkegaard was rediscovered, that Plato and Augustine were seen as more meaningful than Aristotle and Aquinas as guides for understanding how we live. It was then that Sartre, and Heidigger, Jaspers and the rest made their voices heard, questioning the very ground of being, shaking the philosophical world, disowning the traditional metaphysical categories, and setting the world of rational scientific enquiry on its pompous ass. It was then that the emerging mythologists of our age could make their impact felt. It was then that Alan Watts, that wandering minstrel of Zen and mysticism, could define myth as simply and powerfully as "an imagery in terms of which we make sense out of life."[8] It was then that Freud's reductionism, his use of myths to explain away the depth and power of human experience, could begin to give way to Jung, who now suggested that dreams were visions or *images of meaning rather than symptoms*, that they constitute a magic mirror which could unify and transform our experience.

Perhaps the most extraordinary mythologist of our age is Joseph Campbell. He has gathered together the old tales, maintaining the original richness of much of their vision, and once again raised mythology to its original status of spiritual adventure so profound as to be a matter of life and death. In an attempt to understand what myth is about, Campbell explores four functions of mythology. [9] The first function is the *mystical* or *metaphysical,* in which man attempts a "reconciliation of consciousness with a precondition of its own existence ... the monstrous nature of this terrible game that is life." Within this function are our struggles with the experience of living a life that is fundamentally unmanageable, incomprehensible, and ultimately sorrowful. How is a man to make his way on such a pilgrimage, grappling with his guilt, his bewilderment, his impotence, unless there are myths to redeem human consciousness from its tragic sense of being overwhelmed and lost?

Campbell cites as the second function of mythology, the *cosmological.* By this he means that man needs a way of rendering an image of the universe to make sense of where he lives. The myth formulates such an image that is in keeping with the science and culture of the time; it provides a sense of unity, so that whatever one comes in contact with in this life can be recognized as part of "a single great holy picture."

The third function of the myth, which Campbell calls *sociological,* he defines as a way of "validating and maintaining some specific social order." Possibilities for corruption in this function are apparent as kings and priests can invoke the profound experience of dreams and myths to keep people in their place while allowing those in authority to ever increase their power. So it is that at one point James Joyce has Ulysses tap his brow thoughtfully, and declare "in here it is I must kill the priest and the king."[10]

Campbell's fourth function of mythology, he designates as *psychological.* Here he sees a myth as a guide and support to bear individuals from birth to death through the difficult transitions which human life demands. This is perhaps the major function for Campbell, since he sees sociological and cosmological orders varying and those functions of mythology being contingent on the order of the time. Yet he feels there is an irreducible biology of the species which makes necessary that each man face the same inherent psychological problems. His emphasis is on the overly long period of immaturity and dependency of the human species and the consequent difficulties in crossing the threshold to adult responsibility, the difficulty in the delivery to a second birth, which is indeed a social birth. So it is that Campbell tells us "the fourth function is to initiate the individual into orders of his own psyche, guiding him toward his own spiritual enrichment and realization."

The ways, then, of understanding the functions of myths are many. Perhaps in the long run each way is no more than a contemporary myth--a fairy tale that we tell ourselves to comfort us as we wander through the ultimately unresolvable jungle of a life darker, more dangerous, and more overwhelming than we would like it to be.

As for myself, one of the ways of conceiving such matters which best help me to understand them is C.G. Jung's concept of *archetypes*.[11] For Jung, the archetypes are biological patterns of behavior, modes of perception, and ways of experiencing life which have always shaped man's sense of himself in the world. They are unconscious ways of apprehending life, evident to us only in the effects which they produce. These effects are universally typical phenomenological patterns which can be recognized in the recurring configurations of situations and sorts of figures which "shape the way human beings experience themselves, others, and the world at large."[12]

The familiar motifs which repeat themselves again and again in dreams and in myths include such primordial images as the original Creation, the Great Mother both as fruitful womb and as devouring destroyer, the Great Father as Lord of Heaven, wise old man, and as wrathful judge, and the Child as the link with the past. The insoluble mysteries of the relation of male and female, darkness and light, heaven and earth, the groundwork of existence itself make themselves known again and again, as does the emergence and the adventures of the Hero. The myth of the dying and resurrected hero has long been used as a series of images to express the experience of the living rhythm of natural events such as the rising and setting of the daily course of the sun.

Powerful images such as these have always dwelled in the mysterious shadow of man's collective unconscious, subtly shaping his sense of himself, of his world, of Nature itself. These archetypes are not inherited ideas, so much as inherited modes of psychic functioning, biological patterns of experience. Each man is, of course, subject to the particular experiences which make up his own personal history. But each man also stands in relation to all other men, of whatever other time or place, dominated by transpersonal modes by which all men live. The archetypes which bridge the gap between man and man "resemble the beds of rivers; dried up because the water has deserted them, though it may return at any time. An archetype is like an old watercourse along which the water of life flowed for a long time, digging a deep channel for itself. The longer it flowed, the deeper the channel, and the more likely it is that sooner or later the water will return."[13]

It is possible, of course, to try to understand dreams as nothing more than the epiphenomenal expression of physiological processes, or at most as a curiously fragmented and poetically condensed experience of any man's residue of the day's events, perhaps motivated by unconscious unexpressed childhood wishes of the individual. So too, we can attempt to construct a natural history of gods and heroes, in which "myth means nothing other than the report by ardent enthusiasts of that which has befallen them."[14] But to me, objectifying reductions such as these dilute the transpersonal richness of the human experience which the colorful metaphors of dream and myth so awesomely enhance.

I do not know what it is *really* all about. It has been a long, long time since I believed in Reality. I prefer the loveliness and the terror of my subjective experiences to those coldly scientific explanations which in the long run turn out to be no more real, and far less fun than my own fantasies and musings. And so it is that for me the Jungian archetypes provide a richly dramatic, intensely colorful trip. What more can I ask of any life-enhancing adventure? The meaning of archetypes may not help me to understand the human condition any better than I have up to now. It is enough that they allow me to experience it more deeply, more fully, with all senses open to the quality of my movement through this, my one and only life.

THE TOWER.

Chapter Two

LET ME TELL YOU A TALE
TO EASE YOUR TASK

Black Elk, warrior and medicine man of the Oglala Sioux, tells us that "it is in the darkness of their eyes that men get lost."[1] Looking inward is both wondrous and perilous. The Unconscious which all men share, called by some "the depths of the soul", is that dark realm from which visions of the spirit arise. It is a source of primordial powers, sometimes more awesome than a man can bear to face.

So it is that much of the time, most men avoid journeying into this "dark world filled with fabulous beings."[2] The myths which tell their story are demeaned as mere fancy, as children's tales. Night visions of these dark places emerge, and a man diminishes their significance by saying, "I was only dreaming."

It takes the lightning flash of awareness to pierce the darkness of the Unconscious. In the Tarot card of The Tower, the imprisoning structure of ignorance is broken down as lightning strikes. In the upright position, this card promises an event of enlightening disruption. Dealt upside down, it warns of continuing oppression and spiritual imprisonment.

If only we will look, ready to see whatever may appear, if we will listen open to hearing whatever stirs, we will surely find that the modestly offered gifts from the transpersonal depths are again and again at hand. So it was for the Hindu hero-king of old, whose struggle with the great darkness has been recorded in the twenty-five tales of "The King and the Corpse."[3]

Each day a holy beggar appeared in the court and silently offered the king a piece of fruit. Each gift was accepted by the king without his paying much attention to it, as he handed it unexamined to the treasurer beside him. And each day the beggar left as he had come, in silence, asking nothing for himself.

After ten years of this wordless charade, one day the king playfully handed that day's offering to his pet monkey. As the beast bit into the fruit, a lovely jewel fell from its center. Seeing this the king demanded that the treasurer tell him what had become of all the earlier offerings. It turned out that they had been tossed into the treasure house, the floor of which was now littered with a mass of decaying fruit and priceless jewels.

The king was both pleased and curious. The next day he spoke to the mendicant in private, and for the first time the beggar asked for something in return for his offering. He requested that the king be the intrepid hero whom he sought to help him in a rite of exorcism. The brave king agreed to meet with him on the night of the next new moon, at the great funeral ground, the crematorium of the dead, and hanging place of the criminals.

In the darkness of the appointed night, armed with sword and cloaked to disguise his royal identity, the king fearlessly approached the terrible rendezvous. Charred skulls and skeletons lay scattered about, while ghouls and demons filled the air with a hideous uproar. The old sorcerer was drawing a magic circle on the ground when the king approached to find out what he must do to help. The hero-king was instructed to go to the other end of the burning-ground, to a great tree from which a hanged man dangled. He was to cut down the corpse and carry it to the magic circle.

Crossing the burial ground with trembling determination, the king approached the hanging tree to pluck its strange fruit. He climbed the tree and cut the rope with his sword. As the body fell, he heard it moan. But as he examined the rigid figure to see if it was still alive, a ghostly laugh broke from its throat. The king challenged the ghost, but the moment he spoke the corpse flew back to the tree branch.

When the king climbed up to cut it down again, he made sure to utter no sound. Hoisting the body up onto his shoulder he began to trudge across burial ground. But before he had taken many steps the voice in the corpse spoke into his ear, saying: "Let me tell you a tale to ease your task, O king." The king did not reply, and the ghost went on to tell its tale:

Now, once upon a time there were three young Brahmins who had lived a number of years in the home of their spiritual teacher. All three had fallen in love with their teacher's daughter, and he did not dare to bestow her on any one of them for fear of breaking the others' hearts. But then the maid was stricken with a serious illness and died, and the three young men, equally desperate, committed her body to a funerary pyre. When it had been cremated, the first decided to give vent to his grief by wandering through the world as a beggar ascetic, the second gathered the beloved bones from among the ashes and proceeded with them to a celebrated sanctuary beside the life-giving waters of the holy Ganges, while the third, remaining on the spot, constructed a hermit's hut over the place of the fire, and slept on the ashes of the body of his love.

Now the one who had decided to roam through the world was one day the witness of an extraordinary event. He saw a man read from a book a magic charm that restored to life a child whose body had already been consumed to ashes. Stealing the book, the young lover hurried back to the cremation scene, and arrived just when the one who had gone to the Ganges also returned, the latter having dipped the bones into the life-giving stream. The skeleton was reassembled among the ashes, the charm was read from the book, and the miracle came to pass. The thrice-beloved arose again, more beautiful than ever. So at once the rivalry was resumed, but more hotly now; for each claimed to have earned the right to her; one having guarded her ashes, one having dipped her bones in the Ganges, and the third having pronounced the spell.

'And so to whom does she belong?' said the voice in the

corpse. *'If you know the answer but do not reply, your head will burst into a hundred pieces.'* [4]

Believing that he knew the answer, the king dared not remain silent. He offered the solution that the Brahmin who was able easily to work the charm which restored her to life acted as a father. The one who carried out the pious service of taking her bones to the holy Ganges fulfilled a son's duty. But the young man who never left his beloved, who slept among her ashes, he alone lived the life of a husband-lover. It was to him she belonged.

Just as the final word of this judgment was spoken, the corpse let out a groan of mock agony, flew from the king's shoulder, and returned to hang once more from the tree limb. Wearily the king went back, cut down the corpse once more, and again began his burdensome trek.

Again and again, the macabre scene was repeated. Each time the ghost would torment the king with a new riddling-tale. each time threatening that the king's head would explode if he knew the answer but did not reply. And each time, *the king found his consciousness expanded, filled with wisdom he had not known he possessed.* But, maddeningly, each wise judgment earned him only another tiring trip back to the hanging-tree to which the corpse had mockingly returned.

There were twenty-four tales in all, but only twenty-three trudging returns to the hanging-tree. For to the twenty-fourth riddle, the king could find no answer. No man's wisdom can plumb the great darkness to its ultimate depths. He had withstood the ordeal wisely and bravely, but he could find no solution to this final enigma. Instead he puzzled wordlessly over having found holiness beneath a beggar's robe, having been taught humility by a monkey, having his wisdom expanded by the mocking riddles of a seemingly dangerous stranger. With no answer for the last conundrum, he was able to proceed toward his goal of delivering the corpse to the magic circle. Can it be that he was wiser in his silent musings than in his cleverly logical replies?

The ghost, at least, seemed pleased with the king as he took leave of the corpse, which was now a more reliable burden. But as he was leaving, the spectre offered a warning about the terrible dangers which awaited the king within the magic circle:

'Listen, O King,' the spectre warned, 'Listen to what I have to tell you, and, if you value your own good, do exactly what I say. That beggar monk is a very dangerous imposter. With his powerful spells he is going to force me to re-enter this corpse, which he will then use as an idol. What he plans to do is to place it in the center of his magic circle, worship me there as a divinity, and, in the course of the worship, offer you up as the victim. You will be ordered to fall down and do me reverence, first on your knees, then prostrate, in the most slavish attitude of devotion, with your head, hands, and shoulders touching the ground. He will then attempt to decapitate you with a single stroke of your own sword.

There is only one way to escape. When you are ordered to go down, you must say: 'Please demonstrate this slavish form of prostration so that I, a king unused to such attitudes, may see how one assumes such a posture of worship.' And when he is lying flat on the ground, strike off his head with a quick cut of the sword. In that instant, all the supernatural power that this sorcerer is trying to conjure from the sphere of the celestials will fall to you. And you will be a potent kind indeed!'[5]

By the time the king reached the magic circle, the magician seemed quite pleased both with his own completed ritual arrangements and with the king's fulfilled ghoulish task. The circle was now beset with ground bones lit with burning wicks of corpse fat. The sorcerer took the corpse, set it in the circle and adorned it as he chanted incantations. In this way he compelled the spectre to re-enter the body, and began to worship it as the ghost had foretold. Forwarned, the king did not comply with the command to prostrate himself in this black mass. Instead he used the suggested ruse, and as the sorcerer demonstrated the worshipful pose, the king slashed off his head and cut out his heart.

He presented these bloody offerings to the spectre. As he did, a howl of jubilation arose from the spirits of the burial ground. They had been rescued from the slavery of enchantment which the bloody necromancer had attempted.

The spectre gratefully acknowledged the hero-king's victory over the sorcerer who would have dominated the supernatural powers. He told the king that he would grant him any wish he chose. Wisely the king asked only that the tale of this night should be retold among men all over the world and throughout the ages. The spectre promised it would be so, and so it has been in the Orient and in the West, from Sanskrit to English, yesterday, today and tomorrow. I have done my part in telling you this tale. Be sure to do your part by telling it to others!

Recently in my therapeutic practice a patient and I made a latter-day journey into the great darkness. As did that Hindu king of long ago, we found our mythic venture both frightening and exciting. Together we risked the darkness in search of new light.

She came into her therapy hour that day complaining of a vague but persistent feeling of anxiety, and an aching knot of undefined tension. Despite her usually more ready access to the sources of her discomfort, that day she could find neither meaning, nor cause, nor relief from this distress which left her feeling so awful and so stuck. She tried to relate her pain to problems in her life, but somehow couldn't connect. No associations seemed available, and she despaired of being able to emerge from this morass of unrelated malaise.

I had no more idea than she as to what was going on but intuitively tried to concretize her vague uneasiness by asking if she could localize the feelings in some part of her body. The anxiety turned out to lie midway in her chest, while the knot of tension felt like a belly-ache. It was then I recalled having recently read about an "in-the-body trip" [6] (not unlike Schutz's "guided daydream" encounter game. [7]) The idea of encouraging a patient to fantasize a journey into the great darkness of her own body was provocative, but I had stalled about attempting it up till now out of my own fear of the great unknown.

She and I had been companions in other spiritual adventures, and so with her I dared to risk it. I asked if she wanted me to help her in a way which might demand a good deal of her trust. Though obviously hesitant, she agreed to try. I told her that if she could imagine herself sufficiently reduced in size, I could help her to make a fantasy trip into her body so that she might deal with her unyielding distress.

When asked how she would choose to enter her body, she selected her mouth as the point of access. Like a father trying to engage a child in the atmosphere of an unfamiliar story, I set the mood by describing how vast an ordinary human body would seem to someone as small as the tiny voyager she was to become. Excitement and wonder replaced some of her timidity as through closed eyes, she began to see the Lilliputian vistas I suggested.

Soon she felt small enough to enter, and stood uncertainly poised on her own lower lip. She wanted to enter her open mouth but was almost immediately confronted with the insurmountable obstacle of her own too-tall fence of unclimbable teeth. She simply could not scramble over them, and apologized for having to give up the journey just as it was to begin.

I held her hand and offered to help if she would only let me. With my encouragement, she fantasized a mini-therapist on the lip beside her. With comfortable dependence she was able to imagine my boosting her up over the teeth which had blocked her way. She waited as I scrambled up over the barrier to join her once more. When asked to go on with her description of our surroundings, she had us enjoy the bouncy walk across the "water-bed" softness of her tongue. I pushed past the sexual invitation of this association, urging her to head on down to where the trouble lay.

Soon we stood poised over the black chasm of her throat. She was paralyzed by fright as she peered into the unyielding darkness of the void. No amount of reassurance or encouragement could make her take another step. I told her that if she would only tear her gaze from its fascination with the abyss, and turn to look at me poised there beside her, she would see that I was wearing a large pack on my back. Delighted to be distracted from the impenetrable gloom of her throat, she could immediately see the back-pack, wondering how she could have overlooked it up till then. At my suggestion, she rummaged around in it until she found the electric lantern which I was sure to carry.

Taking it out, she could clearly see how bold and bright a beam of light it cast, and was pleased to see how well it lit the dark tunnel of her throat. Now that we could see ahead, it was not difficult for us to make our way down the steep incline and into the wider passage of her chest.

Fear and discouragement moved into ascendence once more as she began to discern the mass of "anxiety" in the passage ahead. She was sure we were stuck. There would be no way through. I went with her as (at my urging) she approached this new obstacle, examining it with lantern in hand. She described her "anxiety" as a massive shapeless brown glob. The sickened tone of her voice suggested to me that what lay ahead was a great lump of shit, but I resisted my temptation to make this interpretation, lest it carry us out of her body and back into the futile worryings of her head.

I asked her to approach the glob and to use the light to examine its structure for some clue as to how we might get through. Looking more closely, she seemed genuinely surprised to see that it was not as solid as it had first appeared to be. She thought we might be able to get through if only she could push it down and out of the way with her feet. I assured her that this would pose no problem because in my rucksack I had a pair of stomping boots for each of us. Again she was delighted and grateful that I carried just the equipment we needed. And so, without further delay, we put on our boots and stomped on through.

Beyond the glob of anxiety, the passage narrowed once more, but exhilarated as we felt, there was no difficulty in making our way down and through an opening in her diaphragm. And then suddenly, more trouble! Without warning, the narrow dark passage opened on to the vast chamber of her belly. She froze in terror when faced with the cold white emptiness of this unmarked void.

I misunderstood her alarm. Thinking that she feared losing her way, I called her attention to a large boulder off to her right, and suggested she take a look behind it. She went to look but was confused by my instructions to take a look into the garrison box on the far side of the rock. She didn't know what a garrison box was. My metaphor was too male. I tried to describe the trunk-like box with its metal fittings. "It sounds like a sea chest," she said at last. With relief, I agreed that I had been mistaken, that indeed it was a sea chest.

I told her to open the chest so that she could study the maps and charts it held. She found them, looked at them, and told me that they were no help at all. With patronizing impatience, I suggested that they were easy to read, Walt-Disney-sort-of picture-maps, that she should look at them more carefully if we were ever to be able to get out of here.

Patiently she explained to me that we were not lost so much as stuck. The vast whiteness before us was not so much a desolate tundra to be crossed as an impenetrable glacier which blocked our way. With as much anxiety as enthusiasm I assured her that I had many more pieces of equipment in my knapsack, that surely one of them would work. She couldn't find any and asked if I could help.

The first option that I offered was the approach which would have been most natural to me, had I been alone facing my own wall of impenetrable ice. I told her I had in my knapsack, a wonderous warmth-machine which would fill our cavern with a soft golden glow, capable of melting away the forbidding coldness. She replied impatiently, "What else have you got?" It was fine for me but not what she had in mind.

Something more formidably aggressive might do, I thought silently. "How about a laser beam, so that we could cut our way through?" Eyes still closed, she smiled and said, "Pretty good. Is there anything else?"

I knew now I was on the right track. "If you rummage around carefully in my back pack, you'll find a small bottle of T.N.T." I suggested. "I've got it," she exclaimed with delight. I asked if she wanted me to throw it for her. She nodded a vigorous refusal.

Up to that point, she had lay back without moving, talking her way through our adventure. Now, suddenly, she was animated with excitement, drew back her right arm, let fly the fantasied T.N.T. bottle, and shouted a gleefully explosive "BOOM!" The unexpected blast raised me right off of my chair.

The dust settled, and in the welcome quiet I began to wonder how this would all end. "How will we find our way out now," I asked suddenly anxious lest she choose a rebirth struggle through her vagina as our escape route.

She was surprised at my question. "Can't you see?" she said. "Just look where we blasted through the ice. You can see the lovely blue sky, the trees, the grass. It's a beautiful sunny day. Let's go out and have a picnic." When she told me *that* way, I could see it so clearly, I could no longer understand how I had missed it up till then.

The stuck and distressed young woman who had begun this journey through the darkness was now transformed into a warm, joyful, mobile creature. She told of a deep sense of ease and comfort such as she had never known, and was filled with child-like wonder that we could have made such a soul-freeing magical trip. She wanted me to explain it so that she could understand what had happened. Suppressing my prideful temptations to interpret how we had worked with her unconscious hostility, I told her that she already understood all there was to know. She seemed relieved, pleased and relieved to feel sufficient, to settle for staying with the intuitive sense of our adventure.

She was sure that she could not have made the trip alone, and I was sure that I could not have done so either. But there was no convincing her that I too was inexperienced, had been frightened along the way and uncertain of the outcome.

She returned for her next session, having retained her sense of well-being and increased craving for adventure. In the interim she had taken a new trip on her own that left her happy and hopeful. She was so proud as she reported having had her first "unrealistic fantasy" on her own. All her life, her daydreams were Practical-Pig work-plans, ideas to be organized, stressful situations to be rehearsed, and future accomplishment strategies to be dry-run. How she had envied her playfully imaginative younger sister who fantasized strawberry worlds and seemed to have always had so much more fun than she. I asked her to write it all down. Here is what she gave:

"I lay in bed the other night remembering with wonder and happiness the fantasy which Shelly and I had shared in individual therapy, when we took a trip down inside my body. It is to my knowledge the first fantasy I ever had. What I had previously thought of as fantasies Shelly called "plans", and after my trip with Shelly I understood why. I lay there hoping we could do that again sometime. Actually, I knew Shelly would, and I was hoping that somehow I would do it again.

"Then all at once without any warning I was in a huge daisy field with Shelly. We were very small, minute compared to the flowers, and it seemed as if the whole world was a daisy field. Without my planning it we moved from one marvelous caper to another. We made little tunnels through the grass and lay on our backs looking high above us at the backsides of the daisies, and watched the sunlight filtering through. We shinnied up the stems and made our way over the petals and lay down in the yellow centers, soaking up the sun. And then most fun of all, we took turns, with one of us bending a daisy down while the other crawled into the center, and then turning loose the stem all at once, sending the other flinging through the daisy field seemingly endlessly. I don't remember the flinging ever stopping and I don't remember at any point who was doing the flinging and who was being flung; and the best part of all is that it doesn't make any difference —

anymore."

The part I liked best was when she bent the daisy stem, pulled down with all of her might, and then suddenly let go so that I was catapulted somersaulting skyward till I came gliding down on dragon-fly wings. Now her turn had come.

And indeed she was going to see to it that her own turn would not be missed again. During the week she had made arrangements for an extended summer leave from her responsibility-heavy job of running a complex government project. She was to meet her sister in Barcelona. From there on it was to be unplanned fun, back-packing across unknown territory, in search of sunshine, of self, of she knew not what.

WHEEL of FORTUNE.

Chapter Three

THE UNCEREMONIAL NATURE
OF PSYCHOTHERAPY

"Who are *you?*" said the Caterpillar.

This was not an encouraging opening for a conversation. Alice replied, rather shyly, "I --- I hardly know, Sir, just at present --- at least I know who I *was* when I got up this morning but I think I must have been changed several times since then."

"What do you mean by that?" said the Caterpillar, sternly. "Explain yourself!"

"I can't explain *myself,* I'm afraid, Sir," said Alice, "because I'm not myself, you see."

"I don't see," said the Caterpillar.

"I'm afraid I can't put it more clearly," Alice replied very politely, "for I can't understand it myself, to begin with; and being so many different sizes in a day is very confusing."

"It isn't," said the Caterpillar.

"Well, perhaps you haven't found it so yet," said Alice; "but when you have to turn into a chrysalis --- you will some day, you know --- and then after that into a butterfly, I should think you'll feel it a little queer, won't you?"

"Not a bit," said the Caterpillar.

"Well, perhaps *your* feelings may be different," said Alice: "all I know is, it would feel very queer to *me.*"

"You!" said the Caterpillar contemptuously, "Who are *you?*"

Which brought them back again to the beginning of the conversation. [1]

Dissatisfaction with her lot, combined with restless curiosity, have led Alice to tumble into the rabbit-hole. Her fall into the seemingly mad world of Wonderland, and her conversations with its zany inhabitants have provided experiences so disarming as to begin to undermine her politeness, her reasonableness, indeed her very identity as a reliably socialized person.

The presence of other human beings offers a continuous challenge to the face we would present to the world. Each of us has been taught to maintain some measure of constraint of our primitive appetites, to present at least the appearance of sociability and self-control. The virtues of good character (however they may vary from group to group) are supposed to be in evidence. Some element of respect for the other, of cooperation, of candor, and of modesty are expected. A certain modicum of civilized demeanor is demanded, as we play out the masked dance of social accomodation.

We are to act as though we were not driven by powerful biological urges, not haunted by dark primitive images, as though our social identities represent who we really are. In order to maintain this acceptable sense of theater, social interaction is replete with ceremonies, conventions, and ritual dialogues which preserve the gloss of civilization.[2] Infractions and deviations which either intentionally or inadvertently reveal our underlying primitive natures are subject to censure, and quickly corrected by remedial interchanges. So it is that the powerfully primordial mythic images which guide human behavior remain hidden behind a facade of mannered reasonableness.

How often it becomes apparent that our gloss of civilization, no matter how valuable, how well-articulated, how strongly supported by philosophical and religious superstructures, remains a thin and tentative veneer. Modern man, that post-Enlightenment creature, likes to think of his nature as being determined primarily by psychological and cultural forces. But recent investigative and speculative scrutiny of the human species makes it clear that much of man's behavior is as biologically based as that of the rest of the animal kingdom. The writings of Ardrey, Lorenz, Tiger and Fox, Goffman, and Hall[3] all support the image of man as an imperial animal, guided by hidden dimensions determined by evolutionary development and mediated by genetic codes, all of which support instinctual patterns of mating, fighting, play and politics. We would like to view our interactions as being based on higher sentiments, on ideology, on moral principles. Yet very often our behavior can be better understood as a product of territoriality, of unwitting biological patterns, of aggressive animal imperatives. Often we act like the animals we are. The only significantly human expression in many instances is the way in which we explain away our base instincts.

The success of William Golding's best-selling novel *Lord of the Flies* [4] reflected our dim awareness of and fascination with the hidden evil within each of us. This lovely, grotesque tale describes nice, gentlemanly prep-school boys who find themselves stranded on an undeveloped island. Within a matter of days, they become warring primitives, frightening us by acting out the desperate secret needs which most of us meet only in our nightmares.

But this is only a novel, you may insist, merely one man's literary invention. Not so! During the London Blitz of World War II (the "good war"), many ordinary, "normal" British youngsters were evacuated from the city to protect them from the nightly bombing raids. These "Infants without Families"[5] as Anna Freud and Dorothy Burlingham called them, were placed in residential nurseries, in decent, well-run communal foster homes, generated as Colonies of the Foster Parent's Plan for War Children, Inc. Most of the children were placed on a temporary basis only, with full expectation that they would be returned to their waiting intact families as soon as it was safe to do so.

These healthy pre-schoolers were well-fed, clothed and housed, given benevolent adult supervision, but unfortunately made to suffer the experience of life without family. Some of the results were that very soon these children developed inordinate patterns of lying, stealing, fighting and extortion. Other children were soon treated as a menace against whom methods of desperate defense had to be adopted. Absence of family support and protection revealed survival patterns in these youngsters not unlike those of any desperate animal.

The patterns revealed in these British residential nurseries is by no means to be discovered only in *children* under stress. I cite these first only because our sentimental notions about what kids are really like make this data more shocking. But adults, indeed whole cultures, can suffer the similar deterioration. A recent dramatic and well-researched example can be found in the latest work of that superb anthropologist, Colin M. Turnbull. His book, *The Mountain People*,[6] describes his personal experiences with the *Ik*, a Ugandan hunting and gathering tribe. Not long ago these people were a decent, generous, stable society. By accident of African nationalistic politics, they were moved from their supportive, familiar hunting environment to a barren, waterless, game-free mountain territory in which the government decided they should become farmers.

Less than three generations in this alien, inhospitable, punishing setting left their culture in ruins and their "humanity" almost non-existent. "Their mountain villages were far from livable; the food was uneatable because there was not any, and the people . . . (became) as unfriendly, uncharitable, inhospitable and generally mean as any people can be." Compassion, love, community feeling, and family life virtually disappeared. Children were now abandoned at age three, forced to fend for themselves as best they could. Those that survived became devious, dishonest, sneaky adults, who sadistically laughed at the pain of their fellow-tribesmen. The old (hardly any survived beyond twenty-five) were deserted but not before the younger hardier ones (sometimes their own children) robbed them of whatever meager possessions they still had, even forcing half-chewed food from their desperately closed mouths. Though our situation is different, Turnbull wonders about the ultimate effects of contemporary Western stress, anonymity and cold self-interest.

A recent study on "The Psychological Power and Pathology of Imprisonment"[7] serves as a chilling prophecy with regard to the tenuousness and fragility of our enlightened, humanistically civilized ways. Only two years ago a Stanford Professor of Psychology created a simulated prison in the basement of the department's laboratory and classroom building. Normal young men were paid to be experimental subjects and arbitrarily assigned the roles of prisoners and guards. The planned two-week experiment was terminated on the sixth day because of the terrifying results in which quickly the subjects could no longer distinguish self from role in the simulated setting. Many of the "guards" soon became sadistically tyrannical in their arbitrary use of power, and even the "good guards" would not interfere with the abusive behavior of the "bad guards." The behavior of the "prisoners" ranged from panic and depression to ruthless selling out of one another. In both groups, spirit and ethics deteriorated quickly and irrevocably. So powerful was the impact of the results of this experiment, that the findings have been presented to the U.S. House of Representatives Committee on the Judiciary in hopes that they would make more vivid the dangerous influence of the prison setting and the need for radical reform. The civilized veneer of human nature cannot bear the strain.

There are so many comforting parameters of our "natures," our standards, our ways that we take for granted, depend on finding there each morning. They do not seem so reliable to me. I am reminded of (haunted by) an experience a few years back when I entered a hospital for major surgery. I was admitted as a competent, self-respecting adult, a husband-father-friend-psychotherapist-writer, and altogether substantial member of the community. Within days, I was not only a patient but a frightened dependent child and a hapless, dilapidated wreck as well. How could I know when I signed myself in, determined to take responsibility for this segment of my life as well, that so soon I could be moved to tears when told by a nurse whom I did not know that I had a "good bowel movement" that day? There are, I suppose, implications in this also for the development of neuroses when parents give kids very little. When children don't get what they need to survive, then emotional priorities get re-sorted and there is no longer the possibility of the luxury of seeking "higher things." Instead the kids must scramble for survival and are reduced to transforming whatever they can get into what they must come to value.

I would like to be careful to point out here that much of what seems corrupt, evil, brutal and grotesque about the underlying biological patterns is really only cast in that light in contrast to our romantic notions of how wonderful it is to be "human." Even disastrous, desperate survival situations sometimes bring out lovely biological patterns as well, as when in a crisis of fire, flood, or political disaster unsuspected strength, courage, loyalty and devotion emerge. I hesitate to emphasize these parameters first because of my cynical expectation that most readers will grab at those examples which support their most comfortable self-images and avoid the more painfully threatening revelations.

In a group therapy session recently one man was telling of being moved by a television program which depicted night predators through a naturalist's eye. Part of the story was of a pack of hyenas separating a hornless, month-old baby rhino from its mother so that they could bring it down and devour it. The baby rhino escaped. The group was pleased and relieved at what seemed a Disney-like ending to the harrowing tale, but the teller pointed out that the baby had escaped for that night, but at sunset on the following day the hyena-pack would return for another try at the kill. There were concerned murmurs from the other group members for the poor baby rhino. I asked how come no one but me was rooting for the hyenas. It was, after all, "God's way."

Some patients tried to help me overcome my "defensive hard shell." But in truth, I was only playing (in the savage way I do). I feel no more committed to the predator than to the prey, except when I am temporarily living out one or another aspect of my own life. The world seems to me neither good nor bad, but only the way it is, a random entropic non-pattern to which we each bring meaning. I am certainly willing to take on a strong sense of theater from time to time, to pretend that there are heroes and villains, but only to intensify the experience of my journey across this stage that has many exciting possibilities, but yet lacks audience, script, and direction. Like Alice, I make my way as best and as foolishly as I can through this bewildering life.

As with other wonderlands, psychotherapy is an effective interruption of old behaviors partly because of the therapist's willingness to operate without engaging in such remedial work. His personal transparency combines with his limiting his participation in protective social ritual. Unchecked by such constraints, the therapist and patient are plunged into primitive personal intimacy, surging with the emotional power of their surfacing transpersonal mythic patterns.

Among the Tarot cards, The Wheel of Fortune symbolizes the impact of the unexpected turn of events. The unpredictability of the therapist's behavior, like the undreamt of surprises which Fortune brings to each man's life, reveals who he is under disarming circumstances. The ever-turning Wheel of Fortune Tarot card is marked by Zodiac signs and mystical animal forces. As you would guess, in the upright position, this card promises unexpected good luck, but if it is dealt to you upside-down, there may be a turn for the worse.

From the very beginning of his contacts with me, the patient is faced with unexpected ambiguities which resist resolution into familiar social categories. My style of meeting is largely free of the ceremonial lubricants which ease most social interactions. Wherever possible I avoid the ritualized manners which so often afford the appearance of civilized contact of the sort which does not require unguarded personal encounter. The therapist's pointed refusal to provide remedial gloss or impersonal relief does, of course, raise the patient's level of uncertainty and anxiety. This increases the risk of his leaving, but at the same time demands that should he stay, he will have to deal in more deeply personal and transparent ways.

The process begins with the intital attempt of the patient-to-be to contact me. When a call comes in on my office phone, there is no ring, only the blinking of a light (which only I can see) to let me know that there will be a message for me at my switchboard in the lobby. This allows therapy sessions to go undisturbed. The switchboard operator is only to ring through if there is an urgent call from my wife or from one of my kids. There are no other emergencies in my profession.

Picking up my phone messages at the switchboard allows me to choose which ones I will answer. I do not open all of my mail, and see no reason to be any more a prisoner of the phone company than of the postal service. Typically the phone message will read: "Mrs. Mary Smith called to request a therapy appointment," and then list her phone number.

At my convenience I call back, saying, "Mary Smith, this is Sheldon Kopp." This immediately takes the first contact out of the traditional doctor-patient mode, posing us as social peers, leaving the relationship undefined, and requiring a conscious choice of salutation by the patient. If I have free time, I meet the patient's request for an initial appointment with the encouragement that we do get together, sit down and talk, and see if we like each other well enough to decide to work together. I offer a time, a firm offer without accomodation. If the patient balks about its inconvenience (most do), I am ready to recommend another therapist. Most patients find a way to work out being able to make the hour I offer, and so we resolve the initial demand for ceremonial accomodation on my part.

I am quite serious about our choosing each other. During that first hour we must get to know each other a bit, and I do *not* assume in advance that the patient will choose to work with me. I always ask how the patient feels about me and demand that the patient consider not coming back unless he has enough good feeling about our meeting to make him hopeful. At the same time, I will not work with a patient whom I feel could not become personally important to me. Somewhere, late in the first hour I will tell a patient either that I will not work with him, that I am willing to work with him, or that I would very much like to work with him, along with my reasons for feeling the way I do. To increase my own freedom in this regard, I let him know that I will not charge him for that initial consultation, unless we both agree to work together.

In dealing with reluctant patients, those who are uncertain about their willingness to make a commitment to work in psychotherapy, my strategy is to raise the ante. For example, when I find a patient with whom I am interested in pursuing the work of psychotherapy, but whose initial defensive ploy involves his resistance to and hedging on any contract demands which I should make, I increase the demands. Thus if a patient insists that he is not sure that he should come as often as once a week, I insist that if he wants to work with me he'll have to come twice a week. If he feels that he might like to try it out for a couple of weeks just to see how it works out, I insist that he make a three-month commitment. If the patient is unwilling to do so it's fine with me that he leave without prejudice and in fact I make it harder for him to come back by insisting that I will not charge him for the initial consultation if he never calls me again. He can save that money and take from the hour what he was able to learn, just by not getting in touch with me again. Should he decide to meet my contract demands and to come back then I will, of course, charge for the initial consultation as well.

One problem that does arise is the issue of good faith in such a resistant patient. That is, I may get him to agree to a three-month twice a week trial period in psychotherapy, but he might have in the back of his mind that if he doesn't like it he is going to drop out anyway, and there's nothing I can do about it. In some cases I solve this power struggle by insisting on getting a retainer as part of the contract. The patient is, of course, suspicious, feeling that I might somehow do him in and push him to break the contract so that I can keep the money. In order to double bind him around that issue I set up the retainer as money which he will indeed lose if he breaks the contract, but *not* as money that I will gain. For example one such patient recently was a Jewish man married to a Catholic woman with whom he often passively struggled. He was unwilling to make a commitment; I insisted on a retainer of two hundred dollars in the form of a check made out to Catholic Charities, payable only if he broke the contract.

Of course, whatever the unceremonial nature of psychotherapy, patient and therapist are real people, operating within a culturally sanctioned social context, fulfilling an economic contract. Their basic *therapeutic alliance* involves an agreement to work together at a specified time and place, their mutual task being to help the patient to be happier. The therapist is a professional who exchanges expert services for money, the patient a client who pays for help.

But it is not the therapeutic alliance that opens the relationship to the play of archetypal forces, but the *therapeutic barrier*. This transforming barrier is the therapist's prerogative to act at any point *as if* the situation were not real. The patient and I meet as any two free agents might, talking his problems out *between* us. But at any time I may shift the focus onto the *way* in which he is discussing the matter, saying, "You react as if I were your father (or your mother, brother, etc.)"

At one level this interruptive shift is an interpretation of the transference, that is, a focussing of the patient's attention on the old unresolved feelings which influence his behavior, and which in this instance have been transferred onto the person of therapist. But more important, this raising of the therapeutic barrier is one of the many ways in which the therapist undermines the social reality, making the patient more vulnerable to the dark forces which churn beneath the surface, opening us to unexpectedly intense personal intimacy.

Each therapy session begins with my silence. Though he may not believe it, the patient knows best where to begin. Should he choose to wait for me to initiate our exchange, the first thing he is likely to hear (fifty minutes later) is my saying, "Our time is up for today."

Should he begin with an attempt at amenities, such as asking me, "How are you today?" he is likely to get no answer at all. If I acknowledge the overture (should he persist), it is likely that I will do so by wondering, "What do you suppose you are up to?" or by interpreting his behavior as a devious distraction, a desperate stalling maneuver, a shallow attempt at bribery, or some other tactic which he typically uses as a character defense against his anxiety. Or, if he is sufficiently stubborn, and I am feeling particularly playful that day, I may acquiesce by offering an incredibly detailed description of the state of my health, going on and on until he interrupts in despair.

Within the frame of reference of everyday social interactions, therapy has the kaleidoscopically lunatic perspective of Alice's Wonderland. The topsy-turvy quality of the relationship has been described satirically as one in which the therapist is always one-up on the patient. The reciprocity of their superior and inferior positions is maintained both crudely by the patient's defensive demands and subtly by the therapist's technical maneuvers. The disarming interplay has been described as one in which "the patient insists that the analyst be one-up while desperately trying to put him one-down, and the analyst insists that the patient remain one-down in order to help him to learn to become one-up."

The patient first submits to this uneasy balance by coming voluntarily to seek my help, by seeing me at my convenience and by paying me a great deal of money. He is to say whatever comes to mind without regard to being rational, appropriate, or socially decent. I need say nothing, and often do just that. What's more, we agree at the outset that the patient often will not know what he is *really* trying to say, since he is guided by motives of which he is often unaware, while I am assumed to be an expert about such matters. My reactions to his behavior are "interpretations" while his evaluations of what I am up to are "fantasies."

On the other hand, when the patient accepts that I am there as a technical consultant, I may insist that he must consider my feelings as those of just another struggling human being. I am the detached expert who is just doing his job and who does not care whether or not the patient "gets better." At the same time I am there as a caring person, who offers what help he can, but who doesn't know any more about how people ought to live than the patient does.

The apparent perversity of my shifting attitudes has a hidden meaning but one that would lose its value if directly revealed to the patient. The therapeutic judo of my tactics is aimed at the interruption of both the patient's self-restricting, risk-avoiding character defenses, and of the face-saving gloss of his mannered social interactions. My shift to being present as another vulnerable human being, one who is there to tell his own tale, is my willingness to be a companion to the patient in the chaos which follows these interruptions. I may spin the patient around and turn him upside down by letting him be thrown by his own weight, but when he comes down in the rubble of his life, he will find me there with him as a committed though world-weary companion. And as he undertakes the frightening pilgrimage of a life open to the perils of the dark forces from which he would usually hide, I will go with him, hoping that we may draw courage from one another.

Yet telling him all of this in advance would be futile. Most likely he would not believe me. Why should he trust me until he comes to know me? And what's more, even if for some reason he would blindly follow my instructions in hope of getting what he came for, his efforts would lack the spontaneous vitality of unplanned actions arising in the fire of the moment. I am well-instructed about such matters by the Hasidic Story of the Cape:

A woman came to Rabbi Israel, the maggid of Koznitz, and told him, with many tears, that she had been married a dozen years and still had not borne a son. "What are you willing to do about it?" he asked her. She did not know what to say.

"My mother," so the maggid told her, "was aging and still had no child. Then she heard that the holy Baal Shem was stopping over in Apt in the course of a journey. She hurried to his inn and begged him to pray she might bear a son. 'What are you willing to do about it?' he asked. 'My husband is a poor bookbinder,' she replied, 'but I do have one fine thing that I shall give to the rabbi.' She went home as fast as she could and fetched her good cape ... which was carefully stowed away in a chest. But when she returned to the inn with it, she heard that the Baal Shem had already left for Mezbizh. She immediately set out after him and since she had no money to ride, she walked from town to town with her ... (cape) until she came to Mezbizh. The Baal Shem took the cape and hung it on the wall. 'It is well,' he said. My mother walked all the way back, from town to town, until she reached Apt. A year later, I was born."

"I, too," cried the woman, "will bring you a good cape of mine so that I may get a son."

"That won't work," said the maggid. "You heard the story. My mother had no story to go by."

THE MAGICIAN.

Chapter Four

BEING WHERE THEY AIN'T

Though the settings have changed, man's patterns of relationship are endlessly repeated. People once lived hidden in dark caves venturing out in primitive bands first to gather edible roots and grubs and later to hunt the wild beasts of the forest and plain. Today overcrowded masses reside in technologically improved structures of glass and steel, while making their living by selling insurance and manufacturing parts for moon rockets. Despite these seemingly monumental changes of life style, certain configurations of the human trip endure. Certain fundamental reciprocal human relationships are to be found again and again.

Most obvious among these are the biologically-supported interdependencies of mother and child, father and son, and mating of man and woman. But, in addition, there are continuing permutations of the archetypal motifs of chieftain and follower, guardian and protected one, teacher and disciple. The relationship of *Healer* and *Patient* is another such inherently potential reciprocity of the fundamental ways in which men depend on one another.

In every time, in every place, some men have sought the help, the guidance, the leadership, the healing hands of others. Sometimes the currency of exchange between the two is the easing of physical pain and disease. Sometimes it is the curing of the soul.

In either case, he who is appointed saviour is expected to have powers which transcend the patient's more human foibles. The role of healer, of course, is not just an appointed office but, like town-drunk or village-idiot, it is in part a voluntary position. And so the temptation to play out the corrupting power trip originates not only with the patient's dependent hope to be cured, but also with the healer's arrogant presumption of placing himself above other men.

The inherent danger in the healer's position of power comes through in the prophetic meanings of the Tarot card of The Magician. When this wonder-worker turns up, the fortune of the person for whom the cards are being dealt includes divine mastery and the wisdom and power to bring about marvelous things. But should the Magician be dealt out reversed, then beware of power used for destructive ends, or paralyzed in weakness and indecision.

The start of the relationship between the psychotherapist and his patient has been described as resembling that of a *sorcerer* and his *apprentice*.[1] The patient, of course, hopes to find a good and all-powerful parent, that magician-saviour who will use supernatural powers to work the wonders that can cure all ills, solve all problems, and bring everlasting happiness.

The sorcerer-and-apprentice fantasies of the patient match exactly the power fascination of the guru who would heal others. It is quite likely that for a while they will both go mad, consensually validating the illusion that the therapist knows more than the patient about the most profound parameters of life, and that this wisdom and power will someday belong to the apprentice if only the young supplicant submits, surrenders, and hangs around long enough. Unless they both give up hope of resolving this power game prematurely, their struggle of magic and counter-magic goes on until either the apprentice is willing to recognize that he too is a sorcerer, or until the younger man wanders off into unresolvedly sullen, hero-worshipping life-long apprenticeship.

The forerunners of today's intra-psychic healers are many. The contemporary psychotherapist is foreshadowed in those individual visionaries who were the gurus of other times and other places. The heritage of the contemporary guru includes healing metaphors of the Zen Master, the Hasidic Rabbi, the Fourth Century Christian Hermit Monk, of Wizards, Medicine Men, and Magi. [2] In his earliest and most primordial form, the healer appeared as the paleolithic *Shaman*, the helper, healer and guide of the earliest hunting and gathering societies. Before man planted crops, domesticated animals or settled for one god and his priests, before all of that "progress," he looked to the shaman for spiritual leadership.

As primitive harbinger of later archetypal saviour figures, the shaman was a suffering hero, a wounded healer who had to die and be reborn if he was to be able to mediate the redemption of his community, the other members of his tough-minded hunting band. He begins his own tortured pilgrimage as a fuck-up, a misfit youth. In overcoming his own personal agonies he comes to be in a position to guide others on their spiritual pilgrimages. His source of power is his personal vision, acquired in the solitude of wilderness ordeals, during which he must make his way without instruction or preplanned pattern.

His self-tortured growth-experiences breed sensitivity to the pain of others, and a deep need to turn-on others to the power of their own visions, to be available as a spiritual companion as they undertake their own adventures. But the Shaman is no gentle saint, no milk-sop Christ. Like Jesus in the Temple when He wildly swung chains to drive out the Money-changers, the Shaman is like a titan to a god, a devil to an angel. There is a powerful contrast between "the wild, quarrelsome, dangerous shamans and the people who were so polite to each other that they were like brothers-in-law." [3]

This lustily surging irritability can be frightening, at times even dangerous, but too, it is that very primordial force which is the healer's power source. The principle of personal abandon which powers the primitive shaman, may be found in the mystics, the poets and the artists of more developed cultures. The shamanistic trance is a regressive spiritual flight during which this guru leaves the everyday world behind, discourses with the spirits and wings to those heavens and hells of the soul which are the wellsprings of archetypal potency. Christ himself demands abandon when he advises one who hesitates as though trapped by earthly duties, telling him "Let the dead bury their dead"; so too when he tells the materialistically reluctant rich man, "Sell all that you have...and follow me."

Never mind the rules! Forget conventional wisdom and morality if you would be healed, saved, made free! Augustine says, "Love God, and do what thou wilt!" while Luther admonishes the men of his age to "Sin bravely!"

The classical pre-figure for the healer who must stand against the gods if he is to save the world is that hero of humanistic enlightenment, Prometheus. This fire-bringer was the supreme trickster, the super-shaman. When Zeus hid the fire from man, Prometheus stole it, returning it to earth where man could once again have its power, its warmth, and its light. Indeed Zeus' punitive withholding of the fire was itself an act of vengeance brought on by Prometheus having dared to fool the very gods. Prometheus had served up burnt offerings in which he wrapped in fat the poorest parts of the slaughtered beast, putting the best parts in another bundle and so tricking Zeus into choosing foolishly, leaving the best parts of the meat for man.

In symbolic retribution, Zeus chained Prometheus to a rock and sent an eagle to eat his liver. Poor bastard, his immortal liver grew anew each night only to be devoured by the eagle again by day. And so his torture continued until he was at last rescued by Hercules.

So it is that the saviour-healer has his archetypal forerunner in the trickster-hero. At its worst, the *shadow of the healer is the charlatan.* The evil underlay of the guru is that dark brother who sometimes surfaces as the quack or the false prophet. It is a form of corruption, or chronic temptation to a power trip, which is the daily personal menace of every honest therapist and to which he must constantly be alert. The Trickster-figure [4] in his less sinister forms is merely an imp, a fool or a buffoon, a practical joker of the

Punch and Judy Show genre.

The Trickster appears in the picaresque mythology of settings as diverse as Ancient Greece, Medieval Europe, the Orient, Africa, and the Semitic world. He is the primitive tricky spider of the animal world, the alchemical figure Mercurius, Satan the ape of God, Tom Thumb and Stupid Hans of fairy-tales. He is the peasants' poltergeist, Loki the Norse helper and trouble maker, or a carnival clown. When not a shaman or witch doctor, he may appear as Hermes, the divine trickster of Greek mythology. That particular Guide of Souls was both a God of Wisdom and a Patron of Magic. Later to become the messenger of greater gods, Hermes was cunning from birth. On the very first day of his life, he is said to have both invented the lyre and stolen Apollo's cattle.

As always, he is both benefactor and buffoon, combining the dual image of both creator and destroyer. In his more serious moments, he is a culture-hero who appears in an account of the earth's creation or of the world's transformation. But always, he is a *spirit of disorder*, one who operates with laughter and with irony outside of the fixed bounds of custom, law, and conventional wisdom. He is a hungry, highly-sexed, wanderer who both plays tricks and is as easily duped by others. But "if we laugh at him, he grins at us. What happens to him, happens to us." [5]

He is a shameless arch-deceiver. Among some American Indians, for instance, the Coyote, who is the personification of this Trickster-Hero, is often seen as a mischievous intermix of Eros and Pan. And so a Skagit Indian poem [6] tells that:

> One day when Coyote
> was walking through Snoqualmic Pass,
> he met a young woman.
> What do you have in your pack?
> she said.
> Fish eggs.
> Can I have some?
> If you close your eyes

and hold up your dress.
The woman did as she was told.
Higher.
Hold your dress over your head.
Then Coyote stepped out of his trousers
and walked up to the woman.
Stand still
so I can reach the place.
I can't.
There's something crawling between my legs.
Keep your dress up.
It's a bumble bee. I'll get it.
The woman dropped her dress.
You weren't fast enough.
It stung me.

Sometimes the shaman plays more malicious jokes on people, and is in danger of retaliatory sorcery or black magic. Even the *appearance of evil* is not easily tolerated in one who is expected to be a saviour. I myself have been under continued attack (counter-attack?) since I published a piece of gurumanship which made some of my disciples and even my priestly colleagues more anxious than they could bear. I had written a piece which even one of my young teenage sons could enjoy and by which he could be instructed. In fact, it was he who titled the piece. But since its publication, some of the therapeutic community have renamed me, not quite as Wicked Witch of the West, but rather as "The Fuck-you Therapist." Read now my trickster's piece and see if you can find in it the wild, wanton irresponsibility of paganism, but most of all see if it turns you on, opens you to your own power.

EASY CHOICE [7]

It was a quiet rainy day at the clinic, the afternoon she showed up asking to see a psychotherapist. That's why I saw her without an appointment, and without any preliminary screening. She flopped inelegantly into the chair nearest to my office door, pushed the door shut with her dripping umbrella, and looked at me unhappily through soggy false eyelashes.

I took the clinic identification card which she had filled out for the receptionist, and asked : "How can I help you?"

"I need advice," she said. "My husband has been in and out of mental hospitals for the last seven years. The doctors called him a 'dangerous Paranoid Schizophrenic.' He's really crazy and when he's mad, he gets physical and hurts people. He won't live with me now, but I go to visit him at his apartment every weekend. He threw me out last Saturday, and he says if I go back, next time he'll kill me. Doctor, what should I do?"

"That's easy," I answered. "Don't go back."

"Oh, but I have to go back," she whined. "I love him. What other advice do you have?"

"Why don't you go fuck yourself," I counseled.

Without another word, she jumped up, whirled around, spattering rainwater across my desk, and rushed out of the clinic.

She never returned. I guess I must have cured her.

There were many critical accusations ranging from "quackery" and "neurosis" to "brutality." There were, of course, expressions of appreciation and pleasure as well. One statement stands out from all the rest for me, one poetic fantasy from Don Lathrop, a Jungian therapist from the West coast, a lovely madman whose imagination and sensitivity is sometimes my only life-line in the stormy seas into which I must throw myself again and again. Here is what he published amongst the letters of derision, scorn and outrage; a poem titled "Shelly:"[8]

"I'm scared."
　"It's only fear," I heard you say.
"I can't stand the agony."

"Yes you can," I heard you say.
"I want to do it, but I don't want to
be uncomfortable."
"Then you don't want to do it,"
I heard you say.
"You are a miserable, hateful,
insensitive beast."
"That's right," I heard you say.
"You can't make me do it, not with all
your clever tricks, not with your
uncaring for me, not with your
unwillingness to lend me your
encouragement and support."
"That's right," I heard you say.
"I'll never do it! You'd think you
got me to do it."
"Man, I could care less what you do
and I don't need your excuses.
You are no fun to be with when you
are like this," I heard you say.

Trickery has always been a part of the healing process. By no means need it be sinister. The healing techniques of the shaman of the Nuba mountains, whose patients are tough-minded hunters, consist "principally in the ability to hide about his person and to produce at will small quartz pebbles and bits of stick; and, of hardly less importance than this sleight of hand, the power of looking preternaturally solemn, as if he were the possessor of knowledge quite hidden from ordinary men." [9]

In the contemporary ministry of the healing of neuroses, trickery is certainly not the only mode of approach used by the therapist, but it's not a bad beginning. Lao Tzu[10] advises us to "Be where they ain't" when he counsels that:

What is in the end to be shrunk
Must first be stretched.

Whatever is to be weakened
Must begin by being made strong.
What is to be overthrown
Must begin by being set up.
He who would be a taker
Must begin as a giver.

"Be where they ain't!" is a tactical rule-of-thumb for meeting patients during the opening phase of psychotherapy. Of course, we all understand that any categorizing of the therapy process into Phase I, Phase II, Phase III and so on is merely a playful way of setting up make-believe classifications, a fictional hedge to be raised at those times when we feel that we can no longer stand working in the boundlessly flowing stream of the ever-changing process of live interactions with another separate human being. It offers the therapist the momentarily soothing illusion of order in the overwhelming chaos of ongoing life. Theorizing is only our way of telling ourselves wonderous fairy-tales, just as psychological interpretation is our way of telling comforting stories to our patients. Enjoy my tale if you can. It is not at all necessary that you believe it.

At those times when the entropic ambiguity of my work makes me feel as though I might lose my Self as well as my way, I am tempted to try to understand what it is that I am doing. Those are not at all the best of times. At the best of times, I can enjoy the creative freedom of not even trying to understand. Yet, since there *are* those times when I analyze, theorize, pretend to myself that there is no truth to the Truth that "This is as clear as it ever gets!", I might as well share the experience as not share it.

Most recently the story has gone something like this: Once upon a time all therapy was divided into three parts, called Phase I, Phase II, and Phase III. Phase I, the Opening or Judo Phase, begins with the patient presenting the symptoms which are his ticket of admission to the cosmic light-show which in our day is called psychotherapy. He does his opening number and the therapist fucks up his trip by being where he ain't (more about this below). This phase lasts from a few sessions to several months, during which the patient usually gives up his presenting complaints. He may either terminate at this point, having settled for relief, or go on to Phase II as a function of having become curious about his life and wanting a more intimate relationship with the therapist.

Should he enter Phase II, the Middle or Intimacy Phase, he and the therapist will be rewarded by a period of several months to several years of continuing closeness, having come beyond the struggle over contract, and well into a period of love and soulful adventure. For some such couples the healing of wounds gives way to the excitement of a pilgrimage of spiritual growth. One of my many impossible wishes is to become successful enough as a therapist to treat only healthy patients, to leave Phase I to lesser gurus and to restrict my practice to working exclusively with patients who have already been successfully cured.

As Phase II draws toward its completion (in those cases when it does), one member of the couple (almost always the therapist) begins to make noises like "This sure has been wonderful, but there is something spooky or unreal about going on and on this way indefinitely." A brief struggle follows often ending with the patient terminating precipitously, offering the exit line: "You know I love you, Doc, and you've been a great help up till now, but you seem to have gone crazy. I'm leaving."

Should the patient stay, it will be to make his way through Phase III, the Final or Separation Phase. This bittersweet ordeal is so poignantly painful that many therapists make sure to terminate with all of their patients during Phase I or II rather than risk ever going through it at all. Phase III lasts from a few weeks to several months, often with an alternation of false stops and starts along the way. If it is completed successfully, the therapist and the patient give each other up forever. If not, the therapist is forever haunted, and the patient (though they may never meet again) remains in therapy for the rest of his life.

Back to the issue of Phase I tactics. They have been sensitively explored in the character-analytic work of Wilhelm Reich [11] in which he begins by ignoring the *content* of the patient's complaints in favor of focussing entirely on the *style* in which they are being presented. Or alternately:

In individual therapy we may get the patient to focus on his past history. In group therapy, we may encourage the patient's curiosity about the group process. Some of what occurs as the patient reluctantly takes on these tasks is that he can begin to lose himself in the sense of giving himself over to the assigned work. As this unhooks him from his willful, self-sorry demand for someone to give him relief right now, a new possibility arises: The patient can now begin to experience the therapist and the other patients as real people with selves of their own; as people who have meaning outside of himself, who can therefore be meaningful to him, and who can ultimately put him in touch with the meaning of his own life. [12]

At this point, the therapist is instructing by indirection, helping the patient to unhook from his old stuck ways, opening him to the possibility of new ways of living (whatever they might turn out to be). The perverse guideline for this instruction is *"Be where they ain't!"*

The patient who begins with immersion in his own history, the therapist must draw back again and again 'to what is going on in the here-and-now. The hysterically emotional, overly impulsive patient must be slowed down to stopping and thinking-over what he is doing, while the obsessionally paralyzed thinker can be met with non-rational responses which finally get him too upset to hold back any longer. Patients who are initially too hard on themselves are to be treated gently and indulgently while self-sorry whiners must be confronted with harsh demands which leave no quarter for excuse-making.

This phase can be really hard work, calling for a great deal of self-discipline on the part of the therapist. Ironically, once a young therapist gets the hang of it, it can be a great deal of demonic fun as well. There will, of course, be present the corrupting temptation to simply be clever and manipulative, to succumb to the healer's power trip. I find that the best protection for my avoiding the charlatan in myself is to keep aware of the patient in myself, to renew again and again the image of myself as "the wounded healer." [13]

When I do, I am in the best position to trust myself, to follow Carl Whitaker's advice about responding to patients. Don't feed the baby just because the baby cries that he is hungry unless it is a time when the milk is overflowing from your own nipples.

To those who demand clarity, speak metaphorically. Only those who would keep things muddled demand direct confrontation at this stage.

Zen literature provides a handy source-book of such Phase I tactics. [14] Here are a few examples of the Zen Master's response to the young monks who sought his instruction by asking for help in their unenlightened ways.

1. Monk: "What is the idea of the Patriarch's coming here from the West?"
   Master: "Ask the post over there."
   Monk: "I do not understand."
   Master: "Neither do I." [15]

2. Monk: "This ground where we sit is a fine site for a hut."
   Master: "Let your hut alone; how about ultimate things?" [16]

3. Monk: "I have come from a distant place with the special intention of seeing you. Will you kindly give me one word of instruction?"

Master: "Growing old, my back aches today."[17]

4. Monk: "What way would you use in the demonstration of Zen thought?"
   Master: Holds up his staff without speaking.
   Monk: "Is that all?"
   Master: Silently throws down his staff.[18]

Lao Tzu makes it all so very clear when he tells us:
Straightforward words seem paradoxical.[19]

Of course the beginning of instruction (whether Zen or psychotherapy) is not the only point at which the Healer offers the patient/pilgrim the treat of trick or trick. I'm reminded of an example of such trickery which I offered in a group setting to a patient who had come further along the way. The therapy group began in an ordinary mode that afternoon with a brief initial silence followed by each of us doing his number. Melvin was really into himself, luxuriating in the low-keyed anguish of obsessing about how he was doing. "It's all just no use at all," he whined. "All these months of therapy, and still I'm never really myself." I pointed out that that was the one problem no one could have, as it was never possible for a person not to be himself.

He seemed pleased at the opportunity to go on and explain, to go on and on and on. He described at length how he could not be spontaneous, could not get past his hang-ups with expecting to be inadequate, could not respond in the here-and-now. I offered to help then and there. If he was open to trusting me for a minute, I would teach him to trust himself by letting him experience the here and now, spontaneously and competently. Offered the opportunity to solve his problems, of course, Melvin was understandably reluctant. He eyed me suspiciously but responded to group pressure to at least try.

I was holding a lit cigar in my hand during this exchange. The moment Melvin agreed to trust me, I flipped the smoking butt across the room straight into his lap. Suddenly his whiningly lethargic, gelatinous manner gave way to alert and angry action as he fielded the hot cigar expertly, shouted "God damn you anyway, Kopp!" and tossed it back at me with verve and accuracy.

His eyes were wide with wonder and vitality. Uncharacteristically he announced, "I've got some other unfinished business to take care of in this group right now." He blurted out some long-withheld anger toward one of the other men in the group, and then told one of the women how much he cared about her. Crossing the room with clear purpose he hugged her with unrestrained tenderness.

In the midst of the embrace, he began to mutter something about how he might mess this up. But when the group told him to shut up and enjoy himself, he seemed pleased to surrender to the moment once more.

Even when the trickster is not being helpful, he is really not an evil figure. More mischievous than malevolent, his clumsiness, impetuousness, stubbornness, and poor judgment result more often in his getting into ridiculous scrapes than in his creating catastrophies for others. "The trickster is a collective shadow figure, a summation of all of the inferior traits of character in individuals." [20] He is the epitome of the fallible human being, a collection of foibles and defects which are the mark of human nature. So it is that he may appear in stories as a jester, a clown, a buffoon, or a fool. It is the cleverness which my mother always zeroed-in on when I maneuvered myself into impossible binds. "Smart, smart, smart, and you're dumb!" she would say, with more sympathy than malice.

Coyote, Spider, Hare, Raven or any of the other trickster figures found in American Indian myths are "no merely horny version of a Disney character." [21] The profound comic imagination which they represent is that of man not yet free from his animal nature. Look what happens when he defies his nature even in a minor fashion:

"As he went wandering around aimlessly he suddenly heard someone speaking. He listened very carefully and it seemed to say, 'He who chews me will defecate; he will defecate!' That was what it was saying. 'Well, why is this person talking in this manner?' said Trickster. So he walked in the direction from which he had heard the speaking and again he heard, quite near him, someone saying: 'He who chews me, he will defecate; he will defecate!' That is what was said. 'Well, why does this person talk in such a fashion?' said Trickster. Then he walked to the other side. So he continued walking along. Then right at his very side, a voice seemed to say, 'He who chews me, he will defecate; he will defecate!' 'Well, I wonder who it is who is speaking. I know very well that if I chew it, I will not defecate.' But he kept looking around for the speaker and finally discovered, much to his astonishment, that it was a bulb on a bush. The bulb it was that was speaking. So he seized it, put it in his mouth, chewed it, and then swallowed it. He did just this and then went on.

'Well, where is the bulb gone that talked so much? Why, indeed, should I defecate? When I feel like defecating, then I shall defecate, no sooner. How could such an object make me defecate!' Thus spoke Trickster. Even as he spoke, however, he began to break wind. 'Well this, I suppose, is what it meant. Yet the bulb said I would defecate, and I am merely expelling gas. In any case I am a great man even if I do expel a little gas!' Thus he spoke. As he was talking he again broke wind. This time it was really quite strong. 'Well, what a foolish one I am. This is why I. am called Foolish One, Trickster.' Now he began to break wind again and again. 'So this is why the bulb spoke as it did, I suppose.' Once more he broke wind. This time it was very loud and his rectum began to smart. 'Well, it surely is a great thing!' Then he broke wind again, this time with so much force, that he was propelled forward. 'Well, well, it may even make me give another push, but it won't make me defecate,' so he exclaimed defiantly. The next time he broke wind, the hind part of his body was raised up by the force of the explosion and he landed on his knees and hands. 'Well, go ahead and do it again! Go ahead and do it again!" Then, again, he broke wind. This time the force of the expulsion sent him far up in the air and he landed on the ground, on his stomach. The next time he broke wind, he had to hang on to a log, so high was he thrown. However, he raised himself up and, after a while, landed on the ground, the log on top of him. He was almost killed by the fall. The next time he broke wind, he had to hold on to a tree that stood near by. It was a poplar and he held on with all his might yet, nevertheless, even then, his feet flopped up in the air. Again, and for the second time, he held on to it when he broke wind and yet he pulled the tree up by the roots. To protect himself, the next time, he went on until he came to a large tree, a large oak tree. Around this he put both his arms. Yet, when he broke wind, he was swung up and his toes struck against the tree. However, he held on.

After that he ran to a place where people were living. When he got there, he shouted, 'Say, hurry up and take your lodge down, for a big war party is upon you and you will surely be killed! Come let us get away!" He scared them all so much that they quickly took down the lodge, piled it on Trickster, and then got on him themselves. They likewise placed all the little dogs they had on top of Trickster. Just then he began to break wind again and the force of the expulsion scattered the things on top of him in all directions. They fell far apart from one another. Separated, the people were standing about and shouting to one another; and the dogs, scattered here and there, howled at one another. There stood Trickster laughing at them till he ached.

Now he proceeded onward. He seemed to have gotten over his troubles. 'Well, this bulb did a lot of talking,' he said to himself, 'yet it could not make me defecate.' But even as he spoke he began to have the desire to defecate, just a very little. 'Well, I suppose this is what it meant. It certainly bragged a good deal, however.' As he spoke he defecated again. 'Well, what a braggart it was! I suppose this is why it said this.' As he spoke these last words, he began to defecate a good deal. After a while, as he was sitting down, his body would touch the excrement. Thereupon he got on top of a log and sat down there but, even then, he touched the excrement. Finally, he climbed up a log that was leaning against a tree. However, his body still touched the excrement, so he went up higher. Even then, however, he touched it so he climbed still higher up. Higher and higher he had to go. Nor was he able to stop defecating. Now he was on top of the tree. It was small and quite uncomfortable. Moreover, the excrement began to come up to him.

Even on the limb on which he was sitting he began to defecate. So he tried a different position. Since the limb, however, was very slippery he fell right down into the excrement. Down he fell, down into the dung. In fact he disappeared in it, and was only with very great difficulty able to get out of it."[22]

At his most powerful, trickster-healer-saviour is "the archetype of the hero, the giver of all great boons--the fire-bringer and the teacher of mankind."[23] He is Prometheus unbound, defiant challenger who takes that he might give, suffers that he might heal, tricks the oppressive gods that he might free men to become what they are. But foolishness and fallability are his other face. And so when in my arrogance as Guru I trick myself, at such times wisdom consists in listening to those voices which would warn me against myself. Sometimes my patients help by not taking me seriously. Sometimes "enemies can be very useful."[24] In some instances only another trickster can see through my games. So it was, that following a turbulent (and for me a triumphant) experience at a Workshop of the American Academy of Psychotherapists, a loving friend and fellow-guru wrote to me, to tell of his response to how I was handling my life amidst the residuals of brain surgery which I barely survived almost three years ago.[25] He wrote:

"The headaches are an indispensable reminder to you of the

central core of your craziness, of the dark side, the side whicn, if left unchecked will destroy you. This was manifested physically in the tumor--with which you are now in symbiotic balance - and psychically (symbols that are translatable) in the psychotic episode. Decode the psychotic episode and you have the answer.

The headaches are the key to your survival. You can see that you have come to tolerate them rather than despise them. When Joen (another therapist) was teaching you to move the pain, I was comfortable right up to the end when she tried to get you to move it out of you. That would be lethal. I think it is a problem of dependency and of who or what we can depend upon. You are resisting God (Self). It's the one area where we are apart. Since you do not yet acknowledge it, Ego must do it all. You (Ego) identify with the archetypal images that are self (God) - and thus *you* must be Moses, The Healer, The Hasidic, The Guru, or whatever. You must build the pyramid--when there are countless willing hands that would help Him. You are not the Pharoah. He lives within you, to guide you, to teach you, to rule you, if need be. You could accept freely only from Roz, The Mother (a third therapist at the workshop). But that is dangerous, for the negative side of that is devouring, incorporation, and death. You appropriately kept a balance there, too.

If there is a Divine Ordering Principle to whom or which you can turn over the task of your life, the world, then you can become a mere worshipper, humbly and obediently throwing yourself at its feet, eyes downcast lest you offend it by "knowing" it (and thus be tempted to try to use the power that rightfully belongs to it).

Good nite my dear, sweet fellow pilgrim.

Don

I still can't rest.

After being with you for five days, I can think more clearly, more simply. I can say "yes" and "no" again.

Jungian analysis/training/theory is capable of being nothing more than lovely embroidery on a pillowcase of obsessive compulsive character made by my Mom and Dad and Western civilization.

You showed me the dark evil in my "tolerance", "acceptance," "patience," and "understanding." In this way I become the Great Mother, enslaving, keeping the world in my belly.

I see a light again in the darkness.

Lovingly,

Don

One recent expression of my personal struggle with the treasure-burden of the healer-trickster role is symbolically written in the growing, wearing, and finally in the shaving off of my Old Testament-Mephistophelian-Psychoanalyst-Magician Beard. Many years ago I grew a full beard, for the fun of it and as a matter of simple vanity. Partly it was my sense of theater at work, taking on a hirsute prop, part of the costume of my trade, much like the leopard's teeth that witch doctors wear around their necks.

I loved the attention it drew at the time, before Madison Avenue turned my stigmata into high fashion. Back then it gave me a small measure of protection, because men who wore beards were not expected to be polite. My fantasy image of my newly-bearded self was that of an amalgam of a ferocious wildman, an untamed shaman, and simultaneously that of an older, wiser prophet and archetypal father. I loved it when a patient said that I looked like a "Santa Claus for the bad children."

Later on when illness turned my life upside down and I returned to therapy as a patient once more, the shifting configurations within me took me to new places, and I knew I had to give up this badge of power. I had found my way once more past my despair and was ready to live again. I wanted to reclaim my innocence, to see what my original face had looked like before I was born. I was ready to be more available, more openly vulnerable. It was scary but one of my sons assured me that if I got into a struggle with someone I could not intimidate, I could show him a photo of how tough I had looked with my beard.

When things occur to me in my head, I most often say them, at times too impulsively. My wife is a far more private person than I. When I talked with her about my decision to shave, as always she supported my wish to do what I chose. She also had let me know that she thought it would be a good thing to let my mouth show so people could see it as well as hear it speak. She pointed out that the sound was more misleading than the sight, since the appearance of my mouth was more tremblingly vulnerable than the strong words which it emitted. And then she floored me (as she so often does) by pointing out that I must have finally come to terms with my grief over my mother's death. I had not realized that it was *that* summer seven years earlier that I had first chosen to grow that stoic mask.

I was tempted to wait and shave while I was away on vacation, but I felt the separation and return to my patients would be complex enough without adding that dramatic and unexpected transfiguration. My patients both individually and in group perceived my changed appearance in a generally consistent way but the meaning they attributed to it polarized them right down the middle. Almost all of my patients saw me as more human, more ordinary, less powerful, but half were delighted, while the rest were scared that they would have to give up their projections and take full responsibility for their own lives and for the ways in which they treated me.

As for myself, I was trying to abdicate as guru, to be closer to others, to let my weaknesses show so that I could ask for and get more sympathy and help. I am weary of making that life-long Moses-trip, tired of leading others to the Promised Land, seeing it only from the mountain-top, and having to remain outside while others enter. And yet I know that I will never be safe from the burdens and temptations of the Healer-Trickster Trek which is my life. At times, I believe that all I am up to for now is learning the most magically powerful and most gently healing trick of them all, *the trick of no tricks.*

Chapter Five

COMMUNITY OF SINNERS

The recurring Father Archetype is experienced in terms of an Old Testament God of Judgment, He who will decide whether we have been good or bad, and if we are to be rewarded or punished. More often than not, He is awaited as a wrathful father rather than as a merciful one. But when Judgment is tempered by Mercy, it is possible to receive a more balanced response, as visualized in the Tarot card of Justice. This Greek goddess holds in her right hand, a double-edged sword which can cut two ways, separating right from wrong. Unhampered by the contemporary blindfold, with eyes wide open, she can read clearly the balance of the scales in her left hand. Dealt upright, she promises that Justice will be done without the preconceptions and prejudices of conventional morality. In the reversed position, she warns of the injustice and inequality meted out by the biased mind.

Each patient comes to psychotherapy believing he is sick, unworthy, or in some way insufficient. He sees himself as the bearer of pathology from which he hopes to be relieved, or of evil which he must overcome. His unhappiness is a neurosis to be cured, his personality a defect to be corrected. He experiences himself as broken and wishes to be fixed.

He does not yet understand that his crazy attitudes and peculiar behaviors began in childhood as sensible and realistic attempts to cope with more than he could bear. They were long ago developed as the only sane strategies which could have saved him from the bewilderingly calamitous world in which he grew up.

These now-incapacitating ways were once all he had to make his survival possible. Now he pays needlessly for maintaining this obsolete style. He fails to see how his adult world differs from the home in which he felt so helpless. He fails to grasp the freedom which has come with finally being able to take care of himself.

His old solutions, once sane, are no longer viable. Because they no longer work, he goes on feeling that there is something wrong with him. He feels peculiar, isolated, out of it. How is he to come to learn that the problems with which he struggles are the same problems with which we all struggle? We are, after all, more alike than we are different. For each of us, the most singular aspect is our common humanity. When a man fails to grasp his place in our common plight, his unhappiness is compounded by unbearable loneliness and self-blame.

Martin Buber once wrote: *"All real living is meeting."*[1] But how is one man to meet another when he feels unworthy of recognition, when he credits the other with being more of a person than he feels he himself is? He lives in a world of life-sized people while he experiences himself as something less than whole. Surely no one else has *his* sort of troubles. Even his attempts at solutions to his problems would seem foreign and unsavory to other people. Shame and distrust discourage him from revealing himself to others. The resulting loneliness and isolation create ever-increasing feelings of peculiarity. The prospect of ever revealing himself comes to be even more painful. But who can accept him, if no one knows him? His hopelessness grows. It is harder and harder to trust until loneliness is all the comfortingly protective a shell such a man has left.

There is, of course, the temptation to project the dark sides of our souls and our self-condemnation onto others, so that we may see ourselves as being good. For a confusing while I lived in fragmented shifting, self-deluding conflict as I began to develop a socialized *persona*, an acceptable mask, a civilized gloss with which to disguise my own dark shadow.

Sometimes my struggle involved moral anguish, as when I was tempted by the escape from pain promised by heroin. At other times "my struggle" was nothing more than a pompous pretense, a smoke-screen to mask my own petty anxieties. One example is the teen-age summer I spent in Bryant Park. Behind New York City's famed Fifth Avenue Public Library is a park commemorating William Jennings Bryant. During the day the people who come to the park are a typical urban amalgam of the brown-bag lunching office workers, the adolescents doing courtship dances, the old, the unattached, the out-of-work, all enjoying the sun and a chance to be with other people without having to encounter them.

But at sundown the scene shifts. The new cast of players are more colorful, more decadent, more flamboyant. The night people who come to do homage at the foot of the statue of "Mother Bryant" are a sub-culture of triumphant male homosexuals, flaming screaming queens, nellie bitches dressed in drag, in satirically exaggerated costume of the envied-despised female. There are of course others as well. Some are called *trade,* men who do not yet know that they are homosexual, who participate purportedly "just for the money." And too there is the *macho* element called *dirt.* The come down to the park to bolster their own uncertain manhood by "beating up on the fairies." But every queen knows that "This year's dirt is next year's trade."

And then there was me, the most peculiar of the lot. Unable to face the fact that I was being drawn to this lavender demi-monde by my own hidden homosexual impulses, I came as a junior psychiatrist, a mock anthropologist. I kept a card file of "case histories." So it was that I was able to indulge my homoerotic voyeurism while maintaining the persona of an incipient mental health professional. It's still embarrassing to remember my fraudulence. Although now I believe I fooled no one but myself.

In the years that followed I became so committed to achieving professional status, to being seen as accomplished or at least as promising, that the vitality which the raw evil of my adolescence had provided began to drain away. I became increasingly intellectual, ponderously ethical, and oppressively into a super-integrity trip. Having lost my shadow, I was now without substance for a period of years.

What was left of me was saved by my seeking the other half of myself by going to work in a Building for the Criminally Insane. I was young and largely unseasoned as a therapist, but what I lacked in developed talent and grace, I made up for in good intentions, arrogant presumption, and a righteous saviour trip.

The beginning was especially difficult. By the end of the first day, all that was left of the afternoon's impressions was a montage of steel bars and cruelly criminal faces. I knew from one of the attendants that "word gets around." Somehow the inmates had been aware of who I was, and when and why I was coming, long before most of the staff knew. Many times in the future I was to come up against this inmate grapevine again and again. But never did I learn how it worked its magic of acquisition and communication of staff plans before they had even gotten beyond the stage of informal conferencing.

It was all the more mysterious and disarming, on first encounter, in that I had hoped to be anonymous on this first visit. Instead, not only did they know me, but several had chosen to kid me about my supervisor's not being there to meet me. They also jibed me about my disappointment over my apartment not being vacated on time.

Then, too, if they knew who I was, they also should have known that I was there to help them. Why, then, did they shout unnerving catcalls about "the new bug doctor" and "the sex class teacher?" Why did they block my path in the cell corridors, waiting till almost the last moment to see whether I would go around them or meet their challenge?

It was not at all the way I had planned it, not at all. I had hoped to go almost unnoticed, to form impressions, size up the men, and make my plans for handling them. Instead, things turned out quite the reverse. I was made self-conscious by their scrutiny, uncertain by their challenges, and anxious by their not wanting to take me seriously.

Nothing was clear to me except my own acute sense of discomfort. My usually keen analytical faculties had somehow been disordered. It was most confusing. Perhaps it was this first encounter with the criminal personality which had done it. After all, I was used to dealing with law-abiding neurotics. It was merely a matter of shifting to this new frame of reference, establishing a new set of norms within which to judge this unknown patient population sample. After all, I could easily imagine myself in the place of troubled clinic patients; but see myself as a criminal . . . ah, that was quite another matter.

It was certainly not that I had never felt the tug of such impulses from deep within my own loins. I was only human. I had these desires, but for me, past early adolescence, they did not get *out of hand*. My mind dominated them, made them know their place and know who was master. Yes, I certainly was the sort of person who could help these offenders on the road back to social control and appropriateness. Not that they need be conformists, mind you, I was too sharp a therapist for that. But they could be individuals in their own right, within the limits of the social system. They could come to have confidence in the rightness of their judgment, in the acceptability of their behavior, even as I myself had. I had rescued myself from my own adolescent journey toward oblivion, and now I would rescue others. Of course, one could not expect miracles. These men came, no doubt, from corrupt and pathological backgrounds and there were limits to what they might be expected to achieve, even with expert help. Yet they certainly could be helped to avoid ever having to repeat their criminal acts. As their therapist, I would have to deal first with their deep sense of guilt, but, all in due time.

By way of experiment, I allowed my fantasies to take me off into *their* world. What crime might I imagine myself capable of committing that could lead to my own imprisonment? Certainly not armed robbery. Murder? Never! A sex crime, perhaps. After all, sex offenders were to be my special area of interest. Let's see. Homosexuality of course, could be ruled out. And certainly I could never do anything as brutal as becoming sexually involved with a child. And the thought of publicly exposing my genitals was too embarrassing, and undignified as well.

Rape! What about rape? Now *that* was more like it! Probably unconsciously over-determined too, since I'd noticed that the title "therapist" can be broken down into the two words, *"the rapist."* Yes, that was it. Rape, the very thing. A crime any man might commit under proper conditions.

So far so good. This was getting easier all the time. I was already thinking my way into their world, and this was just my first day.

Now, the next step. What would it be like to be locked up with such men? This afternoon I had only looked *into* the cells, but not *out from* any of them. I closed my eyes tightly and envisioned myself seated on an unyielding cell cot. The shadows of the bars divided the tiny, bare room into countless bands of light and shadow. I immediately felt the closeness of the walls. But I simply could not expand this smaller-than-life cell in my fantasy. If anything, it crowded in on me more and more stiflingly.

And then, as I again tried to look out through the bars, the front of the cell became crowded with the surly, taunting, sinister faces . . .

My attention quickly returned to my supper. Better not to try to accomplish too much on this first day. Plenty of time for the rest. And, besides, I suddenly felt quite fatigued. It had been, after all, a long and arduous day.

In light of this, perhaps it would be best to drive back to the Institution as soon as I finished eating. That way I could get the groundskeeper to show me to my room before he started his rounds. I could read a bit and then get a good long night's sleep. Yes, an excellent plan. I was feeling better already.

Arriving back at the Institution, I was mildly annoyed to learn that my temporary quarters were in the attendant's wing of the Building for the Criminally Insane. True, this section was locked off from the part of the building in which the inmates were housed. Still, it seemed an uncalled-for imposition, even for temporary quarters. For just a moment, I regretted my impatience in not delaying my arrival until my apartment in the staff's building was available.

Oh, well. What I needed at the moment was privacy and a place to sleep. I'd almost begun to feel like myself again by the time the off-duty attendant showed me to an unoccupied room and hoped tnat I'd be comfortable there.

Thanking the anonymous man in white, I stepped into the bare, gray room, blinking my eyes against the harsh glare of the single naked bulb overhead. My belongings had been piled on the mirrorless, metal institutional dresser. It was as unattractive as the other two pieces of furniture, the heavy, wooden armless chair, and the uninviting metal, cotlike bed.

I changed quickly into my tailored pajamas and argyle slipper socks. There, that was more comfortable. Lowering myself gingerly onto the uncomfortable squeaky bed, I could almost feel the net of rusted springs pushing through the lumpy two-inch mattress. Lord, the furnishings were as inadequate as those with which the inmates had to contend. How did the attendants put up with it? Perhaps they were permitted to make the rooms more homey. As is, no picture graced its walls. No rug softened its gray stone floor. Only the bars were absent.

Hurriedly, I picked up my well-thumbed copy of the mammoth volume which I always kept at my bedside, much as other men kept their Bible. Mine was titled, *The Psychoanalytic Theory of Neurosis.* Turning quickly to the index, I made careful notes on the page references under the categories of criminal behavior, robbery, homicide, sexual deviations and the like, and their relations to superego-id conflicts, the Oedipal Complex, and other reassuringly familiar realities.

But as I tried to understand my new patients in these terms, I found myself too uneasy and distractible to concentrate. The room seemed very bare and unappealing, and what is more, I suddenly became aware of how terribly, terribly small and cramped it was, as if crowding in on me. Strange, I had never before in my life suffered from claustrophobia. I decided to make a note of this phenomenon for future self-analysis.

However, for the moment it was clear that my best bet would be to get some of that much-needed rest. I had to be fresh and clear-minded in the morning if I was to do my best with the Medical Superintendent and other important figures to whom my supervisor would be introducing me. After some sleep, I would be fully prepared. No sense putting myself at a disadvantage because of fatigue.

With a final effort, I pushed away all the shadows of vaguely disturbing thoughts which threatened my complete and ready relaxation into restorative rest. Reaching up, I pulled the string which turned off the unpleasantly bright light. I closed my eyes wearily, sank back against the unyielding mattress, and let myself down into the comforting pool of deep sleep. But, quite atypically, I did not immediately begin to sleep what I usually half kiddingly alluded to as "the well-deserved sleep of the innocent."

Something tugged intermittently at my eyelids, refusing to let them rest, to allow retreat into the deep soft darkness behind them. On first reopening my eyes, I could not tell at once what it was that was bothering me. Only gradually did I become conscious of the beam of light which slowly crossed and recrossed the single, small, high window of my room, casting diffuse but disturbing light through the shadowy depths of the cubicle.

Leaping from my bed, I hurried to the window and looked out onto what unexpectedly turned out to be the empty maximum security yard in which the inmates took their daily recreation. From towers in two corners of the high three-foot thick wall which bordered the yard, enormous searchlights criss-crossed their beams, as if to ferret out any inmate who might be trying to escape. It was the light from these beams which had disturbed my sleep. Now, wide awake, I could imagine the cold-eyed tower guard, crouched over some heavy caliber, lethal weapon, with the safety catch off.

It was to be a week of long and difficult nights, filled with disturbing dreams. But somehow, I could never quite remember them as I hurried out of the room very early each morning.

I could think of myself as being "good," but I knew no peace. Some of the troubled view themselves as being good, others as being bad. Each trip has its own high price. The bad become patients. The good sometimes become therapists.

Ironically, for some such troubled souls, group therapy is a less pressured setting for the beginnings of personal transparency and change than is the more demanding one-to-one confrontation of individual therapy. In the individual setting the patient bears at least half of the responsibility for what happens during each hour. In the group, he is one of eight other patients and may gain time and strength and encouragement by sitting back in quiet trembling while the psychological space is filled by those patients who early demand attention as a way of distracting themselves from their loneliness.

No matter what support the group provides, there are, of course, false starts and discreditings of whatever is accomplished. I remember when many years ago I began running an institutionalized group of male sex offenders. Early on in our coming together there was a mock sense of instant-community born of the newfound hopes of each of these social pariahs. Till then, each had led a secret, shameful life of perverse, offensive compulsive acting out. Each was isolated by his terrible and dangerous secret, a secret which was guilty and exciting, a hidden piece of himself which he masked from all others for many years.

Now as they came together as prisoner/patients in a State Building for the Criminally Insane, the first thing they shared was a self-serving confession of secret crimes. I was too young, unseasoned, and self-important to realize that producing such credentials was easier for each of them than letting himself be personally known, committed and vulnerable. After all, they already all knew it was a sex-offender treatment program. They needed only to make sure that they could tailor a mitigated somehow justifiable confession of homosexuality, rape, child-molesting, exhibitionism, incest, or the like. Yet out of that *appearance* of openness, quickly came a mock sense of belonging, of mutual trust and respect. I so much wanted this sort of "progress" to occur that I closed my eyes to its shallowness. My way of making myself known was after all just as inauthentic and devious as any of theirs. Rather than reveal myself as another struggling human being, I displayed an appearance of expertness. It all came to a short-lived success as we exploited each others' fears and vanities.

My own professional status was actually that of a trainee, but I had masked that as well as I could, especially from myself. The older therapist with whom I ran the group was amusedly tolerant of my self-importance. When he told me that he would be out sick for a couple of weeks, he gave me every opportunity to cancel the group sessions in his absence. Feeling patronized by his support, I stubbornly insisted that I could handle the situation. Surely he was wrong in believing that the group had not yet jelled. He decided to let me learn for myself; curse/bless him.

On my way to my first solo group session, I was distracted by the unwanted epiphany of an inmate message-runner who always managed to get under my skin. The runner swaggered down the institutional hall with all the arrogance of the hipster, he who is with it, while most of the rest of the world is not. As he drew near, the sing-song of his simple greeting, as always, disrupted any calming confidence and concentration which I had mustered and on which I was prepared to rest. The runner's never-changing salutation, offered with a taunting drawl, was, "Hey, man, what do you know...*for sure?*" I grimly nodded a reluctant greeting, muttering silently to myself, "Bastard."

At that point I knew I would never remember how the last group therapy session had ended. I comforted myself by remembering one of the advantages of being a psychotherapist. I could make it the patients' responsibility to remember what had gone before. And, in any case, it was just as likely that someone would begin on a new topic, or reopen an older one. I would have a chance to recall the last session if someone brought up related material. When I did not push myself, I usually found that earlier described feelings and experiences of patients, which related to what was going on, flowed into my mind as if by magic. Some powers are best accepted, I thought, lest they disappear in the face of scrutiny.

I realized that my preoccupation with my own thoughts had made me start involuntarily as each of the series of heavy metal doors clanged closed behind me. Although Tier Nine was on the third floor, I had a sense of descending more and more deeply into the bowels of the earth.

At last I arrived. Finding my place among the already-seated men of the group, I sensed some underplay of unfitting feelings on the seriously set faces. No doubt, they were uncertain as to the older therapist's whereabouts, and this was reflected in their subtly mixed facial expressions. I felt that I should begin by allaying their anxiety.

"Good morning, men," I began slowly. "I'm afraid the other therapist is out sick. But, no need to worry. It's nothing serious. Just an old fashioned case of . . . "

"Yeah, we know," Ross broke in, "measles." Ross always seemed to be the *real* group leader. His interruption threw me completely off stride.

Again, the inmate grapevine allowed them to know things they could not possibly know. But at least they would not know how I felt, if only I could hide my doubts. To the men, I said, "Well, no need for things to be any different just because he is out sick for a few days. Let's begin the session."

In the past, I had sat through the periods of silence with which therapy sessions often begin, and done so quite patiently. But never before had the quiet seemed so long, nor so ominous. I decided that I would just have to wait it out. And so, I waited, silently searching the men's faces for a lead, a clue, some way of knowing what lay behind their eyes. I waited a long, long time, it seemed, but when I surreptitiously glanced at my watch, only a scant few minutes had passed.

All at once I understood. They didn't know if they could

depend on me. They were afraid I was too young, too inexperienced, unready to take over. At least *that* was a problem I could solve. I would interpret their feelings, especially the unconscious ones. Repressed impulses always made for the greatest resistance.

"I know what the trouble is, men," I began brightly. In my own ears, my voice seemed to echo inanely through the empty silence of the stone corridor. Nonetheless, I went on. "The other doctor has been a kind of father substitute for all of you in therapy, and so, naturally, you feel that no one can replace him."

More silence. The men neither moved nor spoke. They just sat, and stared. For a moment I thought I saw a trace of a smile on some of the men.

"What I mean is," I went on hurriedly after a few moments, "that when you were children, each of you idealized his father. Though you feared him, you identified with him. Now, all of those feelings have been transferred on to him. Do you see what I mean?"

Still no response. And then, from Ross, with mock seriousness, "No, *Doctor. You* tell *us* what you mean."

"Oh, I get it. You *resent* my taking his place. Is that it? Well, I can accept that. Why don't you just tell me how you feel. After all, it's O.K. to say whatever you want to here." Then I sat back, sure that I was on the right track at last.

"Bull-shit," Tommy said flatly. He always talked straight when he was mad.

"That's it, that's it. Go on," I encouraged.

"Just bull-shit, that's all."

This was still not going right. "How about the rest of you?" I asked, "You resent me, don't you?"

The other men spoke to Ross rather than to me.

"Tell him, Ross."

"Yeah, go ahead."

"Tell the Doc."

"Go, man."

"Well, now," Ross began, drawing himself up and speaking

with increasing confidence. "I guess I've been appointed spokesman. We don't want to turn this into a gripe session, but we do have a bitch to pitch. And we want to know what *you're* going to do about it."

"It's how you feel about my taking over, isn't it?" I said knowingly.

"No, man. It's how we feel about Red," Ross contradicted. He pointed toward the uneasy-looking red-headed patient who was a recent addition to the group.

Ross went on. "And our feelings about Red ain't repressed, and they ain't unconscious. We want to replace *him* with somebody else ... *anybody* else. And I don't mean my father."

I was bewildered, and the men knew it. "Well ... uh ... uh ... tell me about your feelings?" I stumbled weakly.

"He's a rat," Tommy threw at him, " and we don't like rats."

"Yeah, yeah. Tell him." the other men catcalled.

Ross took over again, obviously enjoying the role. "We got a rule in group, Doc. If you'd been a shrink long enough, you'da known it. 'What goes on in group, stays in group.' And if a guy wants to stay in group, he don't go shooting off his big fucking mouth all over the yard." Then, he turned on Red. "You get that, you red-headed rat?"

"Now you just wait a minute," I pleaded. But I felt that the session's course had already been irrevocably set.

Red was obviously becoming more and more frightened as this went on, but he was determined to defend himself if he could. "Yeah, wait a God-damned minute, you guys. I got as much right to be here as the rest of you. I committed a sex offense too, you know."

"Yeah, you *had* a right to be here," Don said slowly, "but you gave that right up when you sold us out."

"I didn't do anything to anybody," Red protested. "Who said I did? Whoever it was, he's a God-damned liar."

"Oh, yeah," said Ross, taking over once more. "Well, if he's a liar, so are the other six guys who knew what went on last session. I have a list of names and the evidence right here on this paper." He reached into his shirt pocket.

Red tried another tack. "O.K., O.K. So I said something. Everybody's entitled to one mistake."

"He's got a point there," I offered weakly.

"Over-ruled," Ross pontificated. "He's been warned before."

"That's the Gospel," Charlie called out. "I told him myself when I caught him ratting in the yard after his first session."

"So what?" Red broke in. "What's the diff' who knows? You all made the papers when you got busted."

"Yeah, we made the papers," Ross threw back angrily. "That was enough hurt to us and shame to our families. Why should we go through it again? The other guys in the Building know we're in for sex crimes but they *don't* have to know any more than that."

Red was ready for that one. "Ah, you're just touchy because you're a queer and these guys might want a piece of your ass."

"At least that's better than being a baby-fucker," Ross spat at him.

"Cut that out. You just cut that out," Red answered, his face flushing. "I'm in for Carnal Knowledge of a Minor. That's all."

"Baby-fucker, baby-fucker, baby-fucker," Ross taunted. Some of the other men joined in the catcalling.

I had finally had enough. Now it was make or break. "Now, you guys are all being defensive," I commanded. "Insulting each other isn't going to accomplish a thing. You wanted me to help. Now, let's see if I can straighten this out."

"You can straighten it out all right," Ross cut in. "Just drop this rat out of group."

"Yeah, yeah," echoed the other men.

"Now, wait a minute. I want you to stop." I was shouting now, all vestige of composure gone.

"We took it to a vote. He goes out, and that's that," Ross interrupted with finality.

I couldn't let this happen. Groups such as this one had been a going concern for years under the older therapist's direction. I couldn't let it be shattered now. I *had* to remain in charge. "No that's not the way it is," I said as firmly as I could.

"Yeah," Red chimed in, at just the wrong moment. "and there's not a damn thing you guys can do about it."

That tore it. At Ross' signal they were all on their feet, heading for Red with clenched fists.

I leaped from my chair to shield Red, but not before Ross had caught Red with a stinging slap to his already flushed face. I forced my way between the trembling red-head and the seven other angrily menacing group members. The men stumbled into me pushing my tie awry and messing my carefully combed hair. All of this was done as if by accident in their efforts to get to Red.

I felt weak and bewildered before their senseless cruelty. My voice betrayed my helplessness, even as I tried to find victory in defeat. "Men," I said wearily. They stopped to listen with obvious pleasure. "I've decided that it might be best to take Red out of group after all. But just for a while."

Red was silent and downcast, but the other men offered cheery sarcasm to each other.

"Yeah, he's a reasonable guy."

"He's in charge, you know."

"Yeah, and when he makes up his mind, he does what's best for everybody."

Finally, Ross said with great formality, "We all want to express our appreciation to you, Doc. And as you therapists say, 'I guess the hour's just about up; maybe we can discuss these feelings some more next session'."

The men trooped out, horsing around and laughing loudly to each other. Red and I were the only ones left on the Tier.

"I'm sorry, Red," I said softly, "truly sorry."

"Yeah, well, I guess we're *both* pretty new at this game, Doc."

When the older therapist returned, he heard me out, shook his head slowly with the closed eyes and wry smile of a father faced with the mess made by a loved son trying too soon to play at being daddy. The other patients did not seem surprised when the older therapist had Red rejoin the group. It was awhile before they talked over what they had been up to, and even longer before I was able to understand how I had invited the confrontation.

I had been so anxious to feel competent, helpful and in charge that I had quickly bought their simulation of community. But the mere fact that they were all sex offenders was *not* what they had in common as human beings. In fact, it turned out that beneath their good will and community as perverts was each man's deciding that at least *he* was not as low a form of offender as some other group member with whom he had chosen to compare himself. And I myself was perhaps the worst pervert of all. It took time and pain for me to learn that I could not encourage community without committing the participation of my own vulnerable self to the others. The therapist who sets himself above his patients is no therapist. The therapist who does not see that he is merely the most experienced patient in the group has no group.

Much of the time now (although not always) I am in a different place with my patients than the brash, under-ripe therapist I once was. Ironically, a recent experience of the human community of those fortunate strangers who make up a therapy group was again precipitated by the temporary absence of a co-therapist. For a number of years, following my training, I chose to run groups by myself. Now I never work alone in a group. During the tough times when the group is defining itself over against the person of therapist (whether adoringly or belligerently) I want someone else there whom I can count on, someone who really loves me. Though this becomes less often important as I become a participating member of the group, my co-therapist remains a visible emblem of my loneliness and my dependency, a sign that no one of us stands completely alone.

This group evolved in a private practice setting, the first months having been spent in the patients trying to get some relief from their pain while jockeying for favored positions with the therapists. My co-therapist, Barbara, and I were running a group together for the first time, trying to see if we could translate the affection of our friendship into those reciprocities of risk and competence necessary to doing such therapeutic work in concert. We related alternately to individual members of the group, to each other, and to the group process, sometimes wisely and well, sometimes with only fumbling good intentions. All in all, the experience was often fun, our efforts gave promise and the waiting for results seemed worthwhile.

The session that Barbara missed was a lively one. Like Daddy and the children alone in the house with Momma away on a long shopping trip, we all played more raucously than usual, sometimes hurting each other unintentionally in our new-found joyful roughness, but mainly sharing a noisy closeness free of our usual constraints. Only Laurie seemed disturbingly uneasy, uncharacteristically brittle, and irritably ready to argue with any man in the group. Laurie was a bright, articulate, sensually lovely woman in her thirties, unhappy over the failure of her marriage, and chronically deprecating of her worth as a human being. She could not say what was wrong, but seemed distinctly relieved when Barbara returned the next session.

Laurie had hinted at some dark secret in her past. The group was sympathetic about her burden, but no one pushed her. She had asked for help with her "stuck feelings" toward her mother, and I had earlier suggested that she write a letter to mother, a letter she need not ever send. Laurie had stalled, and we had all gone on to other things. Then one day shortly after Barbara's absence, Laurie came to tell us that the session had been an ordeal of panic for her, one which had plummetted her back into the self-torture arising out of her own mother's unavailability to her. And so, she decided to write her letter, to come and read it to the group, to reveal her terrible secret.

She began to read with a show of strength born of counter-phobic bravado, but the wailing undertone of her voice broke through so clearly, that the rest of us listened with the palpably open silence of one person's respect for another's pain. The letter began:

Dear Mother,

Let me begin by thanking you for all the shit you gave me--gave me under the guise of love.

I'll begin at a time long before I understood what love was about, at a time I desperately needed love, and a time you felt desperate about grandma's death. The despair you experienced became my despair, but we never worked it out. Looking back in time, I see that my brother Warren was equally affected by your emotional absence. You needed someone, and so did we. So we found each other. For years, starting out at age five, I existed to satisfy Warren's pleasure. In return, I received attention, pleasure, comfort . . .

The price I paid was enormous . . . Living in a secret world . . . Breaking the secret taboos. "Thou shalt not make love with thy brother . . ." You thought I was such a good kid.

All I wanted from you was to be taken care of. You said to me when I was five: "Take care of yourself."

Over and over again, your actions and words reinforced the notion that women existed to please men . . . that we had no right to feel . . . but yet we had to understand how a man felt. I had no privileges as a human being. My only privilege was existing for a man.

So I fulfilled your dream beyond your expectations, but you never knew. While in junior high and high school, I was attractive and had lots of friends. I was a good kid, for I was getting my kicks with Warren.

I have wondered how I could maintain my relationship with Warren, and never tell you. I realize now that my relationship with you is a myth that I created in order to survive.

You always worked hard, helping out at daddy's store, cooking and shopping . . . I interpreted all your hard work as love. I needed your love so much I refused to acknowledge that you gave me so little. If more was given to my brothers, Allen and Warren, I accepted that, for I was a girl. But you loved only Allen.

When I was younger, I tried so hard in school and at home to get some attention for doing outstanding work. But you lived by old superstitious rule: "To compliment a child will bring down the wrath of God." Your other rule was, "Never kiss a child unless she is sleeping."

At this point Laurie broke off. Her bitterness and vengefulness was not sufficient to suppress the underlying helplessness and guilt. Some members of the group began to respond by sympathetically supporting her resentment. Laurie begged them to first listen to all of her painful guilt about her sexual hunger. She and her brother had continued their sexual relationship for a dozen secret years. And then, a few years later, Warren died, leaving Laurie to live alone with her shame. She began to read fragments from the yellowing pages of a diary, scrawled in tortured solitude during her college years:

Tonight I hate myself--that is what I discovered. If I cannot change this year, I will hate myself forever. Laurie, you must live with yourself. You must learn to love yourself . . . or at least learn to tolerate yourself. What are the traits you hate? Rid yourself of them now. Wash your body clean. Open your soul and heart to sweetness and brightness. You can mend yourself. You asked for love. Well give it to yourself . . . You can make yourself into the person you want to be. You can create this woman from this young girl. Teach her. Show her. Punish her. Mold her. Then you'll love her . . .

You know, Laurie, the traits we want to rid you of. It is not so much ridding yourself of the trait as learning one important characteristic . . . you must learn CONTROL. To control your mind, wants, habits, desires. You must do what is best for you rather than what you prefer. Accept responsibility! Carry out your plans!

Control your base desires and you'll rid yourself of them . . . it is simple. Like cutting a cake. Like saying "No" to a boy. You can control your base desires and emotions with others but fail with yourself. But spring is here. Tomorrow is a new day and I am a new woman. Thank you. I might love you after all.

Goodnight. I'll study hard. I'll get high marks next term. I'll read--and visit museums--and you dear book will hold the secrets to my life. You and I will walk with our heads high, our feet firm, our shoulders squared, facing ourselves as we face the world. We will build a wonderful woman. Thank you God for awakening me before it was too late. To prove my worth to you--as well as to myself--I'll build that woman: an Eve, a Ruth, a Rachel. A woman who loves herself, not because she is Laurie but because she possesses the traits, the strength, the character she envies in others, she respects in others. She - I - Laurie = Woman = Ideal. Goodnight. No more will be said against her. There will be no need.

She sobbed out the old pain. We could all feel that curious amalgam of familiar adolescent romantic strife, made heavy by the sense of personal shame which only Laurie bore. Members of the group thanked Laurie for sharing so much of herself, offered comfort for her sorrow, told her that they loved her. It was left to me to tell her *how glad I was* that she had been wise enough to have sex with her brother through all of those empty early years. At first she could not believe that she had heard me right. The group met my statement with appalled silence, tempered only by the hope that I could be trusted. I told Laurie that though her relationship with her brother was obviously a conflict-heavy source of lingering pain, it was also a desperate reaching out for love. Her secret struggle was a kind of dark self-affirming vitality through which the best of her had survived.

My own old pain was evident as I told her of my own demonic struggle against despair. As a child, it was made clear to me that I was bad. Even in the womb, I had given pain to my mother, and anguish to my father. Once born, I was nothing but trouble. If not for me surely, my good parents would have been happy. There seemed to be nothing that I could do or say which did not hurt them.

I was desperate to learn to be good like all the other children. I watched them and tried to do what they did, so that I too might learn to please. Seeing this, my parents would say, "See how hard he tries to be good, that bad boy." By the time I reached adolescence, I gave up. It seemed that the only thing I really knew how to do was to be bad. And so, with vengeance, I got to be really good at being bad. I gave up passively finding myself in trouble, and began actively to pursue the evil urge. My flowers of evil blossomed in the fertile demi-monde of drug addicts, fighting gangs, prostitutes, pimps, and hustlers. I narrowly missed the abyss of heroin, prison, and death by violence.

Laurie began to see that we were much alike. I reminded her that when I first met her I was drawn to her by her compelling seductiveness. It was her bridge to relationship. I was grateful that she had kept this longing for contact alive in her. Other group members recognized my own demonic residuals, my toughness, outrageousness, irreverence. It had been their bridge to being with me.

Others joined our confessional communion. Ray told of his secret homosexual degradation. Others could see how it was that his stubborn seeking of humiliation had given me the first promise of his strength. The best of him was turned in on itself, vitality without an object. How fortunate that he had found his shameful assignations, rather than let that spark of life go out.

Phyllis had survived her heart-breaking loneliness first by a pietistic immersion in a Southern Fundamentalist church, then by an impulsive ill-starred marriage to a stranger, and finally by becoming the most promiscuously available belle in the stifling small town in which she was trapped. We all agreed that she was one of us. Only her religiosity seemed more sinful than our delinquencies.

We were all painfully human, all glad to have survived, each a bit less lonely for being with each other. God pity those poor lost souls who had chosen to let the fire in them die rather than feed it as satanically as we all had. This community of sinners burned with a black fire. If we had not shed light, at least we had kept warm enough to survive. And now we no longer had to feel so ashamed and alone for having yielded to our human longing for love.

Chapter Six

THE TUNNEL AT THE END
OF THE LIGHT

Of all the forces of darkness, surely death is the darkest. And now I would speak of that dark force of death, of my own death, of the death of loved ones, and of enemies. I would speak of my death, and of yours.

The Tarot image of this darkest of all the archetypes is the mysterious black-armored, skull-faced horseman on the Death card. Everyone is equally powerless before the inevitable onslaught of this dark rider. Upright, this Tarot card promises destruction followed by transformation and renewal. Dealt in the reversed position, it bodes only unchanging stagnation.

When I began writing this book perhaps one year ago I did not know that I was soon to die. I had three years ago undergone brain surgery for an acoustic neuroma during the writing of my first book.[1] I have written earlier of the pain and terror of that ordeal. The operation left me deaf in one ear, burdened with daily headaches as a result of the scar tissue, and subject to unpredictable losses of balance, compensated only at the cost of loss of stamina and excessive fatigue. And too, because the surgeon was not able to remove all of the tumor without killing me, I faced uncertainty as to my future. Would the tumor grow again? Would I face further surgery? Would there be more pain and handicap? Might I even die?

My apprehension and anguish about these matters will be evident to those who have read my words. Again and again my preoccupation with these awful experiences and about my uncertain future occurs gratuitously and redundantly throughout my writing.

When I first began this present book, its working title was *Patterns: The Guiding Myths.* I had read and been influenced by the Jungian literature in recent years and hoped to share that perspective with my readers in my characteristic style of story-telling and personal exposure. I intended to explore the value of dreams and myths in seeing the transpersonal patterns of our common humanity, despite our differing histories and personality patterns. It was to be a long hard look at the helplessness and hopefulness of being human.

Somewhere along the way, my sense of where I was going thrust toward the Forces of Darkness, the same materials of all-too-human yet transcendental patterns seen in a Jungian perspective, but with a heavier emphasis on turning unblinkingly toward the dark side, the shadow, the underbelly. I am sure now that this was given to me in part by the approach of, the immersion into, and the aftermath of my second bout of brain surgery in March of this year.

Soon after beginning the writing of this book I found myself frustratingly burdened with increased daily experiences of profound exhaustion. At first denying the implications of what I knew must be there, I attempted the superficial solutions of rearranging my schedule so that I could work less, indulging in daily naps, and even having a physician prescribe some chemical energizers to keep me awake.

The latter, of course, fucked up my head so badly that I quickly had to give them up. Finally, when I could no longer pretend to myself, I called my neurologist in Boston to tell him what was going on, hoping that he would say that I shouldn't worry, that it was merely some variation of the clinical syndrome of the aftermath of intercranial surgery. Instead he said I should come right up to Boston so that he could take a look. A brief examination led him to say that we would have to try some more exotic (his word for painful) diagnostic techniques. And so he scheduled me for a pneumo-encephalogram and an angiogram and suggested that just in case further surgery was needed we could schedule the operating room and the surgeons to be on hand after the diagnostic examinations. It was clear to me then that there would be no turning back.

The tests clearly showed that the tumor had grown again and that surgery was again necessary. Again the surgeon hoped to remove the tumor completely, and again after twelve hours of surgery he had to give up because part of the tumor was still so embedded in my brain-stem that I could not possibly survive its removal.

In some ways I got off easy. The psychotic aftermath was brief and more benign than my first experience, the handicaps no more extensive, and the daily fatigue considerably relieved. Unfortunately, what the surgeon had to tell me was that the tumor would certainly continue to grow and that I would now face surgery again every two to five years. Having been through two such operations I asked him how many more he thought I could possibly survive. He told me that he knew of one patient who had been through five such operations.

And so, now I know that further surgery is inevitable. I may well suffer an increase in chronic pains and handicaps in the process. I will have to pay for further years of life in the currency of ordeals of pain and terror. And it is clear that at some point, I will die during surgery. My life has been shortened and much of it is a bummer. But I am committed to getting all I can out of what I have left, to pay the costs as I must, to bitch as I need to, and to go on being as much of who I am as I can possibly manage. This book has clearly been reshaped in just these terms.

While still in the hospital I wrote a brief offering so that people who cared could know where I stood. I did it partly just to get myself together, to get beyond the post-surgical double vision and difficulty with hand-eye coordination. But mostly I did it to get my head and heart together. I titled this personal news note, The Whimperings of a Wounded Lion.[2] This is the way it went:

As I first began to think about writing these notes, I was uncertain as to my intent. However, I soon allowed myself to recognize that one reason that I am prolific is that I never write anything without some intention to publish. I've chosen the *A.A.P. Newsletter* this time because in a way this is simply a news note. By now I assume word of my ill health has gotten around through the grapevine of the patient/therapist/encounter group network which undergirds the formal professional communications media. It is my wish only to make things clear, both for the benefit of my own standing in the therapeutic community and out of concern for some worried others.

My brain tumor has grown large once more. I have undergone and survived another bout of neuro-surgery, another ordeal of pain, confusion, and terror. Fortunately, there have been no catastrophic consequences, but again it was not possible to remove the entire tumor, so far enmeshed has it become in my brain-stem. And so I get yet another reprieve on my life, though I must go on living with this time-bomb-with-no-clock in my head. The surgeon tells me it will surely grow again and again. It's rotten luck, but that's the way it is. Again the surgeon saved my life, as again my wife saved my spirit. But there is more. I have never been surprised when my writings and practices have touched off furor, consternation, and anxious dialogue, but this time I received many messages that let me know that I matter more in loving ways to more people than I dreamed was so. I am touched--overwhelmed-- though more grateful than comprehending. Many good vibes have strengthened my heart. They have come in the form of tears, thoughts, prayers, chanted mantras, offers to watch over those I love, even in one instance as an offer to guide me on a preparatory psychedelic trip.

Outside of my immediate personal contacts, I had informed no one except Don Lathrop and Vin Rosenthal. I told Don because he and I have always had the strange power to give each other the capacity to trust ourselves when we most needed it. Don, of course, offered to come and see me through the post-surgical psychotic reaction. I did not let him come but his offer gave me much to sustain me. I told Vin because I had been into supporting some of his lovely literary efforts and did not want to cop out without his understanding that I had to. He called me at the hospital and then sent me the poems which follow. I had been girding myself against my ordeal. The smilingly-helpful, straight-world of the hospital is not a place for me to be emotionally open. Here are Vin's lines:

As the sun rises,
I sit: not knowing whether
Spring will come this year.
(March 8, 1973 for Sheldon Kopp)

March rain--yet I know
Each drop brings us
 a moment
Farther from the snow.
(March 9--after talking with Shelly)

Only my wife, Marjorie, and my eighteen-year-old son, Jon, were in the room when I read these lines, and so I was free to cry. It was good.

I thank you all.

Shelly Kopp

I had been returned once more to the light of life but now it must be lived more clearly over against death's dark shadow.

This was not my first personal confrontation with the dark shadow of death. When my wife and I and our three sons moved to Washington at the beginning of 1961, we underwent a pivotal change in all of our lives. During the first three and a half years, first my wife's mother died and then my father and then her father and then my mother. It was like a series of hammer-blows to the head. At age 35, I suddenly felt like an orphan. Our prolonged grieving, our sense of being alone in the world, and the recognition of our own impending deaths, were all compounded by my wife's and my own independent decisions to give up contact with the remaining members of each of our own families after the deaths of our parents. Those other relationships had turned out to be more emotionally destructive than sustaining.

When my father was dying I was deeply pained but could not stay at his side to the end as I would have wished. He had developed acute leukemia and died within three weeks of the onset of obvious symptoms. He was confused by everyone's lying to him to the effect that he was merely suffering from a curable form of anemia. I talked to my mother about telling him that he was dying, but she felt that that was a bad idea. Since he was her man, I did not feel that I had a right to interfere. It was very painful to see his perplexity and confusion when in the terminal stages there was a blood seepage into his brain resulting in typically aphasic difficulty in word-finding and resultant frustrated outbursts of temper.

In a more lucid moment he called me to the bedside and asked me to explain to my mother that he really did not want to argue with her, but that he was having a terribly difficult time getting his words straight. I promised him that I would try to help make her understand and I did. Soon he was dead.

My father had been generous with everyone but himself. I remember how proud he was at age 58 when he finally bragged to me that he had bought two suits of clothes at one time, more than he absolutely needed. At 58, he had finally bought two suits. At 60 he was dead. I took the few thousand dollars that I eventually received as an inheritance from him and went out and bought a big new, red, air-conditioned Riviera automobile.

Two years later my mother also developed acute leukemia. I remember at the hospital that a resident stopped me in the hall and asked if I was indeed the son of a father who had died two years ago of acute leukemia and a mother who was now dying of acute leukemia. I said that I was. He said, "You have a very interesting genetic background." He looked frightened and confused when I told him to get away from me before I killed him.

The entire clan of aunts and uncles and cousins were at the hospital day after day. One of the things my family does well is conduct a death watch.

I was deeply pained to see my mother dying, to see her hurting and afraid, to anticipate my own loss. Curiously I found as well that I was upset that this should be happening at the beginning of the summer, realizing that it might ruin my vacation. It was enormously helpful to me to get beyond my guilt, to forgive myself for so humanly trivial a bit of self-concern.

My mother was having a very difficult time because she felt just awful and was very frightened while everyone was telling her that she was doing just fine. I spoke to the doctor, who was also an old family friend, and he advised strongly against telling my mother that she was dying. The family was outraged that I should even consider it. I decided it was up to me to choose and that with my father gone I needed only to check with my sister. I asked her what she wanted to do and with usual conviction and support she said, "You decide."

And so I went to my mother's hospital room and did one of the most difficult things I have ever done. She was complaining about how everyone was treating her. I told her that the trouble was that she didn't realize what everyone else knew, that she was dying. I knew that in her own way she had tried to live well and now I told her there was a chance for her to die well.

I guess she really knew, because all she said was, "Well maybe I can do it if you just tell me how long I have to go." I told her she had two or three days. We cried a lot and held each other.

Those three days were the best days of all the time my mother and I ever had together. She was straight and strong and beautiful. She called in each of the people that she loved, told them that she knew she was dying, and tried to get straight with them about what they meant to her and how much she would miss them.

At times it was tough for her. Not only the fear but the pain too was overwhelming. At one point she asked me to bring her some pills so that she could kill herself. I was torn, but I refused, asking her to live with her pain a bit longer so that I would not have to live for the rest of my life with my pain of having helped her to kill herself. She forgave me, but I don't know that I have yet forgiven myself.

The night of the day she died, the night before the funeral, I dreamed that I had come to visit one of my cousins, the one I like best of all my family. I visited her at a private mental hospital which symbolizes my familial compound. I came as a relative rather than as a therapist. As we walked around an inner courtyard, talking, she reached over as if to kiss me on the cheek. But instead she tore a piece out of my cheek with her teeth. It was then that I awoke and decided never to see the family again after the funeral. They had some things that I wanted but their destructive prices were too high. It's been almost ten years and I haven't seen any of them since then.

I still miss my mother and my father at times. The death of loved ones is a painful aching in the chest, sobbed out in fragments, in bits and in pieces. And just when you are sure that you've gotten it all settled once and for all, you turn an unexpected corner and run into another chunk of longing.

But the death of enemies is a far different matter. The death of an enemy is a time for celebration. I can still savor the delight of learning some years ago that a man who had spat out hateful words all of his life had died of cancer of the mouth. He was a destructively bigoted Southern Senator who had projected onto Blacks ("niggers" he called them) all of the attributes of himself which made up his own unexamined shadow. His death filled me with pleasure.

Facing my own death is so very different than witnessing anyone else's death. At times of pain and weariness, it offers some small promised comfort of relief at last. But too I spent many weeks crying, as if grieving my own death as the loss of someone I love. At times I have found myself intrigued and frightened by fantasies of life-after-death, but each time I give them up. Without knowing for sure, I know for sure that death will simply be the end of everything that is me. The greatest pain is in having to give up everyone and everything I love.

For a while beginning with my first operation, I struggled to deny my helplessness by trying to do something about the money so that I could take care of all of them even after I died. I suddenly realized that I had too little insurance and far less in savings. I struggled to rectify things only to be turned down as a bad risk by one insurance company after another. Finally one company offered to insure me on a high-risk policy which would cost a ridiculous amount of money to pay the premiums. Ignoring the fact that I would be setting myself to work too hard in the time that remains to me, I was seriously considering taking the policy. That night I dreamed I was building a Pyramid. I woke to realize that I was denying my mortality, and in so doing throwing away what life I had only to construct a posthumous memorial to my own greatness. Instructed by the dream, I recounted it and told my feelings to my wife and my sons, and informed them that I had decided *not* to take out the policy. They were beautifully loving in supporting the shadowy wisdom of my dreaming self.

Instead I try to face my helplessness and have turned myself as I can, toward enjoying life as it has been given to me, by being myself as much as I am able, and giving myself over to the pleasure of being with people I love and doing things that have meaning for me. I'll take what I can get and make of it what I can.

Many years ago I remember there appeared on the front page of the *New York Times* an article announcing the prediction by a number of astronomers that in several million years the earth would approach so close to the sun that all life on this planet would surely be destroyed. The item caught my interest and I discussed it with a number of people. To my amazement, many of the people to whom I related this prophecy reacted with despair, most often expressed by exclamations such as: "Then what the hell is the point in working so hard and trying to plan for the future!" So focussed were they on the final outcome, that the precious immediacy of each moment of their own particular lives had become obscured.

Sometime ago I began playing the Game of Epitaphs with my patients. So many of them seemed to be looking only toward outcomes that they were living out their lives in a style set up primarily to prove to others that they were good enough, or to prove to themselves that they could somehow win. Their anxiety about results sullied their enjoying the experience of who they were and what that felt like.

As a way of summing up in a terse but tellingly poignant way what that particular person might be missing, I would ask them what they would like to have as a final gravestone comment. The patient would then offer an epitaph and sometimes I would offer an alternative capsule memorial. Some of the epitaphs patients wrote for themselves were: "She took good care of others," "He never let anyone down," "At least she wasn't a burden," and "He never lost an argument."

At that time several years ago, when this graveyard game began, my own head had been into concern for recognizing that I myself was sufficient whether or not anyone else approved. Because of that, as my way of doing my job of showing patients that they had other options (whether or not they chose them for themselves), I would often offer my own chosen epitaph: *"He did his best."* Later on, as I learned to be easier on myself (and so on my patients as well), I amended my own final after-death description to: *"He did his best...when he could."* But since my recent immersion in confrontation with the imminence of the ending of my own life, even that seemingly self-accepting epitaph feels too rooted in results and effects to be a fitting capstone to my own brief but just right existence. Now, were I to bother to choose an epitaph, it would better be: *"He died as he lived...his own way."*

In the end, death comes to all men, as it is coming to me, and as it will surely come to you, putting a period to end each man's story. But to the extent that any man has become who he is, then he may die as he lived, being his own person, "And death shall have no dominion."[3] Just as with the way to live, the way to die is *your own way*.

Let me speak of one particular man's death by retelling the Hasidic tale of Bontche the Silent One.[4] At the time when Bontche quietly died many years ago in a small village in Poland, no one seemed to notice his passing. Who knew whether this simple, uncomplaining, unassuming man died of a work-weary broken back or a world-weary broken heart?

Quietly had he lived, and quietly did he die. All his life he had suffered his misfortunes in silence, gone his way in a barely noticeable manner of peace, humility, and hard work undertaken without complaint. When kindness toward others was a possibility, he gave freely but unobtrusively. When he himself was in need, he accepted help but never demanded it. He was silent in life and silent in death, speaking not a word against God, not a word against men.

And when he died, he was met at the Gates of Heaven by Abraham himself. Welcomed by an assemblage of angels, Bontche could not believe that their warmth and admiration were meant for him. They smiled and coaxed him insistently, until in silent bewilderment, he entered the Heavenly Court, fearful that his poor feet might sully or mar the perfect beauty of the gem-studded alabaster floor. It took a great deal of angelic urging and persuasion to convince Bontche that the Lord had indeed taken smiling notice of his silent self. And not only that, but God had issued a Divine Order that Bontche was to dwell in Heaven for all of Eternity and to be given anything and everything that he desired. Convinced at last, Bontche smiled and replied, "Well if that is to be so, could I have maybe a fresh roll and a glass of hot tea?" Hearing his wishes the angels looked down, a little ashamed.

The death of Bontche the Silent One is as touchingly unassuming as was his life, but even the cantankerous dying of a man who has lived cantankerously befits *that* man in his own particularity. That sullenly removed philosopher of history, Georg

Hegel, for example, died as he had lived, cantankerously:
…on the very point of death (surrounded by his disciples, he) only raised his head a little. 'I had one pupil who understood me,' he was heard to mutter; and while everyone present became alert to hear the venerated teacher pronounce the name, his head relaxed again to the pillow. 'One pupil,' he went on, 'who understood--and he misunderstood.' [5]

I myself am neither as sullenly removed as Hegel nor as unassuming as Bontche. I am no lofty abstract philosopher, nor could I ever be described as a humbly peaceful Silent One. I am deeply involved in intensely intimate relationships, a singer of songs, a teller of tales, and easily given over to fighting the good fight, caring more for the struggle than the outcome. Like Cyrano, when Death comes, I shall meet him in my own way:

Let the old fellow come now! He shall find me
On my feet---sword in hand---
…I can see him there---he grins---
…that skeleton
---What's that you say? Hopeless?---Why very well!---
But a man does not fight merely to win!
No---no---better to know one fights in vain!…
I knew you would overthrow me in the end--
No! I fight on! I fight on! I fight on. [6]

Surely I will be defeated by the Forces of Darkness. I want only to lose in *my own way,* being myself though beyond hope of victory, without concern for the results, but only because it is yet a last instance of *becoming who I am.*

Chapter Seven

THE KARMA OF PERSONALITY

Fairly early on in my work as a psychotherapist I came to agree with what I had learned from the writings of Carl Rogers about diagnosing patients. It is clear that to diagnose a troubled person who seeks my help means to confirm in my own mind and in my attitudes and behavior toward him that I am the doctor, the authority, and that he is the diseased medical case. Diagnosis of mental "illness" is at worst a form of social control, whereby the establishment is able to label people who express dissident (that is, power-threatening) opinions, and/or unusual (that is, anxiety-inducing) behavior. In the extreme, such diagnosing can lead to involuntary lifetime incarceration. In its milder forms it can at least stigmatize an individual in a way that turns him every way but loose in his attempts to make his way among other men.

In psychotherapy, diagnosis and labeling of symptoms put a judgmental barrier between the therapist and the patient. It accords the sense that the therapist is more powerful, wiser, and therefore also more responsible for the well being of the patient. It discourages the patient from exploring who he is without fear of criticism, evasion of being judged and consequent attempts to "improve." In making such judgments, the therapist is turned from the immediacy of his own spontaneous response as another struggling human being who would know and become known to that troubled pilgrim who is his patient.

I have learned to give up the clinical diagnosing of patients for which I had been trained. Occasionally I am still called upon to label a patient for the purposes of meeting the demands of the establishment which issues medical insurance. In this country some forms of emotional suffering are still viewed as medical problems.

This does offer to someone seeking psychotherapy the advantage of being able to get the government and the insurance companies to pay a part of his way. Therefore I participate in this hokum. My inclination at such points is to diagnose all of my patients as having "neurotic depression." My reason is that this is the psychodiagnostic category which comes closest to describing their real problem, that of personal unhappiness.

Despite my best intentions, I do, of course, judge my patients from time to time as I do everyone else whom I encounter, including myself. I believe that there *are* some ways in which conceiving of myself and other human beings as belonging to given behavioral and attitudinal categories helps me to bring temporary order to the chaos of human interactions.

Perhaps man is inherently a creature who forms concepts, or maybe we merely learn to categorize our experiences in order to simplify our lives and satisfy our appetites. I'm less interested in *why* I make judgments than I am in *how* they may help or hurt me. As a psychotherapist it sometimes seems genuinely useful for me to think of people as being of one sort or another, even at the risk of dehumanizing categorization, personal rigidity, and downright intellectual foolishness. And so it is when I talk about knowing myself and others I think sometimes in terms of personality types. These types at least lack the ennobling and pejorative connotations of diagnoses of mental health and mental illness.

Attempts to categorize people into types according to personality or temperament goes back to some of man's earliest efforts to understand human behavior. Aristotle attempted to describe human conduct in accordance with Hippocrates' fundamental categories first established four hundred years before the birth of Christ. Beginning with the conception that there were four basic essences (earth, air, fire, and water), the doctrine was extended to hold that four basic "humours" or liquids made up the body (blood, phlegm, black bile or melancholy, and yellow bile or choler). By the advent of medieval physiology, the temperaments held to be determined by the differing proportions of these bodily fluids came to be described as: *sanguine* ("quick, predisposed to pleasant emotion, but weak, and inclined to change quickly from one interest to another"), *phlegmatic* ("slow, lacking in vivacity, but calm and strong"), *melancholic* ("predisposed to sad emotions, slow and weak"), and *choleric* ("predisposed to anger, and emotionally quick and strong").[1]

Certainly there are some marked differences between the naive Aristotelian classification of human temperaments into four basic humours, and the later sophisticated Freudian categorization of human beings into neurotic characters, fixated at various levels of psychosexual development (oral, anal, phallic, and genital). But they have some things in common as well. Each of the many scientific, astrological, literary, aesthetic, and philosophical systems of categorizing people according to behavior, attitude, and personality is sometimes useful, often misleading, and ultimately fanciful.

At this point in my life, when my own attempts to understand myself and others lead to my categorizing people in comparable ways, I tend to describe them in terms of Jungian Psychological Types.[2] This system seems to me as good and as bad a set of metaphors as any of the other imaginative styles of categorization. Jung's theoretical model of psychological types sometimes makes the differences, difficulties and delights of dealing with other people more vivid for me. Perhaps it can for you as well.

Before describing this particular typology, I would like to examine some of the risks and advantanges of considering imposing *any* type theory of personality. Most dangerous, it seems to me, is the risk of dehumanizing people by pigeon-holing them into conceptual categories. We must be sure to look clearly at every uniquely individual human being, invoking a concept of type only as a guideline, never as a final definition of any man's immortal soul. Next, we must beware of the exaggerated purity of the types of personality established by any particular theoretical category. Each is no more than a conceptual abstraction from which any given real live human being will certainly vary.

Another caveat is that we must remember that all classifications are arbitrary, that is, that some other aspect of behavior could be used in its place. Jung himself, when describing his own behavioral criteria for classifying people, points out that "any general characteristic can be chosen as the basis."[3] And on the simple ground of compassion, we must be wary of type theory limiting the hope of change for any given individual. Yet as a therapist, I believe that each patient's only hope for improving his lot rests on his recognizing the true nature of his basic personality configuration, surrendering to it, and becoming who he is. More about that later.

There are, I believe, more obvious reasons for using a type theory of personality. No matter what our area of study, when confronted with a great number of cases, or pieces of data, or unhappy human lives, we *must* generalize in order to begin to understand. Some system of comparison, some set of referents or compass points are needed if we are not to be overwhelmed and finally lose our way. Personality types offer guidelines for beginning to comprehend the wide variety of attitudes and experiences among people. The categories which are chosen must reflect characteristics which everyone has, in differing proportions. The vividness of the extremes set out by the theory may help us to understand what we may expect from individuals showing different configurations of any particular personality functions.

Perhaps more important, if we have a sense of people having differing types of personalities, we are less likely to ask people to be what they are not. Type theory can help increase the acceptance of differences among people, facilitating our being able to see the other person's point of view. We may be able to see more clearly that many interpersonal problems are at heart simply a matter of differences in personality type, experience, expression, and orientation. At such times, neither party in a conflict need be judged wrong or right, healthy or neurotic, mature or immature. And in psychotherapy in particular, an understanding of psychological types helps the therapist to approach the patient in the patient's own terms, and to keep from setting up his own value system as a model for the patient.

For a type theory to be both fair and useful, it must depend on categories which do not imply better and worse sorts of people. It must be O.K. to find yourself in any one of the types described. There are as many acceptable ways to live as there are personality orientations. The evaluative question is not "What type is he?" but rather "How good is he at being himself?" However, because personality type also implies a way of viewing the world, there is no way to look at another human being totally without prejudice. And so my own descriptions should be read with questions in the reader's mind about my own biases. I'll try to help by disarming myself along the way, by describing what I see as my own personality type with its inherent advantages and disadvantages. To the extent that any particular reader can classify his own outlook and partial out my distortions, I believe he will find Jung's Psychological Types useful, fun, and freeing in dealing with other people.

The most basic difference in people's personalities that Jung describes is that of *Extroversion* versus *Introversion*. I would like to describe this dichotomy in some detail to compensate for the way in which the values of contemporary Western society have reduced and distorted these concepts to the vernacular sense of the *extrovert* being the successful, outgoing realist, while the *introvert* tends to be viewed as the peculiarly awkward bookworm. Like most persistent misconceptions these notions are perhaps most dangerous not because they are wholly false but rather because they just miss the mark.

Jung described these two types as being equally valid psychologically, and in fact as needing one another. He was more angered than he might have been by current prejudices because, like myself, Jung was an introvert. Extroversion and introversion are general modes of behavior, overall subjective views, and thorough-going life styles. Each orientation does, of course, have its shadow, and implies an underlying unconscious, compensatory underside of the opposite type which Jung calls the *inferior function*.

The balanced interplay of these polarities of personality (the superior and inferior functions) brings harmony to life, as visualized in the Tarot card of Temperance. Here the Archangel Michael is shown pouring life's essences from the silver chalice of the unconscious into the golden cup of consciousness. With one foot on the land, and the other on the waters, he brings together spirit and matter, tempering the one with the other. Dealt upright, this card discloses the promise of the successful combining of opposing forces. Reversed, it warns of discord and disunion, and hidden conflicts.

Before exploring such conflicts in depth, let us first begin with an unsullied view of separate polar personality funcions.

Extroversion is a mode of being, a personality orientation, a style of living in which the person's attention, interest, personal investment and responsiveness is directed primarily toward the experiences provided by the people, objects, and stimuli of his surrounding environment. He wants most to be a part of what is going on around him, to meet and to be met, to give importance to and to gain meaning from the world in which he lives. He is outer-directed, field-oriented, and group-influenced. At best he responds with warmth, optimism, and positive conviction to his surroundings with little interest in examining his own inner life and underlying motives. As a result he can be enthusiastically active, living empathetically through and with other people, a materialistically-oriented realist; a hail-fellow-well-met.

Even as a small child, the extrovert adapts quickly and easily to this world, shows great interest in those about him and in his impact on them. His rapid development has a confident, risk-taking air as he actively responds to objects, challenges, and other people.

In the adult, this general attitude of extroversion makes him open to being impressed by people and events, and anxious to make an impression on them as well. He is likely to have many social relationships, with adjustment and accommodation as his guidelines. Altruistic, prolific and community-oriented at his best, he may at his worst be superficial, compromised by fashion and public opinion, or pushy and meddlesome.

Introversion, in contrast, is a way of life centered around the individual's private inner life. The introvert is interested not in his surroundings, but at best, in his own personal response to the people, things and happenings in his life. Rather than join in, he retreats to the world within. His dislike of distracting hustle and bustle, his distrust of those about him, his subjective world-view seem to the extrovert a mark of the introvert's peculiarity and failure to adapt. How hard for his counterpart to understand that he merely finds the inside of his own head more interesting than the outside world.

I remember how poorly I fit in when first I worked as a staff psychologist at a large state mental hospital. It was easier for me to identify with the patients than with my colleagues. There was a pleasant snack bar on the grounds called "The Trading Post" to which we might go for a break in the day's work of stamping out mental illness. How often I entered and was invited to sit with the happy-to-be-together extroverted psychiatric residents or social workers, to join them in coffee and conversation. Almost as often, I refused, choosing to sit alone and drink my coffee instead, preferring my own thoughts and feelings to their company and amiable talk.

I have often felt or been made to feel uneasy about my shyness. For a long while it seemed peculiar that I did not like parties, small talk, acquaintances, or social responsibility. I experienced that guilt which is no more than the secret resentment of unwanted obligations. I was uncertain about wanting so much to do things in my own way, to be uninfluenced by those about me, to be so opposed to being moved by the way most people saw things, by the sound of martial music, by the sentiment of "Lassie" movies. For years, I experienced the needless pain of someone who thought he was an unsuccessful extrovert. My brusque manner put people off and the strange things I had to say were most often misunderstood. How much happier I am to recognize that I am no flawed extrovert, but rather a very satisfactory consummate introvert.

The problem began early, when as the typically introverted child, I was thoughtful and reflective, awkward in my slowly forthcoming dealings with my environment, and much into wanting to do it all by myself and in my own way. This made my parents anxious as I did not fit their extroverted ideals. Because they loved me and wanted me to be happy and satisfactory "like everybody else" they discouraged my inward turnings, and pressured me to wear the ill-fitting mask of an inadequate extrovert for years afterward. The mask was suffocating, unappealing to others, and terribly painful. It feels so good now to wear my naked face, even with its eyes turned inward. For me the real world is inside, and there is nothing wrong with that, my natural view, so long as I remember that for many other people, for "them," for the extroverts it is different. Yet despite my recognition of the equivalent reality of their external world, I am usually inclined to follow the admonition:

TRUST NO ONE BUT ONE'S FELLOW PARANOIDS [4]

Implied in this uneasiness are the dangers of introversion at its worst. While it can be a highly creative way to live one's life, to take one's own trip, to be deeply immersed in the private pleasures and spiritual highs of the private contemplative life, it can be a painfully isolated drag as well. The exotic flowering of paranoia may yield moments of smug self-satisfying superiority in exchange for its hyper-critical, pessimistic put-downs of those about it, but it is heavily burdensome to feel forever menaced, peculiarly unlike everyone else, and ever fearful of appearing ridiculous.

I know less about the burdens of extroversion when that posture is not working well. I suppose the hysterical pressure to respond, to have impact, to be with it, and the underlying dread of feeling helpless, of being ignored, of facing the inner loneliness must be the equivalent torture. Surely everyone's pain hurts as much in its own special way. One clear difference is in the timing. Introverts like me have a long hard time of it earlier in life when the emphasis is on making it with other people. I was sustained only by the hope that someday it would be different. For people like me the second half of life is easier and more rewarding, a time for spiritual turning toward the richness of my own soul, now that I have made my way and established my place in life. For extroverts it seems that they must find the more youthful climb and building of social relationships easier, only to founder on the issue of life too often seeming meaningless once the outside work is done. Yet, I am sure each of us would choose no other troubles than his own.

Jung points up *extroversion* and *introversion* as the two *basic types of general attitude,* and then goes on to explore their variations in the *personality functions* of *judging* and *perceiving.* The perceiving functions (which he misleadingly terms "irrational") are *sensation* which tells us what stimuli are offered up to us in experience, and *intuition* which puts us in touch with past and future implications of the meaning of what we can otherwise only perceive directly through sensation. By way of the concrete perception of objects, people and events, sensations tell us *what is,* while intuition seems to look beyond to tell us about *what is not* given directly to the senses.

The judging functions (which again Jung mislabels, this time as "rational") include *thinking* which makes evaluative ideational judgments about experiences, and *feeling* which expresses the emotional value of the happenings in our lives. Thus thinking tells us *what things mean* and feeling tells what *personal value* they have for us.

For a human being to manage well in all kinds of situations all four functions should be available to make their needed contribution:

Thinking should facilitate cognition and judgment, feeling should tell us how and to what extent a thing is important or unimportant for us, sensation should convey concrete reality to us through seeing, hearing, tasting, etc., and intuition should enable us to divine the hidden possibilities in the background, since these too belong to the complete picture of a given situation.[5]

But the point is exactly with these four functions (just as it is in the case of the two general attitudes) that in each person one or another function *predominates*. This imbalance is what leads to those different personality configurations which we call psychological types. So it is not only that each person is either more or less of an introvert or of an extrovert, but additionally he will be primarily a thinking type, or a feeling type, or a sensation type, or an intuitive type.

There is always an underside or shadow to personality functions. Those aspects of being human which are most unconscious have their most powerful impact just to the extent that anyone is unaware of them. This *inferior function,* [6] this repressed aspect of personality emerges under stress or when we are off-guard, expressing itself in the strangest, most unpredictably primitive, infantile, archaic and inappropriate ways.

The superior and inferior functions will always come from the polarities of the more critical pair of opposing functions (thinking and feeling, or sensation and intuition) while the other pair will serve as modifying or auxiliary functions.

If a given person is a thinking or feeling type, there will be a secondary or auxiliary development of the intuitive or sensation function. Should one of the perceiving functions predominate in another individual, one of the judging functions will serve as an auxiliary. In the interests of simplicity and communication, I will in the main omit any description of the variations brought about by auxiliary functions. Instead I will simply offer descriptions of introverted and extroverted examples of each predominant function. My emphasis will be on the major surface characteristics and on the shadow underlay of the inferior function.

A particular extrovert such as Richard Nixon will operate primarily in the thinking mode. We would label him as an Extroverted Thinking Type with a primitive sense of right and wrong as the *inferior feeling function*. In Nixon's personality we can see a secondary mode of Extroverted Intuition (not unlike General Custer whose intuitive hunch playing and primitively impractical inferior sensation function resulted in his memorable "Last Stand").

The inferior function is by no means merely each man's individual sore-spot or personal brand of foolishness. To the extent that we come to know our shadow side, our wholeness as human beings can be dependent on the compensatory nature of that which is hidden from consciousness. What is lacking in consciousness may be found in the unconscious. That is why our dreams inform us so well when we understand them and upset us so much when we do not.

I will describe the eight basic psychological types and explore the dramatic implications of their inferior functions. In attempting to understand any particular human being in this regard, not only do the omitted auxiliary functions have to be taken into account, but in addition it would be necessary to assess the ways in which the live person varies from pure type. This system of types will certainly create as many problems as it solves. Any time we come to feel that we completely understand any important aspect of being human, we're making a big mistake. With these limitations in mind, I will go on to describe some of what personality variations are like from the Jungian standpoint.

1. EXTROVERTED SENSATION TYPE with *Inferior Introverted Intuition:*

At its worst, the Extroverted Sensation Type is a Nero or a Charles Manson, but such men are so extreme and rare as almost to be allegorical. Their coarseness, brutality, and decadence are corruptions of the active sensory appetites of less extreme examples.

At the lowest end of the profile are those who are simply solely concerned with objects and concrete facts, without any desire to dominate or exploit. These people range from the soulless engineer's down-to-earth, matter-of-fact, hyper-practical " I only know what I see" attitudes toward his intense interest in immediate experience on the one hand, to the highly developed gourmet and aesthete on the other. Oscar Wilde is an interesting example of the latter.

At best this type is a master at noticing details, has sensitively developed good taste, a zest for living and boundless energy. The dangers arise of course from his Inferior Introverted Intuitive function. Because this function is inferior and introverted and intuitive, under stress such people develop dark forebodings about themselves, and project wild jealous fantasies. They may then be reduced to peculiarly compulsive behavior as a defensive shadow counterpart to their surface easy-goingness. At his most disturbed, such a type will shift between outbursts of cruelty and inept attempts to regain control by manipulation of others, between morbid concerns of terrible things happening to his health and fortune, and compulsively frantic pleasure-seeking as a means of denying such eerie premonitions.

2. INTROVERTED SENSATION TYPE with *Inferior Extroverted Intuition.*

Most other people would describe the Introverted Sensation types as "the strange ones." They wander around as if in a trance (or simply looking dumb) but in reality they do not miss a thing that goes on around them. What is misleading to the outsider is that this type reacts very slowly and only in intensively subjective terms. It is somewhat like dropping a stone into an unexpectedly deep well. For a seemingly long while nothing happens, and then spookily up comes the delayed echo of a far-off impact, a strangely other-worldly response which is anything but the clean fast simple splash which was anticipated.

The responses of this type range from the delightfully original and creative to the almost bizarrely remote and unlikely. I ran into an example of the refreshingly creative sort this summer while on vacation on Martha's Vineyard Island. You will remember that the *extroverted sensation type* which I first described reacts to the call of the world of things about him, moved by the compelling demands of the environment, like the mountain climber who ascends to the peak "because it was there." But the Island farmer whom I came across this summer was, in contrast, an *introverted sensation type* whose distant drumming is only the subjective echo of an outside call. This fellow had planted a mile-long row of dramatically towering sunflowers on his land. Realizing that these plants would obviously produce far more sunflower seeds than he could possibly need for feeding his meager collection of livestock, I asked him why ever had he planted a mile of sunflowers. After a silent delay (I thought he hadn't heard me), he replied, "Because they weren't there!"

For such people, reality is what they see. While they readily pick up all of the subtleties around them, what they arbitrarily make of all this out of their own intense removed subjectivity is their only measure of the appropriateness of their responses. They are often surprised at anyone else's surprised reaction to their quite "natural" mythologically saintly or demonic responses.

Like his counterpart (the Extroverted Sensation Type), such a person too has dark forebodings, but unlike him, they are focused not on his own well-being, health and the like, but rather on possible menace from those about him. The result is paranoid suspiciousness under stress, weird hunches about what others are up to, morbid fantasies about everyone else's dangerous and destructive intent. This preoccupation is compulsively demanding often resulting in symptoms of exhaustion. His best protection against such turmoil is his somewhat zany, semi-whimsical viewing of the world as something of a comic charade.

3. EXTROVERTED INTUITIVE TYPE with *Inferior Introverted Sensation:*

Like General Custer, other extreme Extroverted Intuitive Types are often appealingly passionate, impulsive rascals who enliven any situation they come upon, wreak romantic havoc, and often come to a bad end. More moderate examples of such types lack such intense colorfulness but are also focused on their own intuitive hunches about external events. Their ability to see hidden possibilities and focus on the new and promising often makes them competent promoters, enthusiastic advance men, and sharp speculators.

Unfortunately for them, however, they are so easily bored by the familiar, grow so impatient to move on, that often they do not hang around long enough to reap what they have sown. People who depend on them sometimes end up feeling that they have been carried away by the false charisma of essentially irresponsible psychopaths. But often enough, this type lets other people down not because of evil intent, but because of the breakthrough of the unrealistically adventuresome spirit of their inferior function. Their introverted sensation is unconcerned with day-to-day practicality. As a result, under stress, in ventures that have almost mystical appeal for them, such types overlook their own physical needs and may literally work themselves to death.

Their orientation toward future possibilities leads them to overlook the hard facts of life. At best, this lends a dramatic fire which inspires courage in more timid types. At worst, like Custer, they march others off to foolhardy, needless self-destruction. With thinking and feeling function poorly developed, and realistically-oriented sensation repressed to the status of an inferior function, such types sometimes have little in the way of available resources against which to check their intuitive commitments. As a result, because of his ruthless sense of superiority over objects in his life, such a man may mislead himself into a compulsively stuck unsuitable relationship with a woman over whom he rides rough-shod without realizing it, and for whose responsive suffering he may be made to suffer for years. His self-neglect, on the other hand, may be unconsciously compensated by strange phobias and hypochondriacal ideas.

4. INTROVERTED INTUITIVE TYPE with *Inferior Extroverted Sensation:*

The Introverted Intuitive Types are entranced with the

possibilities of archetypal experiences which arise from deep within their own unconscious. They include mediums and mystics, prophets and poets, shamans, seers, and saviors. This clearly being my own psychological type, I find myself to be numbered among the Christs and the crackpots. It behooves you, the reader, to decide where I am to be found along this charismatic continuum.

It is not surprising that I am a deeply committed teller of tales, for one of our characteristics is that we feel compelled to communicate the travelogues of our own inner journeys. Our unconcern with the outer "reality" of facts leads us to be heedlessly embellishing of the truth, transforming our accounts in the service of some "higher" inner reality. Often I am asked by others whether or not I have made up some tale. I can only answer that everything I make up is absolutely true.

The compelling visions of the Introverted Intuitive Type are no mere fancies for him. They lend symbolic value to questions of how he is to live his own life, just as they invite charismatically fascinated discipleship from others. The subjective language of one crying in the wilderness tempts both the guru and his followers to make him bigger than life, to take him more than seriously. Such a personal power pivot is fraught with temptations to corruption. [7]

Another danger is, of course, the erratic emergence of the inferior extroverted sensation function. Intemperant instinctual excesses are the rule. Fortunately, I have gotten away with overeating and some hypochondriasis. As a youth experimenting with drug experiences I completely avoided ever trying heroin, intuitively knowing that I would have become a great stone junkie in a moment if I tried even one taste. The inferior function's compulsively-experienced sensations in this type easily over-ride the contradictory conscious avoidances, leading to ecstatic sensory experiences fully comparable to the mystical inner trips. Ironically, this gets turned around in some such types whose ascetic avoidance (fasting and the like) turn them toward an addiction to inner-space trance-like visions. Psychedelics are tempting bridges which mediate compulsive ties to both inner and outer objects.

It becomes clear from my description of these "irrational" perceiving function types (both extroverted and introverted sensation and intuition types), that the lurking dangers in their inferior functions are those of dark forebodings (among the sensation types) and reckless overlooking the hard facts of life (among the intuitives). In exploring the "rational" judging types (both extroverted and introverted thinking and feeling types), we will find that their destructive shadowy counterpart threatens rigid dogmatism (among the feeling types) and overwhelmingly negative moods (among the thinking types). For each type, functions that serve as creative resources when they are at their best, become thorny frailties when things go awry. Certainly it is true that "One's crown is also one's cross." [8] One part of becoming whole requires that each of us learn to recognize and accept the dangerous primitive potential of his own inferior function.

And now let us go on to consider the judging types in more descriptive detail:

5. EXTROVERTED FEELING TYPE with *Inferior Introverted Thinking:*

There is some temptation to classify men most frequently as thinking or sensation types, more often ascribing feeling and intuitive functions to women. This inclination seems loaded with potential unfairness, confounding foolishness, and the danger of supporting politically oppressive socially stereotyping myths. Even so, I feel that sexist prejudice (like other forms of bigotry) are most dangerous because they are half-truths. It would be easier to dispel them if they were completely false. Instead they are misleading distortions of observations rooted in a more benign observation of cultural differences.

In the Jungian literature, the Extroverted Feeling Type is most likely to be described as being predominant among women. At least let me describe this type and see if you can understand how women may often be pushed into this mold (whether or not it fits a given woman's basic psychological type).

The Extroverted Feeling Type is well-adjusted, easy to get along with, makes friends readily and places a high value on the love, appreciation, and approval which others may offer. This amiable type generates an atmosphere of agreeable acceptance and enjoys making other people happy. Independent thinking is avoided lest it turn out to be improper. While this type may seem a bit manipulatively theatrical, they are really quite genuine in the sacrifices they make for others, often with no more ulterior motive than the pursuit of their own positive feelings and the avoidance of underlying melancholy.

It is equally important to look for the excesses which bespeak of fraudulence and underlying unhappiness. In some such people we experience an abundance of expressed feeling but it lacks a personal quality, more a matter of exaggerated erratic mood swing than emotional fluidity. A stubborn avoidance of any attempt to think anything out is also often in evidence. And when the introverted thinking of the inferior function does emerge, this type's logic is most often aggravatingly negative and made up of overly-critical thoughts about whomever is engaged in the struggle, infantile, seemingly guided more by spite than by reason. Everything is dogmatically black or white, "nothing but" one thing or another. In combination with the hollow-sounding gushy feelings, this becomes classical hysteria at its most frustrating.

For such a feeling type, the only dependable self-protection comes of recognition and awareness of these usually unconscious negative thoughts. Otherwise, such people may be tempted to sell their souls in exchange for others' constantly reassuring approval, lest they have to contend with the sadness and rage which accompany their underlying repressed feelings of worthlessness and loss of hope.

6. INTRODUCTED FEELING TYPE with *Inferior Extroverted Thinking:*

This is the psychological type that I find it hardest to give a satisfactory account of, and I do *not* believe the fact that I am married to such a person is by any means the *only* reason for my difficulty in articulating an example of such inner intensity. It is of such people that others most often say "still waters run deep." These are quiet people, hard to understand because they reveal themselves only indirectly. The deep currents which move them are usually hidden. People around them are profoundly affected by the tone they set by their very subtle presence, but they themselves seem shy, inaccessible, and are rarely moved to explain what they are up to.

My wife is the soul of our family. The rest of us appear to carry on as though we were ignoring her standards and running things our own way, but it is really her powerful secret influence that sets the ethical and emotional tone within which we live. I shamanize aloud my trance-like metaphorical messages about what we all mean to each other, but her silent loyalty pervades and sustains without directly calling attention to itself. Rilke's wonderful line states most clearly where she stands. He once wrote: "I love you, but it's none of your business!"[9]   And when in my hunger for confirmation of my charisma, I demand more explicit statements of appreciation from one who already gives me so much in the way that she lives, she answers unperturbedly, "No, I give you enough; that would be like doing double-duty."

Such people at times fall victim to emergence of their Extroverted Thinking Inferior Function. The result is an obsessive involvement in the details of so many external facts that they are overwhelmed by too much material. Making lists helps, but only as a temporary hedge against a flood of confusion and depression. If this is not fended off with intermittent despotic bossiness and freeing outbursts of negative feeling, the result is a kind of emotional exhaustion.

As a self-proclaimed Shaman I am, of course, fascinated with the secret powers with which the spells are cast by such a "Who, me?" low visibility, notoriety-disclaiming sorceress. I am intensely aware of the moving enchantment of her hidden sacred commitments, of her unexposed poetic sensitivity, of her ambitious secret longings, but only of their silent impact, rarely of any explicitly stated content. It seems to be absolutely crucial to trust her without being able ever to know exactly what it is to which I am committed to surrendering.

7. EXTROVERTED THINKING TYPE with *Inferior Introverted Feeling:*

At his best, the Extroverted Thinking Type is a competent, realistic, clear-thinking organizer, who successfully grounds his convictions in objectively established standards. Such men are often high-powered administrators who have incorporated modern scientific method in their ambitious ventures. Their hard-driving exacting precision can be tempered by a theoretical commitment to social reform and a self-styled altruism.

Exaggerated postures of this sort in which feeling has been too successfully repressed result in more stubbornly aggressive ruthless tyranny in some, and more dry materialistic, pedantic, hyper-conventionality in others. In either case there is also the danger of hidden inferior function manifesting absolute feelings of being absolutely right, in the worst tradition of martinet who feels he is beyond criticism. In the service of their infantile sense of right and wrong, they do not shrink from any piece of brutality or deceit in attempting to defeat their enemies.

It seems clear enough that Richard Nixon constitutes an Extroverted Thinking Type. I suppose it would depend on where you stand politically as to how you would evaluate how much of his inferior function is showing.

8. INTROVERTED THINKING TYPE with *Inferior Extroverted Feeling:*

The Introverted Thinking Type also values ideas over emotions, but his attention is inner-directed and consequently results in more abstract, theoretical and analytic speculations, often of a highly original nature. Such people may be superficially polite but they are not really very much interested in involvement with other people, and so are often misunderstood or patronized. A benign example is the apocryphal tale that automobile drivers in Princeton always stopped their cars when they saw Einstein ambling absent-mindedly down the block, his head buried in a book, or lost in thought, knowing that he would cross a busy street without ever noticing just where he was.

The impractical, absent-minded professor appears to be a child-like misanthrope, fussy when distracted from his inner musings, and open only with intimate friends who share his intellectual interests. If his inferior extroverted feeling function is roused, he may display the crochety, emotional touchiness of the intellectual hermit, or he may form unlikely irrational positive attachments which have an almost mythological coloring. Examples come to mind such as Einstein's sense of his enchantment with Israel, Whitehead's love affair with a universe made up of friendly bits of throbbing consciousness, or the tragi-comic affair of the professor and cabaret vamp in the German film, "The Blue Angel."[10] In this film a middle-aged bachelor schoolmaster, gives up his life work to pursue the Marlene Dietrich floozy-enchantress, degrades himself to be with her, goes against all customary reasoning, and ends up a bedraggled clown in her cabaret entourage. Unwitting destructiveness to self and others is always a danger for such out-of-it abstracted types.

There are many fascinating permutations in any particular individual, depending not only on his given psychological type, but also on both his deviation from the pure type and secondary configuration brought about by which auxiliary functions predominate. And too, much of the conflict between people of basically different types (who are of course drawn to one another) can best be understood in these terms. Jung cites the example of when an Extroverted Thinking Type argues with an Introverted Thinking or Feeling Type. He points out that "A capital error regularly creeps in here, for instead of recognizing the difference in the premise one tries to demonstrate a fallacy in the conclusion."[11]

The advantages and disadvantages of such typological intermixes was recently described to be by a young woman who is an artist married to a psychiatrist. She is an Introverted Sensation

Type and he an Introverted Thinking Type. Their collisions have been occurring around the project of decorating a new home. She suggests unusual color schemes which often work out beautifully, though he goes along only reluctantly with annoyed protestation because there is no way she can explain them to him in advance. On the other hand, she would tend to be unrealistically extravagant in her home-furnishing purchases, except that she has become wise enough to pay attention to the instances when he is worrying about their finances. Instead of going off the deep end at such times, she has learned to respect his inner sense of order when it comes to financial planning. But, as she puts it, "I never know that it's time to worry until I see him worrying."

THE DEVIL .

Chapter Eight

WHAT EVIL LURKS
IN THE HEARTS OF MEN

And the soul,
if she is to know herself,
must look
into the soul:
the stranger and the enemy, we saw him in the mirror.[1]

"Beauty and the Beast"[2] is a lovely fairy-tale variant on the perennial human theme of the merging of opposites. Sometimes its message has been diluted to the shallow sentimentalization that "a true heart is better than either good looks or clever brains." But the intuitive response of my own dark soul tells me that its lasting truth has to do instead with each Innocent's need to lay claim to the Beast within himself.

Think back over the years to the time when you believed all the tales of wonder which you have since become too rational and mature to appreciate. Can you recall that Beauty was the youngest and most beautiful child of a once-very-rich merchant who had six children, three boys and three girls? The other daughters were vain, while Beauty was the innocent. While the other daughters sought husbands she thought herself too young to marry and instead chose to live devotedly with her father. When the merchant lost his fortune the family all had to go live in a small cottage in the country. Of all the children, only Beauty could accept her fate with humility and devotion. She worked hard without complaining while the others indulged themselves with breakfast in bed. When occasionally fortune treated them better, Beauty asked for nothing for herself while the others made all sorts of outrageous demands. When their father insisted that he wanted to bring something for

Beauty, she said she would be happy if only he would bring her a single rose.

On his way back from his journey the father had gotten presents for the children, but since it was midwinter he had difficulty in locating a rose for Beauty. Wandering through the dark night, cold and hungry, he came upon a great house. No one seemed to be at home. He entered, ate, and slept, hoping that the master of the house would forgive him. When he awoke late in the morning, he found a handsome new suit of clothes laid ready for him to replace his own torn, soiled garments. He thought he must be in the home of a good fairy who was taking care of him.

After breakfast he went out into the garden and took a bunch of roses to carry home to Beauty. Just then he heard a loud noise and saw a beast coming toward him, a beast so frightful to look at that he almost fainted with fear. The Beast was furious that the man had rewarded his hospitality by stealing his roses and told him that he would soon die for his transgression. The merchant begged for mercy, explaining why he would gather a rose for Beauty at any cost. The Beast told the merchant he would let him go if only the man would bring one of his daughters to replace him. If not, then the man must return in three months to be done in. The merchant pretended to accept the Beast's terms so that he could get back and see his children once more. He promised. The Beast agreed and gave him many lovely things to take home to his family.

When the merchant returned home and told his children of his plight, the other daughters blamed Beauty for the mess he had gotten himself into. But Beauty said, "It is not necessary that my father die. I will give myself up to the Beast and prove my love for the best of fathers." The brothers objected and said that they would go out and search for the monster instead. The father did not want any of the children to suffer and said no, he would go back and give himself up to the Beast. But Beauty stubbornly argued her love and insisted that she would go. After three months, Beauty made ready to go to the castle of the Beast. The other daughters pretended to be upset, but Beauty herself went willingly.

When Beauty and her father arrived at the castle, they were well fed. Beauty suspected that the Beast had a mind to fatten her up before he ate her up. The Beast appeared and asked Beauty if she had come of her own accord. When she replied that she had, he answered, "Then you are a good girl and I am very much obliged to you." Beauty and her father were bewildered. The merchant left sadly and Beauty went to her room to sleep. During the night, Beauty dreamed that a lady came to her, saying "I am very pleased, Beauty, that you have been willing to give your life to save that of your father. Do not be afraid; you shall not go without a reward." Beauty was amazed to find that the Beast had done what he could to make her accommodations lovely and pleasant, and now she knew that he did not want to hurt her. As they got to know each other, Beauty had to admit that the Beast was very ugly, but also that he was very kind. The beast admitted his ugliness and also claimed to be very stupid, but Beauty told him that very stupid people are never aware of it themselves.

Gradually, Beauty became so responsive to the Beast's kindness that she began to forget how ugly he was. At one point the monster said, "There is many a monster with the form of a man. It is the better of the two to have the heart of a man and form of a monster." Eventually the Beast asked Beauty if she would marry him. She was frightened but always truthful and she said, "No." He seemed sad, but not angry. Over the months her sympathy and affection for the Beast grew. Eventually she began looking forward to the time he would spend with her. The only thing that bothered her, besides missing her father, was that the Beast again and again asked if she would marry him. After a while, she asked the Beast if she might go home and visit her father, feeling that his heart must be breaking with grief over their separation because he loved her. The Beast said that she could go, but told her that if she stayed away he himself would surely die of sorrow. Beauty assured him that she liked him too and that she would return in a week so that she would not cause him any unhappiness.

She went home, delighted to be with her father again, and again found herself in the envious competitive struggle which her sisters forced upon her. Beauty was happy once more being at home with her father, but toward the end of the week she dreamed of the garden of the palace in which the Beast lay dying of sorrow. She felt awful at being tempted to treat the Beast so cruelly when he had been so kind to her. She even thought, "Why do I not marry him? I am sure I should be more happy with him than my sisters are with their husbands. And I want to do nothing to make him unhappy."

She got up, put on the magic ring which would return her to the palace and in the morning found herself back with the Beast. She called out to him, "Beast, dear Beast," but there was no answer. Finally she remembered her dream and rushed to the garden and saw him lying there looking as though he were dead. Forgetting his ugliness, she threw herself on him and seeing that his heart was still beating she fetched some water, sprinkled him, and wept.

The Beast opened his eyes. "You almost forgot your promise, Beauty," he said. "I was determined to die since I could not live without you. I have starved myself, but I shall die content since I have seen your face once more."

"No, no, dear Beast," Beauty cried out passionately. "You shall not die, you shall live to be my husband. I thought I felt only friendship for you, but now I know that it is love." At this the palace was transformed into a place of loveliness and the Beast was well and strong again.

As he rose to his feet, he changed from the ugly Beast to a tall, handsome, graceful young prince who thanked her with tender expression. But Beauty sobbed, "But where is my poor beast? I only want him, nobody else." And the prince replied, "I am he," and went on to tell of how a wicked fairy had condemned him to this form and forbade him to show any wit or sense until a beautiful lady would consent to marry him. And since Beauty had judged him neither by looks or by talent, but by heart alone, then he was now again free.

But we must see that not only does Beauty's tenderness bring the terrible Beast to fulfillment. We must understand too that her acceptance of his ugly animal nature brings her beyond her own too-good-to-be-true virginal ever-readiness to sacrifice her own longings. Coming to love the primitive, untamed being of the Beast is equivalent to Beauty's coming to terms with the powerful instinctual forces within herself. The result is that she emerges as a flesh-and-blood woman with a handsome, virile beast-man all her own. No longer Daddy's little girl; clearly Beauty is about to get laid.

The Beast of the story is an archetypal motif, a metaphor for the disowned dark side of our heroine, a side which seems ominous and to be feared, but only so long as its true nature remains hidden in the darkness of the not-me, the land of the shadow.

The Tarot visualization of the Shadow Archetype is The Devil card. A horned, tailed man and woman stand chained to the half-cube (the Throne of partial knowledge) on which Satan sits. This is the card of black magic which foretells of the emergence of dark forces and revolutionary violence. Reversed, this card promises healing and the beginning of spiritual understanding.

The shadow is the negative side of the personality, not necessarily a bad or undesirable side, but those aspects of the self which do not fit within the idealized self-image which we each develop to make living as an imperfect human being more comfortable. Jung himself remains somewhat mired in the moralistic morass which is the residue of the provincial, ministerial childhood background trap against which he rebelled, and from which in many important ways he successfully escaped. As a result, his moralistic emphasis undervalues some of the positive value of the shadow. But he does make the negative face of the shadow powerfully vivid, and indeed has the inspirational courage to urge each man to come to terms with that potent underside of his person from which he would flee.

Unfortunately there is no doubt about the fact that man is, as a whole, less good than he imagines himself or wants to be. Everyone carries a shadow, and the less it is embodied in the individual's conscious life, the blacker and the denser it is. [3]

There is something terrifying about the fact that man has also a shadow-side to his nature which is not just made up of small weaknesses and blemishes, but possesses a positively demoniacal impetus ... a delirious monster ... the blood-lust of the beast ... Out of a dim presentiment of the possibilities lurking in the dark side of human nature, we refuse to recognize it. We struggle blindly against the healing dogma of original sin ... [4]

In other words, it is quite within the bounds of possibility for a man to recognize the relative evil of his nature, but it is a rare and shattering experience for him to gaze into the face of absolute evil. [5]

Jung instructs us well about the evil of which we are all capable. But I find him even more helpful when he emerges from the Victorian perspective which so often limited Freud as well. In such moments of illumination, Jung helps me to stay in touch with knowing that nothing that is human should be foreign to me, that the issue is not just that of accepting evil as well as good, but rather of more modestly and lovingly simply coming to terms with *what is,* regardless of how it fits with any given conventional morality. It is this aspect that he illuminates when he points out that:

If the repressed tendencies--the shadow, as I call them--were decidedly evil, there would be no problem whatever. But the shadow is merely somewhat inferior, primitive, un-adapted, and awkward; not wholly bad. It contains inferior, childish, or primitive qualities which would in a way vitalize and embellish human existence ... [6]

One woman's struggle against the delightful aspects of her shadow is transparent in a series of dreams which highlight the inner journey during her pilgrimage of psychotherapy:

I dreamed I was in the courtyard of a resort hotel, wearing a long, slinky skirt split up the front so that my legs were exposed. A friend of my father's was there watching me appreciatively. I recalled how I despised him. He was better educated than my father, and more assertive; and though they both held similar jobs as engineers for the State of Alabama, the other man was always upstaging my father. Though they liked each other to some extent, my father also disliked the man intensely, something he told me but no one else.

As I stood in the courtyard, I moved about seductively, feeling very confident that he wanted me. We went inside his hotel room and I took a bath. I didn't have my own toilet articles, so I used the soap, sponge, bath oil, and towels that belonged to his woman. The things were a lovely shade of pink, and I enjoyed them for that reason, and because I enjoyed taking her things and feeling that her stupid, fat old man wanted me. As I was in the bath, a friend of mine, a woman with whom I had been involved in a close sexual and emotional relationship, came into the room. We laughed together about my seducing the man, and had an extra big laugh about "even using her things!" Then a young man came into the room. I got out of the bath and walked over to him. He held me close to him very tenderly, and I felt very gentle and loving toward him. I don't know who the young man was, though it feels right for him to have been a young man in one of my therapy groups toward whom I feel very loving and tender.

Next I dressed and walked from the bathroom into the bedroom. There were a lot of people in the room, having a party. I felt very beautiful. Everyone became quiet, and an engagement announcement was made. The engagement of the stupid, fat man and his woman. She was wearing a garish, hot-pink satin dress; her hair was "salt and pepper" gray; and she was fat. I felt contempt for them both, and felt very superior, beautiful and smugly aware that the man wanted me, not her.

That night, the night of this dream and several nights afterwards, I dreamed of weddings, with me as the bride dressed in white, and of having a family with several children. The strangest feeling I was having in the dreams was an awareness of a lack of excitement and vitality. I was getting married; I had a family; everything was as it should be; and I felt bored.

She struggles against the shadow of her own lusty, sexy-bitch sensuality. It is reflected in the flashy aggressive older man who was her father's friend in life, father's own slightly-disapproved-of shadow, a companion he needed but with whom he could not fully identify. While still in the process of exploring her shadow-self, this woman must temporarily restore the balance of her idealized self-image with the duller series of virginal, doughty, bridal dreams. Some day soon she will be whole, owning her shadow, living with all of her lovely self. My own struggle with *my* shadow has been no different, no less confusing, exciting, and ultimately rewarding.

Partly in order to free your understanding of the shadow from its usual embeddedness in the stultifying moralism in which we have all been raised, I would like to tell of someone else's meeting with the *child* who is her own secret self. Ann's unexpected encounter with her child-shadow occurred in the setting of one of the psychotherapy seminars which I run each week.

My attempt has been to humanize therapy supervision. The shallow mock-myths of contemporary medical and behavioral science have cast unhappy human beings as "sick patients," their spiritual gurus as "doctors," and exploration of what goes on between them as "case conferences." For several years I conducted supervisory therapy seminars as traditional case conferences. In each group of psychotherapists, we began by focusing on the group process and on the presentation of tape-recorded individual and family therapy sessions.

After a while, I began to feel that *respect for the patient* under discussion demanded that he be *present* and *participating*. Both the therapists and the supervisor became more humanized in the process.

Eventually we were working with two to four patients present, in what turned out to be an exciting, sometimes scary, ultimately rewarding growth arena. At first I was flying by the seat of my pants and tempted to bravura excesses. But as we came to trust each other more, we could clearly see how the impasses belonged to the "betweenness" of therapist and patient, of supervisor and therapist. We were each able to observe how the other really worked, instead of lying to each other about what we thought we did.

Instead of the therapists "presenting cases," therapist and patient came in as a "couple" who wanted help in learning how to get more out of their time together. The patients began each session frightened and bewildered, but most often came away touched and enlightened. And, these patients taught me a great deal. They turned out to be wonderful consultants, seeing through another patient's deadlock with *his* therapist from a perspective we therapists too often lose.

On this particular day, a therapist named Ann was scheduled to bring in a patient. This account of what transpired will be an amalgam of her impressions and my own. It all began on a day when the patient did *not* show up. Ann had been a member of the seminar group for several weeks. From the outset, she had seemed scared. She wanted very much to be a good therapist, to give, to be appreciated, to be the strong parenting one.

> *Within minutes after I first came into the seminar, Shelly dealt with the protective game of my anxiety. He asked me what I wanted of him. I told him I wanted to be tougher as a therapist. He told me I may never be. He told me I would have to fight hard to make a place for myself in the group to get what I wanted. I felt listened to and heard.*

During the following sessions other therapists brought patients to the seminar. I gave almost nothing. Shelly told me he did not care if I chose to remain retiring. Jack said he would like me to stay retiring, so much like his mother, and he enjoyed that. His looking so much like my son, my dead brother and my dead father made his comments all the sharper. Barry said he did not want me there if I was retiring; he wanted something from me. Gerry said I was probably a good therapist but hadn't opened up. Marcia, too, questioned my doubting myself in the group. Will, my co-therapist, said he had worked with me one and a half years and was getting more from Jane with whom he had never worked before. I came away feeling immobilized, stuck.

Then it was my turn to ask a patient to come to the seminar. I had put this off as long as I could. I invited a young woman, with whom I also felt stuck. The day and hour came. She did not. She was to tell me later she came ten minutes late, had waited an hour past the end of the seminar. She had not thought of knocking on the door.

Her session became mine. I think it was Barry who suggested I had selected someone I knew would not come.

I had been acutely anxious about my patient's not coming. I denied that her not coming made me anxious. In the waiting room I had been sniping at Will about another patient we both saw in our group. I had not realized it was sniping. I was angry about a turn of events related to this patient and the co-therapy group. I was not dealing directly with the anger, or my anxiety about the seminar.

When Shelly heard about the co-therapy problem, he told me I am nasty, vicious, and controlling. He told Will he didn't have to keep me, he could get rid of me. I thought you had brought her here for me to make love to, to get her off your back [Shelly to Will]. Jack too spoke to Will about the bitchiness of "your woman."

Jane said she was uncomfortable. It seemed I was being

picked on because my patient hadn't come. Shelly asked the group if they saw how I had got things in an uproar. I was still unconscious myself of what I had done. At worst I could see only hard banter on my part.

Shelly asked Will why he didn't deal with me when I was vicious. Will explained he is reluctant to, that whenever he does, he himself gets hurt.

Shelly again talked to me about how controlling I am. He gave to me, talking about the transferential elements involved in my patient's attitude toward Will and my over-control against hers. I could not tell Shelly clearly I had worked with the transference nor could I tell him I felt I had acted more decisively than my custom. I couldn't say these things and remained bewildered he couldn't understand my feelings.

By this time Shelly had commented on my imprecise use of words--I "brought her to the group," to "put her in the group" to finally, "I asked her to come to the group." He asked why I was playing with my hair. I didn't answer him straight. He pointed out I control by questions.

I was hurt and confused. I felt helpless. I could not escape the truth of what he was saying. To be "vicious" hurt the most. I had even prided myself, self-righteously as I see now, on not being vicious. But there it was, I had been vicious. I did not want to look at Will. I could not deal with how bad I felt. Instead I said I was glad I was strong enough to hear the criticisms and take them. I said nothing about being hurt.

Barry wanted to know why I didn't cry when I was hurt. I said there was a time when I might have cried but I had cried all week and wouldn't cry now. Jack asked how many chances like this did I get. [To work with Shelly, the group, to get something for myself is what I heard.] Only a few I said. All the better to blow it he said.

Jane spoke to Jack, you and I could see she went to the brink and stopped. I'm pissed off with you, [Jane to me], for not going on.

I was an emotional blur of hurt, anger, bewilderment--and resolve: I would not lose the moment, the encounter with Shelly. I turned back to him. I'm overwhelmed I said. That's the first honest thing you've said. Shelly looked at me and waited.

I'm lost.

I know.

I want something from you and I don't know what. A pause. I respect you and want your help. Nothing from him. I knew terrible desperation. This man was waiting to hear from the center of my soul.

Another pause! Gerry smoked his pipe and then--You're going about this as if it's something you could learn from a book; I'm not that way. And more--I think you know what you want.

Shelly spoke. He sounded gentle. You have so much longing. It's what I like best about you.

Tears were close. To be understood frightened me. I struggled on. I like you and want you to like me.

Why do you water it down like that? said Shelly.

No place else to go. Still so difficult to say. I love you and want you to love me.

Do you really love me?

Tears began. I could only nod.

And you want me to love you?

Yes, but I can't control that.

I didn't know you knew that.

Tears again.

You have to let me know you. His voice was softer.

Is your longing for your mother or your father, he asked.

My father.

Where is he?

Dead.

Where is he buried?

In Shenandoah, Virginia--I could hardly say it.

I want you to call your father loudly enough that he will hear you, and plead with your father to love you.

And I called to my father, dead, in a valley town in Virginia. Please love me!

I don't know what came next. I remember only anguish and tears. I think it was then Shelly told me the group was being quiet out of respect.

Shelly asked me to ask the group for something.

She had finally been willing to define what it was she wanted there in the group. She said, finally, as though confessing, "I like you and I want you to like me," and that was a rather bold confession for someone as timid as she. I responded by saying, "Why do you water it down like that?" She flushed and became uncomfortable but this quickly took her into the recognition that what she was really talking about was not "liking" but "loving." She experienced this as some sort of contemporary response to what sort of teacher-guru I was. I knew that it was a transference response, a very old one, a little girl longing for acceptance by her father. As we began to work with this there was a good deal of group interaction because the transference was so powerful. I purposely shunted the focus of her attention away from me, to another therapist, Jack, a strong male in the group about whom she has somewhat similar feelings, but to whom her positive transference seemed less intense. I was, after all, not doing therapy at that point. After some strugglingly reluctant exchange, she was then talking about wanting to get Jack to help her, to respond to her.

I turned to Jack. I anticipated asking Jack would not be easy. Jack in his blondness reminds me of my son, who had called a week before to tell me his wife had had a miscarriage of their first child. I was still grieving--shared my son's and daughter's pain, grieving for the grandchild I hoped to have, and for lost opportunities to be mother again but this time round more open, honest, direct, more the person I hope to be and regret I was not, as I had not been that day with Jack in the waiting room. I had not understood his absence the week before when he said he had not attended the AAP conference in New York after all. When he volunteered no information, I did not ask where he had been, just said, oh, you stayed in town, in an aloof and bitchy tone that I let take over sometimes when I am unsure and angry. When I learned his wife, close to delivery of their first child, had asked him to stay with her, I felt ashamed.

So I first apologized to Jack, I'm sorry for what I said in the waiting room. I would like to know you and you to know me.

No answer.

All the day's hurt and pain and longing and grieving was a knot inside me. I asked to be held.

Nothing.

At one point I leaned back close to tears. I want to be held.

No answer.

This was a teaching seminar and so in addition to my own concern about where this woman was going as a human being ... her struggle was honest, intense, important ... since this was a teaching seminar I thought that I would try to have the group learn something in the process in addition to participating in this human experience. It is curious to me how once you are well into an intense human interaction emotionally, it doesn't matter how intellectual or didactic you get. It is always the feeling that carries the exchange. And so indeed I did go on to intercede in the group technique that I had seen used and that they might try out in order to get us past this impasse.

The technique I talked about was this: There is a drug rehabiltation group for junkies in New York called Daytop Village, a residential treatment center where veteran ex-junkies treat recent defectors. It has a good reputation as being a somewhat effective, residential hangout for curing addicts, with all the usual limitations of substituting one sort of dependency for another, I suppose. Their techniques are bold and powerful. In the Synanon-type group they tend to use punitively confrontational techniques in which people excoriate one another, which has its own power to tear away social defenses. But there is another technique at Daytop, which is the one that I was interested in relating to the seminar.

In order to raise funds and to educate, Daytop has a traveling theatrical group. The plays they do, or at least the one I saw, have been developed by and are acted by people who have been in the program, and are ex-addicts. The theme of the play I saw in Washington was the experience of a number of addicts going through the program. What happens, of course, is that they get into these small encounter groups and they make their excuses. "It's not my fault," "Nobody should blame me," "How can I help but be on heroin?" "Besides it isn't such a bad thing," all the bull-shit-resistances of self-support systems which allow people to continue to use heroin and throw their lives away.

At a certain point within these small group confrontations, the new member is emotionally backed-up against the wall by the others. The group gets him in touch with the fact that what he really wants is someone to love him, and that it does not feel clear whether anyone should or could love a person like him. But the groups gives him to understand that possibly they could love him if that's what he is longing for. But only if they could really hear him, clearly enough to be moved to respond to him.

Then follows a very torturous exchange in which the person who is on the spot first says, "Oh yes, I would like someone to love me," then the group tells him that they don't believe and can't be moved by that kind of bullshit tone and so he goes on and says, "Well, how can I get it," and they say, "You kind of have to really ask for it." He says, "O.K., well, would you please love me," and somebody says, "What?" and he says, "Would you please love me." And somebody says, "I can't hear you, man." Finally the exchange goes where it might; the guy on the spot is revealing his anguish openly, is disarmed, totally vulnerable, saying, with his heart in his hand, "Please love me. Won't someone please, please love me?" And if he can touch the group, if he can get people to really react out of their guts then he can have the acceptance he seeks.

Now I described all of this to the seminar group simply as a suggested group process technique. You'd think that since I was describing it as a technical strategy, that there would be no way in which we could all lose ourselves to the experience. I don't know whether such techniques simply have such strongly emotionally compelling qualities of their own that they sort of take over ... or whether it's the fact that I'm really a pretty good story-teller so that I'm not just lecturing but inviting them on a trip with me.

Shelly told a story. At Daytop ex-addicts plead to be loved and if anguish is clear enough maybe they'll be loved.

I spoke to Jack again. I'd like you to love me.

I know that.

I plead with you to love me. The difficulty of pleading for what I want most began to flow through me in anger. God, I can't plead!

Come back next week he said and turned away.

The group talk moved elsewhere. Who talked and about what, I don't know. I knew only desperation. I tried again. Are you still there?

He looked at me.

I plead with you to love me. Now it was a plea. I put the coffee cup down and in terrible pain, please, please love me.

He reached out his hand and held me. I cried and cried and cried. So much grief for so many losses, so much relief at being accepted by Shelly and Jack and for the hope that others too could accept me, love me. It's all right he said which I heard as you are all right. I willed myself to stop crying, and gave another gift. Do you want to cry some more? And I did, the anguish less and the comfort more. When I went back to my place on the sofa Barry held my hand for the rest of the session. I was no longer crying, but I was still past words. I could only listen, sometimes in dumb confusion, as when Jack said to Shelly, thank you, I always like to try new things and Shelly said he could count on the quality of Jack's work. Another spin of the mind to a Kafkaesque grotesquerie while feelings said no, what they gave is real. While I had been crying, I heard almost sublim-inally Shelly say many things of reassurance. You have taken many criticisms today, it will be downhill for you now. And, this time [the seminar] is one of the times I most look forward to each week and other giving words my mind cannot recall but my emotions have not forgotten.

We did pick it up from there, and the group (particularly Jack) began to move Ann toward having either to say in some honest, open, moving way just how much she wanted to make a claim on the group, or to leave the child in her vulnerable. And if she couldn't do it that way, then no one was going to fucking bother with her.

The pitch grew and I encouraged Ann to go on, while at the same time I discouraged Jack from settling too cheaply. He hadn't been here before and inclination was to give in easily, when she began to ask, to *demand* to be loved, held, cared about, given to, and the like. Because of the mothering healer in him (the archetype from which he works), he was ready from the outset to say, "O.K., fine, you can have it all right away." But I discouraged him at each point, until Ann was really up against it. She had stubbornly dug in her heels masking the shadow of the hidden child in her behind righteous parental demandingness. But, bless her, she stayed with it, struggled to reclaim her child-shadow until finally she could cry out her need in a way that touched us all, grabbed each of us somewhere in the emptiness of his own heart.

And when her anguish was at a pitch so intense that it was in no way demeaning to her to respond, Jack came through. His way was to say, "Sure," when she finally begged to be held. She climbed onto his lap, and he held her as she cried and cried and cried for a long, long time. By then each of us was crying, some for her and some for ourselves. We talked about it in many ways. Ann told us later that she had really become a part of the group at last. Her gratitude was open and abundant for all to see and feel. Changes came about in the rest of her life as well from this experience. She went back into treatment herself as a patient to try to clear the clutter and to get all she could for herself. We were all touched, pleased for her and for ourselves.

When I stopped crying Shelly told me my stubbornness is my power. I had never experienced with so much awareness what good things stubbornness could help me find and had not identified this as a possible strength. He spoke to me about my anger. I had experienced that pleading is not pleading until I give up the anger.

Shelly thanked me for trusting him.

Several times he told me, you are worth struggling with. To be worth struggling with! Treasured words.

Everyone in the group embraced me as I left. Barry said everyone is lining up to hug you. I drove to my office twenty miles away, tears streaming down my face. To be known and loved, and to know and love. What else is there?

The next week I told Shelly how confused I am. I hope you stay that way he said. I tried to explain how different my work and my life seem to be. He asked what was I really saying. Of course it was thank you, and I love you.

Then I had a dream and felt much closer to Shelly because I had killed him. I don't know how I had done this, memory draws a blank. He lay in a state on a polished black stone slab. His head and face were covered by a white lace ski-type cap and mask. I could not tolerate his being gone. I brought him back to life. As colleagues we sat and talked. I remember how comfortable this was. We talked about my journey, where I was to go next. We were on the third or fourth floor of an office building, it could have been the seventh floor, as Shelly's office is. He told me the only way for me to go now was out the window. That's crazy, I said. And I jumped. There was a tree below, a beautiful tree, with a strong limb. I

*caught the limb with one hand, holding on, swinging, feeling
light and free. Then I drifted gently to the ground.*

*Shelly told me he would not analyze the dream. He
accepted it as a gift. I felt the greatest pleasure. I had wanted
to give Shelly a gift. I had seen the dream as rich in good
things for me but had not seen clearly it was a gift for him too.*

For me the most important aspect of this was that we all must
somehow face our demons, go the distance, without hiding,
shading it off, deleting it, or understanding it. We have to face the
power and the anguish of what any given experience offers us as an
opportunity to be in touch with the primordial things in ourselves.
And so I was especially touched when a couple of weeks later Ann,
after having read a manuscript of mine, wanted to give me
something in response. And when she returned the manuscript
there was in it a Xeroxed copy of a poem titled *Ithaka* by a
contemporary Greek poet, C.P. Cavafy,[7] whom I had not known
before, but it seemed just right and it was as though I had been
looking for that poem without knowing it existed. I was pleased
that Ann in particular, out of the depth of her own intense soul
and the sensitivity of her own dark nature, would know that this
would be just right for me and that she would be generous enough
to offer me this part of herself. And so I thought this poem will say
some of what I want to say in my new book, about facing all of
life's pilgrimage, the darkness of its shadows as well as the warmth
and brilliance of its light.

When you set out for Ithaka
ask that your way be long,
full of adventure, full of instruction
The Laistrygonians and the Cyclops,
angry Poseidon--do not fear them:
such as these you will never find
as long as your thought is lofty, as long as a rare
emotion touch your spirit and your body.
The Laistrygonians and the Cyclops,
angry Poseidon--you will not meet them

unless you carry them in your soul,
unless your soul raise them up before you.

Ask that your way be long.
At many a summer dawn to enter
--with what gratitude, what joy--
ports seen for the first time;
to stop at Phoenician trading centres,
and to buy good merchandise,
mother of pearl and coral, amber and ebony.
and sensuous perfumes as lavishly as you can;
to visit many Egyptian cities,
to gather stores of knowledge from the learned.

Have Ithaka always in your mind.
Your arrival there is what you are destined for.
But don't in the least hurry the journey
Better it last for years,
so that when you reach the island you are old,
rich with all you have gained on the way,
not expecting Ithaka to give you wealth.

Ithaka gave you the splendid journey.
Without her you would not have set out.
She hasn't anything else to give you.

And if you find her poor, Ithaka hasn't deceived you.
So wise have you become, of such experience,
that already you'll have understood what these Ithakas mean.

The openness of the members of that seminar group to their
own dark shadows encouraged me to share a dream with them, a
dream which is a signpost along the way of my own ominous
pilgrimage.

One night I dreamed that I was on Cape Ann, that's the north cape of Boston Bay. My own cape, the place where I most often spend my summers, is the south cape, Cape Cod, and the lovely islands which surround it. The southern cape is warm and rich and green and soft, but not so Cape Ann. The north cape is very different. I've been there and it has qualities that draw me back, but for the most part it has been a place that I have avoided. Cape Ann is a dark, rugged, craggy seascape; angular, covered with scant, scrubby foliage; dark, windblown, dangerous-looking territory--in its own way a strikingly beautiful seascape, but very ominous.

My dream began with my having emerged from a small rugged beach cottage such as one might find on Cape Ann. I stepped through the doorway of the cottage and out into the night. I don't know where I was headed, but I began to walk slowly across a great open barren wilderness, a vast tundra. I followed the ambling footpaths; there were no roads. I wandered for a while and had come quite a distance from the cottage.

Suddenly the night became very, very dark. I don't know now whether I realized this in the dream or whether it came as an explanation to myself after I had awakened, but it seemed to me that the moon had suddenly fallen behind dark clouds. As I stood there in the sullen darkness, unable to see which way to go, a piece of my every-day anxiety suddenly flooded the dream. One of the difficulties in my life, a residual from brain surgery undergone three years ago, is that my balance is very uncertain. I am inclined to topple over, to be taken by the inertia of my own movement. My body compensates for this during the day and although I suffer from some fatigue as a consequence, I can make my way. But at night when it's dark my own kinesthetic feedback is limited, distorted, betraying; without daytime's visual cues, I need either to carry a light or to hold someone's hand. Holding someone's hand was a difficult thing for me to surrender to. For a while I stubbornly resisted that. I no longer do so.

In the dream when I found myself in the darkness, I suddenly felt like a fool and I said to myself, "What the hell are you doing out here without a flashlight? How stupid to leave the house without the light that you needed." For a moment I stood there and debased myself for having made a mistake. Then I decided I must go back to the house, I must get a light, I am simply not going to be able to manage. I was afraid I would stumble and fall and hurt myself, or worse yet that I would get lost forever or that vast dark plain. I moved my feet, shuffling them about, trying to find the footpath. In doing so I found that I couldn't really tell where the path was just from feeling about with my feet. So I got down on all fours like an animal padding around with my hands to see if I could discover where the path lay so that I could find my way back to the house.

While I was down there, scrounging around, I became aware of another presence. I was not alone. At first I thought that it must be a dog. I need to say here that I carry about with me some counter-phobic reactions to anxiety about dogs, anxiety which I don't understand, and of which I am only inferentially aware. I don't know it directly, dogs don't seem to frighten me, but I know that I am a bit rougher with them than I need to be; that I try to intimidate them rather than to make friends. At any rate, if it was a dog, it was only a dog, and I wasn't too disturbed about that.

But I was on the alert and as I watched, the beast drew closer. Soon I could see the intense gleam of his glaring, yellow eyes. And then I knew it was not a dog. The beast I faced was a wolf. Characteristically, I reacted as in my waking life. The first thing that occurred to me was, "Oh, I see, now I have to kill this wolf." But then uncharacteristic things began to happen in the dream. I suddenly had a new look at myself and I thought, "That's absurd. It's too crazy! How can I kill a wolf with my bare hands, on his turf, in the darkness, at a time when I can't even walk with safety?"

And then came a second, still more startling wave of revelation. I suddenly could understand in a new way what I must do. I knew then that *I must make friends with this wolf*.

At that point the dream ended and I awoke—awoke to feel that a door had opened to an unexplored part of my life. I do not know where this will lead. I both hope and dread meeting that wolf again, that wolf who is my own savage soul, the terror in my heart, my secret shadow. And yet I *must* learn, God help me, to give up my warrior pose, to surrender that sense of mastery that goes with being able to overcome my terror. Instead I must learn to yield to it, to own it, to make friends with it, to come to love the rest of myself when next I encounter that *wolf* who is *my own dark brother.*

The question then arises, should we not fear Evil? A compelling answer is offered by Dietrich Bonhoeffer, a German theologian and Protestant minister, who knew evil first-hand, living as he did in Nazi Germany. He was at first committed to piety and pacifism but began to see that these forms of goodness were an illegitimate escape from the evil he had to confront during the rise of the Hitler regime. He became an active member of the Resistance movement for which he paid dearly, with years in prison, months in concentration camps, and execution by hanging. In his *Letters and Papers from Prison,* he discusses the ways in which Evil depends on Folly as a mediator for its effective impact:

Folly is a more dangerous enemy to the good than evil. One can protest against evil; it can be unmasked and, if need be, prevented by force. Evil always carries the seeds of its own des-truction, as it makes people, at the least, uncomfortable. Against folly we have no defense. Neither protests nor force can touch it; reasoning is no use; facts that contradict personal prejudices can simply be disbelieved--indeed, the fool can counter by criticizing them, and if they are undeniable, they can just be pushed aside as trivial excep-tions. So the fool, as distinct from the scoundrel, is completely self-satisfied; in fact, he can easily become dangerous, as it does not take much to make him aggressive. A fool must therefore be treated more cautiously than a scoundrel; we shall never again try to convince a fool by reason, for it is both useless and dangerous.

If we are to deal adequately with folly, we must try to understand its nature. This much is certain, that it is a moral rather than an intellectual defect. There are people who are mentally agile but foolish, and people who are mentally slow but very far from foolish--a discovery that we make to our surprise as a result of particular situations. We thus get the impression that folly is likely to be, not a congenital defect, but one that is acquired in certain circumstances where people *make* fools of themselves or allow others to make fools of them. We notice further that this defect is less common in the unsociable and solitary than in individuals or groups that are inclined or condemned to sociability. It seems, then, that folly is a sociological rather than a psychological problem, and that it is a special form of the operation of historical circumstances on people, a psychological by-product of definite external factors. If we look more closely, we see that any violent display of power, whether political or religious, produces an outburst of folly in a large part of mankind; indeed, this seems actually to be a psychological and sociological law; the power of some needs the folly of the others. It is not that certain human capacities, intellectual capacities for instance, become stunted or destroyed, but rather that the upsurge of power makes such an overwhelming impression that men are deprived of their independent judgment, and--more or less unconsciously--give up trying to assess the new state of affairs for themselves. The fact that the fool is often stubborn must not mislead us into thinking that he is independent. One feels in fact, when talking to him, that one is dealing with, not the man himself, but with slogans, catchwords, and the like, which have taken hold of him. He is under a spell, he is blinded, his very nature is being misused and exploited. Having thus become a passive instrument, the fool will be capable of any evil and at the same time incapable of seeing that it is evil. Here lies the danger of a diabolical exploitation that can do irreparable damage to human beings.[8]

I agree, in the main, with Bonhoeffer's emphasis on folly as the mediator of evil. What he described in the sociological problem of the relationship of the folly of the many to the brutal evil of such a monstrous leader as Hitler I see as well in analog as a psychological problem in the individual's foolish denial of the unconscious evil within himself. And in this psychological realm, as in the sociological interactions which he described, I also agree " . . . that folly can be overcome, not by instruction, but only by an act of liberation . . . "[9] So it is that often patients of mine describe what they do as being neurotic or irrational, translate "foolish." In such instances a person will say that he acts in a way that hurts those about him whom he loves but that he cannot help it because he acts out of an unconscious need, or on a compulsive basis, or because he had an unhappy childhood. Certainly he wants to do the right thing and has been trying for a long time to overcome this foolishness, these neuroticisms, but to no avail. He thinks perhaps he should try harder, and seeks out a therapist to help him to do so.

To his surprise, I define what he does as evil rather than as neurotic. Further, I suggest that he should try harder not to overcome such things but to give in to them, that is, to acknowledge them as his own wishes and to try whenever he can to express them, exaggerate them, and enjoy them. The patient, of course, balks at such satanic support.

One way around this resistance is a movement into a fantasy trip. I suggest that he need not worry about the outcome of what he is about to do because it will hurt no one, only we will know about it, and after all it is only an experiment. If the therapeutic relationship is trusting enough and the patient is not too anxious, then we can proceed as I ask him to imagine that he is not hurting others in spite of himself but because the things that he does in this regard are things that he wishes to do. Take for instance a man who is having secret extramarital affairs. He says he cannot help it as it is simply an expression of a compulsive sexual need. He regrets it and feels guilty because he feels he should not do this out of loyalty to his wife, and he fears that if she finds out she will be hurt and angry and there will be trouble for him. I reinterpret his guilt feelings as resentment of unwanted obligations (as Fritz Perls called them). Then I might suggest he explore in fantasy and describe to me his affairs as they could be if he had every opportunity that he wanted to have such experiences, if they could be as pleasurable as he dared hope, and in a manner that I might find interesting and entertaining. As he proceeds to do so, he often finds that the main complaint that he has is that he doesn't have as many affairs or as torrid affairs as he would wish. His fantasy wishes far exceed his actual transgressions. Putting him in touch with a deep sense of pleasure in having his own way in this regard helps him to own his impulses for such sexual indulgences.

Only then can we proceed with the other aspect of it, that is, the ways in which he hurts his wife. This second phase of evil is gotten into by my encouraging him to tell me in detail, and in an exaggerated way (so that I don't get any misconceptions) all the things his wife does that hurt *him*. If he can get into how hurt and angry he feels toward his wife, how trapped he sometimes feels in his marriage, how sexually limited he feels by his commitment to marriage itself, his own hurt and angry feelings will emerge with great intensity.

I tend in response to center on his experience of powerlessness, his feeling that his wife gets her way and that he doesn't get his. A quick shift at that point back into his pleasure in his extramarital affairs with an emphasis on the fact that she doesn't get her own way then, does she? Or that certainly is one time when he gets *his* own way, tends to elicit a mischievous, sardonic, often satanic smile or laughter. We laugh together in nasty gleefulness, and it is at that point that he is most likely to get in touch with the fact that his extramarital affairs hurt his wife (or could hurt his wife if she knew about them) because that is *exactly* what he is up to. He cannot get *his* way with her and so he ends up at least in fantasy seeing to it that she does not get *her* way.

The question at that point involves an examination of his "disloyalty to his wife" as opposed to whether or not he is being *loyal to himself*. However these problems are explored in the therapy session, that patient soon finds that he can no longer define them as neurotic symptoms (that is, as folly). He can see himself as being deeply into the expression of his own hidden wishes to be more sexually self-indulgent and to win the wilful struggle that he experiences with his wife. He can be an evil bastard if he wishes in his marital struggle and as far as I'm concerned he can enjoy it, he need only acknowledge it so that it's clear between us and a greater source of pleasure to himself. But insightfully observed behavior is different from that same behavior carried out as naive folly. And so, often enough such behaviors are briefly enjoyed without conflict only to be given up as the patient turns more directly to face his struggle with his wife on a more open exchange of dialogue. Energy is then directed at those things in the relationship which really anger him and which he indeed may be able to change (or if not, may come to be able to live with without feeling threatened and anxious about them).

Similarly, "neurotic symptoms" or other follies which are not traditionally viewed as misconduct can yield to their transfiguration into acknowledged and enjoyed evil. A woman came to see me recently complaining of unexplained, tearful unhappiness, blank-minded confusion, and forgetfulness. I could get no sense of what she was like as a person as she described her symptoms, except that she was trying very hard to give me the kind of clear description of her symptoms that a good patient would give. She had no idea of what caused them or how they related to her life. A brief discussion of what she was like before she developed such symptoms gave the picture of someone who was "a nice girl," whom everyone could count on to do things for them, and who did not bother anyone else with her own troubles. We talked a bit of how her marriage to her husband was similar to her relationship to her parents, all of whom appreciated how good she was and each of whom told her not to worry (lest they had to pay attention to how bad she really felt).

I pointed out how awful it was that now her unhappiness was evident to everyone, that she was too confused to be independent and had to bother other people to help her, and that her forgetfulness made her (unfortunately) unreliable in doing the things that others wished. She responded that indeed this was awful and this was why she wanted to be cured. She expressed great concern that all of this was a burden to her family. When I suggested that it might be a way of getting back at them she was absolutely horrified, particularly when I laughed in saying so. I went on to say that if this wasn't a way of getting back at them then how in the hell did she get back at her husband? She said, "Oh, by not talking to him and by not having sex with him."

She grinned a nasty grin and the first flash of vitality and triumph appeared in her eyes. We giggled together at how there was no way that he could get her to stop doing that. However, new pressures had come into her life and those forms of retaliation were no longer sufficient, hence the new "neurotic symptoms," that is, this foolishness that incapacitated her. I would like to tell you of how I helped her to acknowledge this folly as evil, to own it, to enjoy it, and to overcome it. But that was not the case.

You see, except for the brief gleeful confession of her passive resistance, she came across as all good, too good to be true. Was it not for at least a hint of evil on the surface, I would have seen her as completely inaccessible to psychotherapy, as the sort of clinic patient who responds only to support and pills. But even so, I don't like her sort of goodness and the tyranny that gets carried out in the name of her touchiness and sensitivity. She gave too little and asked too much and so I told her that I was not interested in working with her. I offered to give her the names of some other therapists who might work with her but she rose in a flurry of righteous indignation, told me "No, thank you," and left the office in a pietistic huff.

Be that as it may, I was aware that I was more glad to be rid of her than I would have been to have had her stay around and have me help her. As a younger therapist I could not abide the feeling that there were some patients whom I did not like and did not want to work with even if I could help them. And so, acting out of the folly typical of many therapists I would try to work with such people and be bewildered by my efforts being so ineffectual and by the patient's soon leaving therapy unimproved.

Earlier I had not yet realized that I had these feelings that I was not supposed to have, that my work in therapy should be primarily a source of pleasure to myself, and that that meant not working with anyone whom I didn't like. Instead I foolishly tried and tried to be good. In retrospect, supported by my work supervising other therapists, I can see how the good therapist who would never think of getting rid of his patients unwittingly does just that by unacknowledgedly evil ploys aimed ostensibly at helping the patient. At this point I choose to be bad and glad that I am rather than to be foolish and unhappy to find myself so. I feel supported in this by Jung's observation:

> The dammed-up instinct-forces in civilized man are immensely more destructive, and hence more dangerous, than the instincts of the primitive, who in a modest degree is constantly living with his negative instincts. [10]

In psychotherapy it is clear that the hidden forces within any given patient are dangerous to him *only* when he is unaware of them. Even the darkest of matters can shed light once they have been discerned and the patient looks at them with unblinking eyes. The difference between the wicked and the righteous is not clear unless seen in the context of how much of the evil within himself a man will face. The Hasidic rabbi of Lublin tells us:

> I love the wicked man who knows he is wicked more than the righteous man who knows he is righteous. But concerning the wicked who consider themselves righteous, it is said: "They do not turn even on the threshold of Hell." For they think they are being sent to Hell to redeem the souls of others.[11]

How can it be, you may wonder, that the acknowledgement of evil can lead to good? I am reminded of a powerful example in the culture of the Shtetl. Among the Eastern European Shtetl Jews, angry argument is a vital part of life with other people. And when these people fight fiercely with family, friend or neighbor, they feel free to denounce the other person for every sin in the book which can be brought to mind during the argument, that is, every sin save one.

No matter how angry a man becomes in an argument he must refrain from mentioning the one thing that would bring the flush of serious shame to the cheeks of his adversary. He may curse the other man without inhibition, colorfully telling him, "You should lose all your teeth except one, and that one should ache ... (or) you should burn like a wick and they should put you out with Benzine." [12] But he is never to drench the other's face in blood by mentioning the one thing that would shame his adversary.

And so it is, no matter how wild the fight may become, if you know that the man has an illegitimate child, or that his brother has broken with the Faith, or that his marriage is unhappy, this you will *not* say to him. You may fight the good fight but you do not hit a man below the belt. By knowing most clearly the most evil way in which you could shame the other man, you take on the responsibility of fighting ferociously and still treating him with respect, of never being so cruel as to strike him in the one place where he would be most vulnerable.

It is not the all-too-human angry fighting that would be evil in such a case, but rather feeling that you are above the other's level and therefore can strike at his vulnerability as though you had none of your own. I am reminded of the irony in the hierarchy in the Catholic Church at the time of the Spanish Inquisition. This was the time when first the Jews and then the Arabs in Spain were told that unless they were willing to convert to the Catholic faith, they must leave the country. At first, those who converted were accepted as new Catholics with the understanding that some of their own old ways would still be in evidence in their lives, that human beings were after all not able to make themselves perfect and certainly not by an act of will.

Later, these very human remnants of their original ways of life became the basis upon which they were indicted, tortured, robbed, and killed. Evidence of remaining Jewish or Arabic customs were denounced as evidence of bad faith and called forth the most horrendous punishment. The difference between the early tolerance and the later barbarism was partly dependent on who was in charge.

The more liberal days took place under the reign of a Borgia pope. He was a lusty man-and-a-half who had gained his position through political ascendancy and manipulation, a man who had been involved earlier in violence and sensual living. And so he was much more understanding and accepting than was Torquemada, a righteous man who took over the administration of the Inquisition. Torquemada was so good that he wore the uncomfortable homespun monk's robe under the fine raiment which his office called for. The pietism of his own hair-shirt way of life made the imperfections of others unbearable to him. And so he treated those poor souls with perfection-demanding cruelty which resulted in his having them tortured and killed to save their souls.

And certainly I am at my worst as a therapist when I am into trying to feel that I am any better than anyone else. At such times I help my patients to torture themselves about feeling that they are not good enough, that they are to blame for all their unhappiness, that if only they tried they certainly could do better. In contrast, at those times when I am most aware of the evil and limitations in myself, I feel most accepting of my patients as other struggling human beings.

This gets expressed in the ways in which I listen to them and often makes me able to see and communicate to them how much of their unhappiness is their asking more of themselves than a human being can do. Every thought and feeling is allowed and no action is beyond imagination if only a man will face the consequences of his acts. Conventional morality is a game and ethics must be embedded in situations, that is, each act must be judged in terms of its meaning for a given person at a given time rather than in terms of laws cut into stone tablets. Like Zarathustra I support my patients' explorations into the darkness of their own souls, saying: "They will call you destroyers of morality, but you are only the discoverers of yourselves." 13

Quite often I find my patients are much too hard on themselves. They come to me with expectations that I will judge them, find them wanting, discipline them, and make them good. Part of this is their own projection. It also has to do with my reputation as being a tough confrontational psychotherapist. Indeed I trust my toughness and at times it is a useful resource in my life and in my work.

Recently I have found myself in a dilemma as to how I should act about a conflict with which I was struggling. Because of my ill health and threat of a shortened life I wanted to raise my fees. I found that in order to do so I had to get permission from a Price Control Board and hired a lawyer to help me to do so. One of the grounds on which I was advised to seek an exception from the fee-binding regulation was that of the change of the quality of my services which my own professional development had brought about. And so one of the grounds on which I made my claim was that sort of bid.

The bureaucrats who were to decide the matter chose to reject my grounds for the change of the quality of my services and instead suggested that if I could obtain a diplomate from a self-appointed board of psychological examiners that this would indeed show my improved status and justify the fee raises. This seemed absurd to me. I had consciously decided a long while ago not to try to obtain that particular seal of approval for it seemed meaningless. Now I was confronted with financial need, with my sense of helplessness about my illness, and with the necessity of working through the Establishment in order to get what I wanted (something I have been long able to avoid doing).

Those people who would have been appointed to judge me

were psychologists whom I would not have accepted even as trainees in my psychotherapy seminars. They are the sort of self-important people who volunteer for censorship boards and committees to confer honorary degrees. Not my sort at all. Now I was confronted with the possible necessity of having to please these people if I was to get what I wanted and felt that I had a right to claim. I struggled (partly with the frustration of my powerlessness) feeling that to give in to such people would be to play the whore. My wife helped me by being of no help. That is, she insisted that we could get along without the fee raise and that if it all seemed too hard for me that maybe I should take it easy on myself and not bother to do it. This put it squarely back in my own hands.

That night I had a dream. I dreamed that I had been elected pope. It seemed to me that my problem was whether to be called Borgia or Innocente. This brief, conflicted dream fragment did not seem so bad at first. After all, the last such dream that I had had was that I had finally discovered what my job was. My task in life was to be God. The only redeeming feature was at the time of the earlier dream, although I was God, I was on vacation.

The present dream was in its own way a bummer. I took the troubled fragments with me to work the next morning and in the course of an hour with a patient with whom I have worked for a long time, I shared my dream. She responded to my anguish by pointing out that I was making the whole thing too extreme, that perhaps I did not have to make a choice as mutually exclusive as being the politically manipulative Borgia on the one hand or the scrupulously moral Innocente on the other. Her interpretation was very helpful and eventuated in my being able to see finally that my real problem was in my having to take on at all the mantle of infallibility of being pope.

Once I realized that, I gave up the impossible chore of deciding how to handle the question of the Inquisition of getting a diplomate in psychology. Instead, I could take my wife's advice, see that the whole thing was too difficult for me at this point, give up, and forgive myself.

I am bad all right, but only as bad and as good as other people. To be out of danger and live in peace with myself it is only necessary that I clearly see my shadow, the dark side of myself. Every bit of me is worth something, even the evil part. The dark forces themselves can be a source of strength if I avoid the prideful sin of scrupulosity, the self-sorry importance of making my evil any worse than anyone else's. We each must learn to look clearly at our list of sins, to take responsibility for our evil urges, and to be able to laugh at ourselves when we take ourselves too seriously.

There is a Hasidic tale that is most instructive:

During his stay in Mezritch, the Rav of Kolbishov saw an old man come to the Great Maggid and ask him to impose penance on him for his sins. "Go home," said the maggid. "Write all your sins down on a slip of paper and bring it to me." When the man brought him the list, he merely glanced at it. Then he said, "Go home. All is well." But later the Rav observed that Rabbi Baer read the list and laughed at every line. This annoyed him. How could anyone laugh at sins! For years he could not forget the incident, till once he heard someone quote a saying of the Baal Shem: "It is well-known that no one commits a sin unless the spirit of folly possesses him. But what does the sage do if a fool comes to him? He laughs at all this folly, and while he laughs, a breath of gentleness is wafted through the world. What was rigid, thaws, and what was a burden becomes light." The Rav reflected. In his soul he said: "Now I understand the laughter of the Holy Maggid."[14]

Chapter Nine

WOMAN BLUES

I guess you could say that my main problem with women is my stubbornness. Although I know better, I somehow never fully give up the fantasy that someday I will get to understand what a woman is all about. Understand, I'm not your run-of-the-mill Male Chauvinist Pig. My wife, Marjorie, has taught me much of what I do understand about what it might be like to be a woman. And it is she who knows me well enough to declare that I am the most liberated man she knows with regard to the issue of women's rights, that is, a man who views women as fully equivalent human beings. Yet she also points out (at the damnedest moments) that at those times when I do *not* seem enlightened, I am quite as lunatic as other men in my misunderstanding of what the hell women are all about.

When I am wise enough I look to women to instruct me about such matters. And so they do, but part of what they teach is that some of what I would learn is beyond my comprehension. Discouraging messages such as these come not only from the obviously militant advocates of female politics such as the Women's Liberation Movement leaders, the Lesbian Gay Liberation spokeswomen, and female writers from Simone de Beauvoir to Sylvia Plath. A simpler, less sophisticated, non-political, anonymous Abyssinian woman offers the following absolutely devastating description of her concrete living of the feminine experience:

How can a man know what a woman's life is? A woman's life is quite different from a man's. God has ordered it so. A man is the same from the time of his circumcision to the time of his withering. He is the same before he has sought out a woman for the first time, and afterwards. But the day a woman enjoys her first love cuts her in two. She becomes another woman on that day. The man is the same after his first love as he was before. The woman is from the day of her first love another. That continues all through life. The man spends a night by a woman and goes away. His life and body are always the same. The woman conceives. As a mother she is another person than the woman without child. She carries the fruit of the night nine months long in her body. Something grows. Something grows into her life that never again departs from it. She is a mother. She is and remains a mother even though her child dies, though all her children die. For at one time she carried the child under her heart. And it does not go out of her heart ever again. Not even when it is dead. All this the man does not know; he knows nothing.[1]

How then can I begin to understand what I might of that creature who both completes and confounds my world, that being who is so much like me and yet is significantly wholly other as well? Frankly, one of my inclinations is simply to try to *use* women to fill my own needs without struggling with the heavy responsibility of keeping in mind that they are human beings with their own sacred souls. I'd like to say that I don't give way to this very often *because* I am deeply respectful of the separate humanity of the women in my life space. But the truth is that mostly I don't try to use women because when I do, I am most open to being used myself. Maintaining the illusion that I am in control is futile, lonely, and in the long run always more costly than the effort is worth.

I remember early in my practice treating men who "used" prostitutes. All they had to do to control these women was to give them some money and they could manipulate them into doing whatever they wanted. They could make a whore not only do any sexual trick they commanded, but could get her to be nice to them as well. If such men couldn't buy love, at least they could rent it. The women needed the money. The men had it. The women had to give in. The men were contemptuous, superior, in control.

Later in my practice, I began to treat some hookers and strippers. They made it clear to me that the Johns with whom they dealt were suckers. Give them a little sexual excitement, and you could get them to pay all the money they had. Men were so easy to control. [2]

The degrading mutual exploitation of prostitution is simply the most obvious form of men and women using each other as objects. The subtler and more deadly things we do to each other are far more common. In the microcosm of European Jewish Shtetl culture, [3] the men spend much of their time studying the Talmud, exploring the Law of the Holy, while the women administer matters of hearth and home. There is much political exchange of seeming to respect the importance of each other's role. But beneath the veneer of such courtesies is deeply felt contempt.

The men really believe that the women are too ignorant, foolish and shallow to appreciate the sacred writings of the Torah. Let them be the servants to man that God intended them to be, cooking and cleaning without thinking or feeling. The women themselves, beneath their public deference to men, see themselves as running the real world of people while the men nit-pick in the world of religion and ideas, like small boys at play. But the loss of a mate whom one can respect and trust is only part of the sacrifice. The loss of part of the self is even more costly.

I remember well a very beautiful young woman, a call girl whom I began treating several years ago. She was no $10-a-trick street-corner hooker. She was class--a Capitol Hill, $100-a-night companion and lover. But aside from the social setting, the emotional dynamics were the same--a hooker is a hooker. She came because she was depressed, with the same emptiness and sense of futility that all hookers carry inside. She was a willful, seemingly self-indulgent, emotionally-detached human being who could use sex as decoration, as an instrument for profit, as a weapon to degrade men (without recognizing that at each point she degraded herself as well).

Over a period of months the work went well and she moved, as she wanted to, from a career as a prostitute to the next level of such work in our culture. She became a cocktail waitress, still trading seduction for cash, still manipulating, still keeping her heart out of it. She would show up at my office during a break in her work, dressed to the nines; usually she wore a low-cut elegant, but a bit too obvious, velvet gown, floor length. It would be split up one side almost to her hip exposing a long, lovely, mesh-stockinged leg and high-heeled silver shoes. In her hair was an overdone rhinestone tiara to set off her rococo makeup and costume jewelry. But when she entered the office she'd drop into a leather chair like a little girl, say "This is the only comfortable chair in this whole lousy town. Can I take my shoes off?" And she'd settle in, and we'd talk of what her life had been like and what it was now. And often she'd cry.

She worked hard, and as things started to work out she even got herself a boy-friend, not a customer, but someone she truly liked. Of course, in the process of transition who would she get but someone who had problems of his own. And so she involved herself with an older, married man who eventually "betrayed" her by choosing his wife instead. She was hurt and furious. She'd let herself be vulnerable and for the first time it was she who was hurt.

She left the office that day swearing revenge; somehow she was going to get him. She returned later in the week for our next appointment absolutely furious at me. She told me that I'd ruined everything, that once she had been able to take care of herself and now she no longer could.

What had happened was that she lured her lover back to her apartment one last time in order to make him feel as helpless as he had made her feel. She went on to describe the scene in which she had gotten him into bed, determined to excite him, to raise him to a fever pitch and then to throw him out. She turned him on in ways that she had learned in a thousand other beds. She was getting things just where she wanted them, and then--she turned to me and said, "It's you, you bastard, you with your therapy. You ruined everything. Just when I had him where I wanted him, *I got excited!*"

It seems as though the only way any of us can "use" another person is by temporarily having to give up a part of ourselves. So be it! It turns out that my trying as a man to deal with women by using them as objects will get me nowhere worth going to. What then are my other options? I'm tempted to go back to where it all began, to the first woman in my life, to mother. In my struggle to make my way through this complex male/female world, it has in fact turned out to be helpful to examine my early mother/child experiences, to sort out the remnants of that personal history, to disengage the impact of its unfinished business from the present reality of my adult relationship to women who are my contemporaries. But there are maternal forces at work in my life that are not the product of that long-ago struggle with my now dead, sometimes missed good/bad biological Bronx mother. There are as well the primordial, dark images which churn out of the Unconscious, which I share with all other men, archetypal images of the Great Mother.

In Tarot, one aspect of the Great Mother appears in the Star card. This naked maiden, pouring the waters of life, inspires hope, and promises that great love will be given and received. The forebodings of doubt and pessimism expressed by her being dealt upside down, threaten loss of love.

In times of great distress, moments of overwhelming fear or pain or weariness, I long for the refuge that a good mother could provide. Though some of us would rather not face that tender hunger deep within us, at such moments the mother-longing inside each of us rises up. For some it echoes a lovely safe time when as babies the good mother was indeed there to provide all of the needed care and nourishment, comfort, warmth, safety and protection that was to be desired. But many of us never had that lovely maternal care, never felt at one with a mothering provider of union, pleasure, and peace. And still we long for such a surcease of pain and anxiety with a powerful nostalgia, as though searching for some state once achieved and now lost.

How can it be then, that a man can long to recapture something that never really existed in his own personal history? How can he miss that which he never had? The personal mother which each of us experienced always figures with monumental significance in the shaping of each of our lives. Not only does she affect us directly in terms of the ways in which her personality and behavior influenced the vulnerable, half-formed children we once were, but too she functions as the accidental carrier of the powerful archetypal experience of the Great Mother image.

So it is that no mother, whether loving or cruel, no matter how dependable or inconsistent, will be experienced by her child solely in terms of her actual performance, or only in terms of what really went on between them. Each mother will be burdened with the child's ambivalent reactions to the opposing archetypal aspects of the Great Mother, she who is both loving and terrible.

Each child imbues his own personal historical mother with the multiple images of the Great Mother Archetype.[4] The kaleidoscopic imagery which elaborates the pale figure of the "real" biological mother (she who raised you) intensifies the experience of each child and haunts the imagination of each adult. These dark, profoundly primitive images are touchingly illuminated in Toby Tate's poem, "Mother of Sorrows":[5]

Infant
Sister
Mistress
Mother
Lady of Mercy
Queen of Peace
Gate of Heaven
Throne of Wisdom
Mirror of Justice
Refuge of Sinners
Comforter of the Afflicted

holding both breasts in her hands
holding one breast and pointing to her loins
arms open to embrace
holding a serpent
holding a flower
riding a bull
standing pregnant
squatting in childbirth
holding an infant to her breast
with rampant animals by her side
crowned with the walls of a city
Mother of Sorrows

For many of us the fundamental importance of the Great Mother has been obscured. We who have been raised in the Judeo-Christian tradition of Western culture assume a myth of creation which begins with the pre-eminence of the Great Father who has made all that is, who created man. In Genesis we find the traditional patriarchal version of a paternally founded humanity with a woman created as a playmate/companion and servant of man.

However, there are other earlier creation myths in which we can recognize the Great Mother as the source of all things. The patriarchal reduction and distortion of her status is reflected in the diminished remnants of her epic which remain in the tale of Eve and the Serpent. So it is that in the earlier Accadian Creation Epic, we are told:

In the beginning the world was without form and void. And our Great Mother Eurynome rose naked from the abyss, and, looking about her, found that she was alone. She danced in the darkness, and by her dancing the air was set in motion. Wind blew upon her face from the north, and she took it in her hands to rub it, giving it the similitude of a speckled serpent.

This same serpent lusted after our Mother and she suffered him to cast his coils about her body, and to know her. But as yet he had no name.

And in the process of time our Mother took the form of a dove
and brooded upon the face of the water and was delivered of a
great egg; which the Serpent coiled about to hatch it, so that
it split open and all things were created.[6]

In all primitive myths, it is the female rather than the male who
gives life.

The longing for the union with the womb-containment of the
Good Mother to which I have referred is merely one aspect of the
recurrent complex themes of the maternal archetype. But it is the
first one, and therefore a fitting aspect with which to begin.
Rejoining the Great Mother is often expressed in spiritual longings
for mystical experiences in which the individual regains his place
as an undifferentiated part of the cosmos. To be at one with the
Universe, as in oceanic experiences, is to know union with the
Great Mother at the time of Beginning without End. Perfection,
wholeness, unmarred satisfaction, complete contentment describe
such a paradisiacal reunion. All is Unconscious, total dependence,
unexamined bliss. We are all haunted by such longings. In each of
us there is the Taoist seeking to be the fish that loses itself in the
water.

My own confusion about the impact of the actual biological
mother vs. the haunting archetypal maternal forces made it easy
for me to be swept up in the recent Family Therapy emphasis.
Seeing the family as a social system in which the identified patient
was merely acting out his or her appointed role by being "sick"
made it seem evident that I should be treating the family as a
whole rather than the fragment of its emotional economy
represented by the individual neurotic patient.

And so it was that several years ago, I began to do work with
the family as patient. That is, I sometimes saw problems the
patients presented as the interstice of the interactions among
mother, father, children, and sometimes even extended family of
grandparents and uncles, cousins, and the like. For a period of
time I saw such networks of people on a regular basis, together in

concert, exploring with them how they related to one another, how each fit into the family's emotional calculus, and how the symptoms of any given person in the family reflected the turmoil of the group.

I worked, I suppose, with as much success and failure as most beginning family therapists. But after the newness of the approach wore off for me, I found my interest recentering once more in psychotherapy with a particular individual.

Today, most of my work occurs in the betweenness of a given single individual patient and myself. Certainly we may at times deal with the patient's relationship with other people in his family-of-origin, but for the most part this is done in terms of the patient's experience, fantasy, wishes, attitudes and desires, rather than by playing out the drama with all the other actors present. I do see marriage as a powerful enough context for most people's lives for me to be unwilling to treat a married person without at least one time meeting the spouse, exploring relationships, giving that person a chance to meet me, and at times opening the possibility of continuing the couple's work in a group. But aside from that particular opening strategy, I do not any longer often see the patient in the presence of other members of the family.

I have, however, in recent years, begun participating in a new episodic adventure. When working with adult patients individually, I will sometimes, if it seems indicated and feasible, invite them to bring in their parents or parent for a single encounter. Most often I do this as a way of short-circuiting the long, slow, resistance of the patient to the taking on of final and irrevocable status as an independent adult who must somehow leave the parents and childhood once and for all.

The greatest difficulty for me in first attempting this was the struggle against my own arrogant presumption that I must somehow make something important happen during that hour. Most often I failed, not only to make something happen but even to allow those things which might evolve to occur of their own accord. To the extent that I have learned to let some things be, I now am able to have productive one-shot meetings with my patients and their parents. Sometimes the patients still live in the same geographical area in which the parents continue to live. In those instances they tend, most often, to need some kind of contact of this sort because they remain embedded in that family network even though they may say themselves that, after all, they only see the parents once every couple of months and the parents don't mean much to them.

In other instances I may have someone bring in a mother and/or a father when the parents are in town for a visit or just passing through. In some instances, patients have, after working through their initial frustrations, worked out a specific invitation or even a request, a demand, a claim for a parent even to come across the country at least once so that they may speak out clearly, see where they stand, and give the parents a chance to say what the patient has been and what he is now in their eyes. Often the patient hopes that one way or another things will be made right, that finally the longed-for closeness and accord with the parent will be reached. I try in preparation for the meeting to make clear to the patient that probably nothing will change between him and the parent. At the same time I insist that certainly this will be a useful experience, an instructive one.

At best the patient, and hopefully the parent as well, will see things as they are, will get some notion of what small changes might occur, and more crucially will see and accept how some things are basically unchangeable. The patient may then learn how he or she is stuck, what that means, how to release himself, and where that puts him with regard to the rest of his emotional life. Of late I am more and more convinced that the most important impact of this work is to help the patient once and for all to differentiate his or her *particular* and *temporary experience with the biological parents* from the *transpersonal eternal return* to the fears and longings associated with the dark forces or *archetypal parental images* which are the *ineluctable human heritage of every man and woman.*

By way of example, let me tell you about one such recent encounter of a mother and daughter, myself and the Great Mother. I have for a while now been treating a woman in her thirties involved in a second marriage, herself the mother of several children, a person who has been very hard on herself. She is a lovely, imaginatively creative woman whose pattern it is to give much to, and for the most part to ask little of, others. Interspersed with this character armor are intermittent outbursts of irrational demands escalated into desperate destructive struggles from which she gains little but a kind of martyred self-justification. Her slow and poignant work with her own grief and rage has, over the months, allowed her to be more self-respecting, less self-denigrating, more realistically able to begin to fill her own needs, to ask for space for herself, and gradually to decrease the need for the destructive episodic outbursts, which caused her and those about her so much pain.

This is a woman who was raised by deaf and dumb parents. She grew up in the heartbreaking silence of a house in which no one could hear her when she cried out, a house in which there were no voices to call her name, to let her know that she belonged and that she mattered. As a child, she finally acquired a small radio and to this impersonal companion she clung, the only sound of seemingly human contact available to her most of the time, but one that could not hear her own voice or cries. It was absolutely incredible to me when first I learned of the setting in which she grew up that her focus was on how hard it must have been for her deaf parents. Certainly life-long silence was a tragedy for each of her parents, a compelling one, hard to bring up one's own needs in the face of. But this woman did not know what to do with my concern for what it must have been like for her as a child. She had been trained not to focus on herself. When finally we came together to look at what her own experience had been, she cried and cried and cried, but unfortunately at each point her grief was stemmed by the feeling that maybe she hadn't done enough, by the notion that if only she had been better, been more responsible, tried more, cared more, then perhaps things wouldn't have been so tough.

The work went well. Eventually she felt strong enough and competent enough to accept my suggestion that she invite mother to come in, so that the three of us could spend an hour together. I felt very frightened at the prospect. I am, after all, a psychotherapist, a man who makes contact by listening and who heals with the metaphor of his own words. I did not know sign language and the patient's mother did not read lips well. The idea of spending time with someone with whom my usual verbal ways of making contact would be futile and frivolous felt overwhelming. But working with this woman had meant a great deal to me. She had given me much. I admired her courage and the depth of her caring as she struggled to make more space for herself in her own life, and so, though I warned her that I might easily fail, I was quite willing to spend the time with her, to give her a chance to have this needed experience with her mother and me. It would echo so much life-long pain, but this time she did not have to go through it by herself.

The afternoon that she brought her mother with her I had the clear feeling that probably I'd made a mistake. It soon became apparent that mother, a woman who had developed the primitive defenses that allowed her to live in a silent world, did not really have any idea what psycho therapy was about. She seemed to confuse it with some kind of medical treatment for physical disease. The patient had agreed to be interpreter, using hand signs to communicate with her mother and translating for each of us.

I began in the way that I usually begin with family encounters, by trying to give mother a sense of why I had invited her to come and by trying to get some clarity about what she wished for and expected herself. The patient did the same. We got nowhere. In desperation I tried to concretise the meaning of what was going on by instructing the patient: "Tell your mother that I love you and that I want to help you, and that I worry about you because you do not ask enough for yourself."

It was difficult for the patient to express herself this directly to a mother with whom she had made only fragmented, frustrating and impersonal contact for all these years, but she tried as best she could. Mother replied by signing that she too was worried about the patient. I brightened. Perhaps we had an accord, perhaps we could do some work. But it soon turned out that mother's worry was a function of the fact that daughter did not write enough or do enough for her. Her worry about daughter was simply a worry about her own needs not being filled.

Okay, then, I centered on how angry she must be that daughter does not meet her needs, but she insisted that the reason was that daughter was busy with the children and didn't have the time. I encouraged the patient to tell her mother what was going on, that is, that she did not contact her often because it was frustrating, unsatisfying, that she felt she didn't matter to mother, that she was not too busy, but that she did not wish to make contact. Mother got confused and insisted that this could not be so, it was simply that the daughter was busy. We were all stuck once more.

I struggled to get through but to no avail. I was reduced to telling mother that I thought she was a liar, that surely she must be angry. And indeed, her anger was clear, in her posturing, arms folded, mouth tight, jaws set, but she would insist with the use of signs that, no, I was wrong, everything was just fine, her daughter was busy, and she didn't know what daughter was talking about. Surely daughter was not really upset.

It became increasingly clear to the patient that the problem was, and had always been, *not* that mother was deaf and could not hear, *but* that she damn well wouldn't listen. Gradually, through the tearful rage of her own frustration, the patient came to see that even if mother had been able to hear she would have given nothing, and what's more that had she, the patient, been raised by a loving deaf mother, things would have been very different. She would have known that she was cared about and felt good about herself.

When her mother left I held the patient while she cried in a new and bitter and final way. The past now seemed to her really to have passed. The face of her real mother was clear, separated from the powerful form of the Great Mother. *Now* perhaps she could get on with her life, less burdened by the Mother Complex which empowered the middle-aged ungiving deaf-mute mother of her childhood, making that withholding lady less important. Perhaps too she could more easily give up her own life in the distorting role of the Good Mother. Disengaged from the Great Mother archetype, her own mother was less important, and might no longer incite this neurotic attempt to show her up by being the mother Mom was not.

You cannot defeat the Great Mother! So long as your adult life is defined over against the biological mother of your childhood, you are confusing her limited importance with the overwhelming power of the dark haunting images of your psyche's active imagination, with the deep-felt shadows of the collective unconscious. These are feelings which we all share regardless of the quality of our upbringing.

At some point in therapy, once the patient has examined present attitudes in the light of unfinished childhood longing, I sometimes turn his attention to his helplessness before the Great Mother. As the patient struggles to finalize his relation to his childhood, I may simply insist: "Like it or not, *Mother won,* and *you lost!*" This confrontation with helplessness often seems intolerable to the patient at this point. He is further dismayed to see that even the ways in which he chooses to fight this helplessness (whether by submission or by rebellion) have been defined by Mother. What is he to make of this defeat by the all-powerful mother when he has already come to see that Mother is just another human being, who herself was raised by her own good/bad mother?

Only his increased courageous awareness can help. He must face the awful ambiguities of adulthood if he is to be free. Moving away from the hope of ever being reunited with the Great Mother means solving your own problems every day for the rest of your life. It's such a heavy responsibility. It doesn't seem fair at all. It's wearying and none of us will ever be completely free of the temptation to try to go back. But facing this awareness is the only way to escape the siren song of the womb/sea of the Unconscious, the haunting call to return to the Great Mother. To make his way, a man must follow the hero's journey. He must move toward awareness by heeding the call to adventure, accepting the aid of magical helpers, eschewing those who would tempt him to give in. He must endure his ordeals, slay the dragon, journey to the underworld and finally return with his new-found wisdom. [7]

A woman's struggle with separation from the Great Mother (and with the men who would defeat her efforts) is analogous but in significant ways, it differs from a man's struggle. Erich Neumann's analysis of the myth of *Amor and Psyche* throws clear light on women's struggle for freedom. [8]

Psyche, like her fairy-tale counterpart, Snow White, is a mortal maid of such unspoiled beauty that she is loved by everyone and adored by every man who meets her. In their acclamation of her, people inevitably compare her with the goddess Venus (Aphrodite) and find the maiden more desirable. Venus, mythic representation of the Great Mother archetype, is goddess of beauty and all else that is female, and like Snow White's "Mirror-mirror-on-the-wall, who-is-the-fairest-of-them-all?" step-mother queen, she is intensely vain, jealous and possessive of the men about her. When she becomes aware of how mortal-Psyche is worshipped, Venus cries out in rage:

> Behold, I the first parent of created things, the primal source of all the elements; behold I Venus, the kindly mother of all the world, must share my majesty and honor with a mortal maid...But this girl, whoever she be, that has usurped my honors shall have no joy thereof. I will make her repent of her beauty... [9]

Venus then appointed her son, Amor (Eros) to be the instrument of her vengeance, instructing him to make Psyche fall tragically in love with the vilest of men. Psyche learns of her projected fate when an oracle prophesizes her death in marriage to a monster. By surrendering to her fate, Psyche finds that she can claim new options and ends up living a luxurious palace-life married to an invisible husband who comes to her only in bed in the darkness of the night.

Her anonymous mate is, of course, Amor who is too taken with Psyche's charms to do her in as mother had commanded him. Yet he takes her in the unenlightened male mating of marriage as abduction and rape. Caught in the primitive instinctual surrender to the male which is the lot of the as yet unliberated woman, Psyche "....unwittingly, yet of her own doing....fell in love with Love." [10]

Psyche's envious sisters appear on the scene, and urge her to disregard Amor's insistence that he not be visible to her, and tell her that she must discover what he looks like lest she be mated to a monster. These sisters represent Psyche's own shadow-side, her wish to be free of male domination. Guided by them, she brings an oil lamp to the darkened bedside of sleeping Amor and discovers that he is no monster. Instead she recognizes him as a god, but one whom she views simply as a beautiful man, once she dares defy him by bringing the light of her own awakening awareness to their relationship. This beginning of higher feminine consciousness requires the support of her sisters, just as it does in today's consciousness-raising groups. By taking a more active role, Psyche both celebrates her own individuality and serves as an archetypal model for all women's emergence.

But in seeking awareness of just who Amor is (as well as clarity about whom she herself has become), Psyche inadvertently burns him with a drop of scalding oil from the lamp of her new-found consciousness, at the same time accidentally cutting herself on an arrow from his quiver.

> Psyche's act leads, then, to all the pain of individuation, in which a personality experiences itself in relation to a partner as something other, that is, as not only connected with the partner. Psyche wounds herself and wounds...(her husband),

and through their related wounds their original, unconscious bond is dissolved. But it is this twofold wounding that first gives rise to love... [11]

Hurt and angry, Amor goes home to the Great Mother, Venus. Psyche's seeking to reclaim her lover evokes further wrath from Venus. To redeem herself, Psyche must take on heroic labors which Venus sets for her. It is not enough for a woman to free herself from male domination, she must go on to reclaim her femininity in new and difficult ways. She must accomplish great things on her own, with courage and independence, but in a way which redeems the best of female power without simply acting like a man. And so she does, staying in touch with the unconscious instincts as she calls upon her earth-powers to accomplish labors as terrible as a journey to the underworld.

Sent on her own way by the Great Mother, Psyche defeats evil by accepting it in herself (unlike the male hero who must slay the dragon.) By bringing together opposing goddesses who represent separate aspects of the maternal archetype, Psyche reunites the Good Mother and the Bad Mother, reclaims the unity of her own female power, and regains her lover in a transformingly new love relationship. In asserting her own independence she reveals Amor's mortal aspect, attains her own divine aspect from the Great Mother, and gives birth to a human/divine child who reflects the delicate yet powerful interplay of the eternal ambiguity of the man/woman relationship.

The whole damn thing of male/female relationship remains both delightfully and exasperatingly ambiguous to me. Militant female liberationists argue that there are no *real* differences of ability and approach between male and female. They contend that apparent role and attitudinal differences are all learned (and consequently can be unlearned), that the seeming sexual differences have been encouraged solely as a means of men's continuing exploitation of women, and that anyone who says different is a Male Chauvinist Pig. Because I believe fully in the need for women's rights to be fully supported, this seems like a hell of a time for me to insist that there may well be inevitable, inherent sexual differences. Yet, aware of the dangers of my being misunderstood (or even of my being unwittingly abusive to others), with characteristic male heroics, I will go on to discuss some of the aspects which I believe differentiate men and women; differences which lie at the heart of both their value and of their danger to one another.

There has recently been a good deal of compelling and worthwhile discussion of female sexuality. Important affirmations and clarifications are available of the equivalence of women's and men's erotic deisres, of the role of clitoral orgasm, of the right not to have unwanted babies, of the woman's body as her own (rather than as "belonging to her man"). The redressing of the implied sexual inequities are women's due and ultimately will be to men's advantage as well. What then (if anything) will remain of the differences which might continue to contribute to heterosexual fulfillment? I continue to believe that men and women are not simply biological variations of the species with mere trivial differences limited in importance only to their specifically sexual and reproductive functions. Male and female seem to me to have reciprocities of attitude and ways of being which complement and complete one another in the most creative ways, though these differences may at times be their greatest sources of conflict. So it is that I see sexuality as a metaphor for creativity in the charming account of male and female separations and comings together in the *Upanishad* of THE CREATION OF THE MANIFOLD WORLD FROM THE UNITARY SOUL:

1. In the beginning this world was Soul (Atman) alone in the form of a Person. Looking around, he saw nothing less than himself. He said first: "I am." Thence arose the name, "I." Therefore even today, when one is addressed, he says first just "It is I" and then speaks whatever name he has. Since before all this world he burned up all evils, therefore he is a person. He who knows this, verily, burns up him who desires to be ahead of him.

2. He was afraid. Therefore one who is alone is afraid. This one then thought to himself: "Since there is nothing else than myself, of what am I afraid?" Thereupon, verily, his fear departed, for of what should he have been afraid? Assuredly it is from a second that fear arises.

3. Verily, he had no delight. Therefore one alone has no delight. He desired a second. He was indeed, as large as a woman and a man closely embraced. He caused that self to fall into two pieces. Therefrom arose a husband and a wife. Therefore this (is true): "Oneself is like a half-fragment," as Yajnavalkya used to say. Therefore this space is filled by a wife. He copulated with her. Therefrom human beings were produced.

4. And she then bethought herself: "How now does he copulate with me after he has produced me just from himself? Come, let me hide myself." She became a cow. He became a bull. With her he did indeed copulate. Then cattle were born. She became a mare, he a stallion. She became a female ass, he a male ass; with her he copulated of a truth. Thence were born solid-hoofed animals. She became a she-goat, he a he-goat; she a ewe, he a ram. With her he did verily copulate. Therefrom were born goats and sheep. Thus, indeed, he created all, whatever pairs there are, even down to the ants.

5. ...(The original male/female soul) knew: "I, indeed, am this creation, for I emitted it all from myself." Thence arose creation. Verily, he who has this knowledge comes to be in that creation of his.[12]

Here, then, are male and female created by the division of the Original Unitary Soul, with mating as a creative reunion born of the need to come together and to become complete once more. Unfortunately, the tale is cast in the image of male aggressive sexuality, of the woman's evocatively inviting insistence of being taken and of male pursuit and ultimate female surrender. Thus the authorship sounds already male-dominated to me, but with less distortion than later patriarchal creation myths. In the

Upanishads, the earliest Hindu teachings, it is still clear that man needs woman as much as she needs him, and that her objection is to being used instead of being treated with as much respect as the male treats himself. Still it behooves us to understand how much we need each other.

Here again Jungian archetypes can be very helpful, particularly his concepts of the *Anima* and the *Animus*. Jung suggests that in the transpersonal unconscious of every man is his Anima, the woman in him, just as within every woman there lurks her Animus, the unknown aspect of her that is male. So it is that men and women not only share a common humanity, but perhaps even the differences between their ways of being are potentially not insolubly alien each to the other. It is only that some modes are more readily available to the male, and some others to the female. Perhaps it is only to the extent that I can accept the woman within myself, that I can ever hope to understand women, to receive all that they have to teach and to offer me.

Yin and Yang are the ancient Chinese vital principles of the universe, the fundamental polar categories which maintain life's state of tension when in opposition and effect its harmony when they work together. Yin is the Feminine Principle and Yang, the Male. The ancient Taoist sage, Lao Tzu, in describing to Confucius his voyage to the World Beginning, tells:

> The mind is darkened by what it learns there and cannot understand; the lips are folded, and cannot speak. But I will try to embody for you some semblance of what I saw. I saw yin, the female energy, in its motionless grandeur; I saw yang, the male energy, rampant in its fiery vigour. The motionless grandeur came about the earth; the fiery vigour burst out from heaven. The two penetrated one another, were inextricably blended and from their union the things of the world were born.[13]

Originally neither of these categories was more important than the other. At first they merely referred to one side or the other of a hill or of a river. Gradually they began to acquire reciprocal characteristics such as darkness and light, such that one had no meaning except in contrast to the other. Yang, the male principle, came to be characterized as sunlike from heaven, bright, firm, creative. Yin, the female principle, represented the earth, the moon, dark, yielding, sustaining.

At first these modes were seen as equivalent primal powers of equal value, both being completely necessary aspects of existence. Some radical feminists would argue that life begins as female and that the earliest and best developed civilized culture was a now-lost matriarchal society, which modern man only both mimics and distorts with his oppressive patriarchy. [14] There is some evidence that the concepts of Yin and Yang may have suffered some comparable distortion.

The earliest known Chinese culture in which they appear is the Shang Dynasty, a hunting people who developed to the pastoral stage, shamanistically-led believers in a world filled with spirits. But more significant in this context, the Shangs were a totemistic matriarchy who believed "the female was the animal of change, the animal that could bring about transformation." [15] But the female power of the mare gave way to the male power of the dragon when, in the 12th Century, B.C., a neolithic Western tribe called Chou invaded the area and replaced the Shang as the dominant power. Perhaps, as is often the case, the god-like figures (or in this case the goddesses) of the pantheon of the conquered people are relegated to lesser and more demonic positions in the spiritual hierarchy of the conquerors. By the time of the Chou Dynasty, Yin began to take on aspects of negativeness, weakness and evil in contrast to Yang's new-found positiveness, strength and inherent goodness.

So far I have suggested only a few of the fundamental characteristics of Yin and Yang. There are far richer images described in the *I Ching*, the three-thousand-year-old Chinese *Book of Changes*. It is a volume filled with fundamental folk wisdom. Like the Bible, it has been used as an oracle, and like the Bible it offers better guidance than prophecy.

In the *I Ching,* Yin appears as broken lines and Yang as unbroken ones. They are combined into hexagrams symbolizing the fundamental interplays of the female and the male forces in their mediation of the way of life. The basic male three line figure is called Ch'in, and the female is called K'un.

Ch'in, the concentration of the Yang force, denotes father and:

> ...suggests the idea of heaven, of circle, of a ruler...of jade, of metal, of cold, of ice, of deep red, of a good horse, of a thin horse, of a piebald horse, and of the fruit of trees. A door open. In Ch'in God struggles. [16]

K'un, in contrast denotes the mother and:

> ...suggests the idea of the earth, of cloth, of a cauldron, of parsimony, of a turning lathe, a young heifer, of a large wagon, of what is variegated, of a multitude, and of a handle and support, among soil it denotes what is black. K'un represents compendious receptivity, and response to Ch'in. K'un completes the great beginnings originated by Ch'in. Think of a door...closed. The greatest service to God is done through him in K'un. [17]

These alternating primal states, the Yin and the Yang, the feminine and the masculine principles expand and contract, grow and diminish, come and go like the night and the day, as "sooner or later everything runs into its opposite." [18] So it is that the cold and the warm seasons give way one to the next. Who is to say one is more important than the other? Unfortunately some men do choose to give pre-eminence to one over the other. So it is that in consulting the Chinese *Book of Changes,* the seeker is urged to remember that:

> The New Year commences in February, before the Spring's Equinox and opens the six months of creative activity which come under the domination of the forces of yang. During this time the masculine pursuits of farming, hunting, building and marrying are all important.
>
> The yang phase passes its peak in June, prior to the summer

Solstice and wanes until it is superceded by the forces of yin, which begin their reign just before the Autumn Equinox in September. During the second half of the year more docile, feminine activities come to the fore; weaving, recreation, the planning of the year ahead, childbirth. [19]

Despite such pejorative distortions of the feminine, it seems to me that there is some basic wisdom in the Taoist doctrines of the Yin and the Yang. Most important for me is the insistent reminder that there cannot be one without the other, that each has qualities needed by the other, that the masculine and the feminine principles complete one another as they alternate as rhythmically as the tides. Their equivalent significance amidst their significant differences is for me the model not only for my relation as a man to a woman, but as a human being to every other human being. Vonnegut points out that it is a grave error to mistake or let:

...old-fashioned writers...make people believe that life...(has) leading characters, minor characters, significant details, insignificant details...lessons to be learned, tests to be passed, and a beginning, a middle, and an end. [20]

There are differences certainly among human beings, and some clear ones I believe between men and women, but it is in our sexual and our human differences that we are perhaps most alike. The Taoist doctrine of differences and similarities which underlies the interplay of the Yin and the Yang (and our foolishness about them) is clearly stated in the ancient parable of "Three in the Morning":

There was a man who kept monkeys. He told the monkeys, one time, that their acorns would be rationed: each monkey would get three acorns in the morning, and four acorns in the evening. The monkeys were infuriated. And so the keeper said, "Look, I am not an unreasonable man. We will change this. Each of you may have four acorns in the morning, and three acorns in the evening." And with this the monkeys were all pleased. [21]

The strong surge of feeling that I have experienced while

writing these last few pages makes me aware that this is my center and perhaps my only real contribution. Whatever specific differences in the sexes that I may come up with will certainly be less moving observations to me (and I assume to you, the reader) than is my sense of isolation in this world of people. In the male/female separation, I feel the loneliness, the terror and the void most clearly. And so only now, in this writing do I come to understand how much of my longing to be a woman, to bring forth the womanliness in myself, is partly my wish to be less alone, to be less firmly imprisoned in my own separate skin.

The neurotic exaggerations of *the simply human* sometimes present in the men and women who seek therapy is instructive. Perhaps, like Jews, therapy patients are just like everybody else, *only more so.*

My experience as a psychotherapist suggests to me that the most comon matching in marriages in our culture is in the direction of the obsessional male to the hysterical female. At best, the obsessional male can be described as logical, thoughtful, realistic, capable of attention to detail and planning ahead, stable and self-contained. At worst, his wife may complain that he is too reasonable, unresponsive, hard-headed, detached, cold, picky and unfeeling. The hysterical female on the other hand may be described at best as warm, affectionate, emotionally expressive, imaginative and capable of deep feeling relatedness. At worst her husband may complain that she is emotionally demanding, greatly exaggerates her complaints, is unstable and undependable, and has no sense of logic whatsoever.

Thus this matching of seemingly gender-bound characteristics brings about the completions of the male by the female and the female by the male that make for the richest and most fulfilling aspects of marriage. Paradoxically, at the same time, this intermesh also leads to the most exquisite pain, misunderstanding, and seemingly unresolvable conflict. As a family therapist, or at least in my work with couples, I have a distinct advantage. My own marriage, you see, can much better be described as the mating of a somewhat obsessional female with myself, a colorfully hysterical male. At my best, then, I have a good deal of the woman-in-myself available to me which makes me much less likely to side disproportionately with the men in the couples, for in my own best view of myself I have little need for logic, much commitment to feeling, and a much greater trust in intuitive understanding than in scientific inquiry.

Be that as it may, from whichever side we approach marriage or mating, it behooves us to seek out people who will complete our own skewed or self-limiting approach to total humanness. Marriage can be viewed as literally seeking, if not the "better half," at least *the other half*. It becomes a way of finding in the other a means of compensating for our own imbalance. At worst, of course, it's a matter of simply finding someone else to blame, but even that has its place in our difficult trek through the world as a single, isolated and only partially-developed individual human being.

It is tempting to try to find some further understanding of the difference between male and female in the homosexual analog. Of course, there too the differences that we find may be more the result of centuries of cultural impact than of some fundamental biological differences between the sexes. Nonetheless, let us take a look and see what we find.

One of the differences between male and female homosexual coupling is that there are among male homosexuals many more brief, faceless encounters, pickups of strangers in public places, which involve fleeting, explicitly sexual interplays without one person getting to know so much as the other's name. This is less true of female homosexual encounters. It is my impression, as well, that male homosexual couples tend to have relationships of briefer duration than lesbian couples. It may well be that the difference is that males bring to their homosexual relationship less of a sense of relatedness, less instinct for nesting, or continuing supportive nonsexual feelings.

This tends to be supported by my impressions of the

differences between male and female homosexual relationships which are brought about in institutionalized settings, such as reformatories and prisons. In male correctional institutions, the typical relationship is characterized by the dichotomy of "wolf" and "punk." The wolf is the aggressive, pursuing male homosexual who exploitively intimidates the younger, more passive male homosexual, the punk. He offers protection and rewards for the punk's co-operation, and brutal punishment for his reluctance. Most of the relationships involve an emphasis on explicit and somewhat impersonal sexual exchanges.

In contrast, the homosexual relationships of institutionalized females are more lasting, social and elaborate. They tend to congregate into "family" groups with designations such as "aunt," "uncle," "niece," "nephew," "cousin," with much more communal-living emphasis. There tends to be much more in the way of getting to know one another, of affectionate and social exchanges, and less of the anonymous and exploitive explicitly sexual interchange, more common to the male homosexual.

All of these observations are in general fitting with the Yin/Yang distinctions and with popular characterizations of men as strong, active and aggressive, while women are often seen as weak, passive, and submissive. All of this then fits with men being viewed as sexually exploitive while women we are told are more vulnerable because of their need for love as a grounding for sex. All of these stereotyped descriptions are further supported by a vision of men as logical, fond of detached abstract thinking, instruments of Logos, with women in direct contrast understood as being emotional, intuitive, mediators of Eros. Women are thus seen as being more in touch with their Unconscious and with the fundamentals of everyday living, as allowing Nature to flow through them rather than actively fighting to conquer it as a man is thought to do.

It seems to me that these caricatures and distortions of gender resist clarification and eradication not only because they serve the dominant male in his political oppression of the female, but because they are *not* totally incorrect. Instead they create as much mischief as they do and are as difficult to dispel because they just barely miss the mark. They are grotesquely subtle distortions of actual differences, which create confusion and irrelevance without being so totally made up out of whole cloth as to be transparently wrong enough to be readily understood and finally gotten rid of.

I can only hope to substitute descriptions of the sexual differences which avoid any suggestion of one being superior to the other. The best recent explorations of these matters which I have come upon are presented by a very wise woman who also happened to follow her career as wife and mother with many creative years as a Jungian psychotherapist. Irene Claremont DeCastillejo in her touchingly profound book, *Knowing Women,* [22] describes some of the differences between women and men in terms of differing sorts of awareness (thus eschewing the popular characterization of women as less aware). Her own writing is a movingly vivid example of female consciousness at its best as she demonstrates the feminine gift for *relatedness* in her enlightening exploration of "meeting" and of "bridges" in the living terms of immediate experience. She explores memorably the differences between man's "focused consciousness" and woman's "diffuse awareness" by describing the "basic woman" as one in whom:

> Everything is accepted, enjoyed or hated as a whole. She feels equally at one with the stars or a drop of dew, a rose or a blade of grass. She does not analyse them nor want to do anything about them. She is simply aware. For man and again I refer to the extreme male, the scent of a rose is not enough. He must learn all he can about it, prune and graft the plant to obtain even better roses. No woman, as woman, does such things. They would not occur to her.

I found Dr. DeCastillejo's awareness incredibly helpful. I am reminded by this of an exchange between myself and a young therapist in a therapy seminar which I run. He was terribly stuck in his work with a patient mainly because he resisted seeing that he was merely involved in the sort of honest errors so characteristic of relatively inexperienced workers in this field. Overly dismayed and threatened by having to recognize his mistakes, he was unable to learn from them and to move on. I told him that though he hated his status, I envied his being a Beginner. So many errors were allowable, so much could yet be learned, and so much help was available, if only he could allow himself to enjoy this childhood of his career.

I told him how awful I felt when Fritz Perls died, forcing me to recognize that there were no fathers left for me in this field, that no one could any longer be counted on to be bigger than myself. The young therapist's concern for my situation helped to free him from his stuck denial of his *pisher-hood*. (*Pisher* is an affectionate Jewish word for a pants-wetting toddler who is too young to be expected to be toilet-trained.) I shared with him that his concern also put me in touch with the realization that again and again I have returned to being a Beginner, each time I ventured into some new area of the work. And furthermore, I realized that the absence of fathers has encouraged me into taking the wise direction in the last few years more and more to look to women to instruct me.

I have three teen-aged sons and am deeply involved in both immersing myself in and trying to gradually relinquish my fathering of them. Of course, when I forget to let go, they remind me that I must. My oldest son, Jon, now at college, pitched our battles in political terms, again and again pushing against .my parental authority on constitutional grounds of human freedom and dignity of spirit. Nick, my youngest son, had to learn to survive a household in which for a long time *everyone* was more articulate than he. And so, by now, when he finds me arbitrarily authoritarian, he simply refuses to listen or to discuss in *my* terms. Instead, he meets my arbitrariness with straightforward obscenity, bird-calls, and satirical imitations of what he finds unacceptable in my behavior. My middle son, David, asserts his own independence more on the basis of logical analysis of our roles, supported by a precocious brilliance of argument. In a recent struggle with him, in self-defense, I called up an old, (I hope) obscure distinction in logical inquiry, the Nomethetic vs. the Ideographic (His and Mine).

To do so, I had to reach back many years into my own more intellectual posturings. He, of course, *was* aware of the esoteric distinction, and so managed another step toward no longer needing parenting. Later, I realized that the Nomothetic/Ideographic distinction seemed an apt metaphor for the differences between male and female approaches. At the time when I first came across it I was less in touch with the woman within me and was somewhat rigidly embedded in an examination of the metatheoretical grounds of scientific inquiry.

I searched the shelves for a book of the sort that I once read avidly, but have since for years avoided. At last, I rediscovered a book with the (for me, now) unlikely title of *The Structure of Science: Problems in the Logic of Scientific Explanation.* In it Ernest Nagel re-explained to me that the Nomethetic approach was that of the natural sciences and some of the social sciences "Which seeks to establish abstract general laws for indefinitely repeatable events and processes." [23] It is the "pure" detached logical attempt to consciously free the mind from the everyday realities in order to establish predictive, controlling, probabilistic concepts of what life is about. It is a *man's* way of dealing with the world.

The Ideographic approach is a powerful metaphor for the feminine psychological approach, as I understand it. It is a prime approach to the understanding of human events, such as in the study of History, more as an art than a science. The Nomethetic "contain few if any references to specific objects, dates or places ... " [24] This abstract generality contrasts sharply with the Ideographic approach in which statements are " ... without exception singular in form and are replete with proper names, designations for particular times or periods, and geographic specifications." [25]

This female *relatedness* is aimed at meeting unique, singular events without concern for formulating general rules about their occurrence. After all, a woman understands that a particular interaction between people happens only once, and that abstract speculations about it deaden its immediacy and cloud our intuitive grasp of its once-and-for-allness. Attention to the feelingful aspirations of the particular human qualities of the people involved makes it irrelevant for the feminine force to try to make up unreal conceptual laws about them. *Masculine* conceptualization thrusts towards *mastery* while *feminine* understanding moves toward *contact*.

I find it difficult, yet absolutely crucial, that I remain aware of these differences in approach of the male and the female without deeming one more important than the other, one superior and the other inferior, one the center and the other the surrounding ground. The reciprocal interdependence of the masculine and the feminine, of the Yin and the Yang is concretized visually in the eternally-fucking black and white fish which symbolically represent the Tao, the uncarved block which is the natural way of life to which it behooves us to submit, the great water of nature in which we fish must lose ourselves.

As a man, I must listen closely to what women have to say if I am to be instructed. Eleanor Bertine (yet another woman therapist of Jungian persuasion) writes of her understanding of the relation of Yin and Yang, of the psychological sense of the roles of the feminine and the masculine principles:

> The two together are essential for a complete personality, the masculine giving the forms, the feminine the color. But the principle of one's own sex should always be in the ascendance, with the other presence in a complementing capacity. [26]

For myself, and others I know, the greater danger of the two appears to be the risk that the principle of the other sex may be totally excluded.

Each of us must allow the emergence of the principle of the opposite sex within ourselves. A man must listen for the voice of his anima, of his woman within. And each woman would be wise to harken to her animus, to the concentration of Yang force within herself which will offer her own masculine resources and balance when she needs them. Bertine stresses the need, at the same time, to keep one's own same sex principle in ascendance. For myself, and most other men I know, the greater danger of the two appears to be the risk that our feminine natures may be totally excluded.

It may be that during this time of women's striving for independence there is some greater temporary risk of their masculine upsurge overwhelming the primary feminine identity. I am reminded here of the rhetoric of Jill Johnston, a militant Gay Liberation Feminist who insists:

Until all women are lesbians, there will be no true political revolution. [27]

And indeed the Lesbian Gay Liberationists have been a significantly supportive factor in the Women's Liberation Movement. A comparatively small group of these homosexual women have brought strength and dedication to the Movement, unimpeded by dependence on the male. Yet beyond a certain point they seem more a part of the problem than of the solution in this critical aspect of human evolution. Woman must come to her own maleness (as man to his femaleness) but we all need to beware the demonic force of our shadow as it emerges from being hidden from consciousness lest the solution be worse than the problem.

Perhaps it is enough to say that for the moment men are more in danger of completely missing the woman in themselves, while women must take care to resist being overwhelmed by the man in themselves. At another time in history, the dangers might be reversed. By way of example of the male side of this struggle, I would like to share part of a letter from a good friend whose life-long struggle with his Anima helps him to understand my own:

I still am not able to separate passivity, castration, paralysis, and defeat from the sweet gentleness of acquiescence. In fact, I experience them as having to co-exist. At the very same time I know I must resist at all costs giving in, that I must hold perfectly still and not utter a single cry of protest as I am being beaten and tortured, at this self same time, I know there is a gentle, loving, comforting companion who never leaves my side although I cannot always see or hear or feel her.

It has been my impression that ever since the brain tumor was diagnosed, this gentleness has become much more evident in you, has occupied a much larger part of your ego. Naturally, I see the tumor as a material manifestation of the negative, devouring Mother. Therefore, I believe a compensatory element has emerged in consciousness, and it is this aspect in you, as in myself that I seek to establish contact with.[28]

By pointing to the risks in finding the rest of ourselves, I do not mean to suggest in any way that they are not risks worth taking. A man out of touch with his feminine side, like a woman who has disowned the masculine aspect of herself, is a caricature of what a complete person might be. And if a person is out of touch with the anima or animus aspect of the opposite sex in him- or herself, surely that person will be an enemy to the personification of that disowned opposite sex when he meets it abroad in the men or women with whom he or she must make a life.

Again I will let a woman instruct me on the matter of knowing that I cannot disclaim one aspect of myself without losing some of the valued remainder of my nature. Here is one woman's dream that tells the story. The dream reads:

I saw a woman sleeping. In her sleep she dreamed Life stood before her and held in each hand a gift--in the one Love, in the other Freedom. And she said to the woman, "Choose!" And the woman waited long; and she said, "Freedom!" And Life said, "Thou has well chosen. If thou hadst said "Love," I would have given thee that thou didst ask for; and I would have gone from thee, and returned to thee no more. Now, the day will come when I shall return, and that day I shall bear both gifts in one hand."

I heard the woman laugh in her sleep.[29]

Chapter Ten

LET OUR DREAMS INSTRUCT US

Wisely enough, man has always been fascinated by his dreams. That is not to say that there have not always existed among us those imagination-stifling practical hyper-realists who would say, "But it's only a dream." Their tone is the same as others who decry the soul-force of myths saying, "They are, after all, only stories." In more recent post-Enlightenment times, scientists have come to believe that "it is likely that the subjective experience we call dreaming is merely a by-product of an essentially physiological process,"[1] just as Aristotle once understood dreams as an effect of the nocturnal coursing of the blood resulting from an imbalance of the humors. Not that I deny the physiological aspect of any part of experience. Rather, I have come to believe that all speculative attempts to resolve the mind-body dilemma are futile. My concern is that the physiological focus not distract us from the treasures of a more phenomenological approach. And indeed, despite these attempts at rational/scientific and tough-minded explanations, men open to themselves have always experienced the power of their dreams.

The shaman, spiritual leader of the hunting and gathering societies of the paleolithic era (as well as among their contemporary Eskimo and Indian progeny), asserted his own inspirational power through the impact of his trance-like visions and dreams. And each young man in the tribe was encouraged to define his identity and his destiny by way of his own personal dreams and visions. The shaman inspired dreams, till the priest-hood emerged to exploit men's visions, transfiguring individual inspiration into group dogma which turned men away from open-ended personal imagination and daring and thrust them toward conformity. No longer to be guided by personal intuition now each person was to be directed by "truths" and reductive explanations which would rob him of his own singular power.

And so it is that Joseph Campbell, modern master mythologist, warns us with his statement: "For myself, I believe that we owe both the imagery and the poetical insights of myth (vision and dream) to the genius of the tender-minded; to the tough-minded only their reduction to religion."[2] His terms "tough-and tender-minded" are misleading unless we see that a special kind of courage is demanded of those who would give themselves over to their dreams. So it is that the old Sioux visionary, Black Elk, points out that "It is hard to follow one great vision in this world of darkness and of many changing shadows. Among these shadows men get lost."[3] He recognized the dangers of the darkness, not the darkness of the inner space of man's mind so much as the shadowy spirit world that surrounded each man.

In the history of dream interpretation, some of the earliest ascribed meanings were non-psychological though it is now possible to re-evaluate them psychologically. For instance in the Old Testament, Joseph speaks to his brothers saying:

Hear this dream which I have dreamed: behold we were binding sheaves in the field, and lo, my sheaf arose and stood upright; and behold, your sheaves gathered round it, and bowed down to my sheaf. [4]

According to the Bible, they understood the dream as a prophecy of Joseph's future ascendancy, a prediction which they sought to undo by selling their youngest brother into slavery. Like all attempts to flee from fate, this escapist act, of course, allowed the prophecy to come true by facilitating Joseph's contact with the Pharoah and his subsequent rise to power. From a psychological viewpoint, it is easier to understand their hatred of him in terms of the unconscious ambition for dominance expressed in his dream.

So too, when Joseph subsequently was taken down to Egypt, the Pharoah's land, it came to pass that no one could interpret the ruler's dream. We might understand Joseph's response either as prophetic or as merely shrewdly and intuitively insightful. The Pharoah's account to Joseph was:

I have had a dream ... : Behold in my dream I was standing on the banks of the Nile; and seven cows, fat and sleek, came up out of the Nile and fed in the reed grass; and seven other cows came up after them, poor and very gaunt and thin, such as I had never seen in all the land of Egypt. And the thin and gaunt cows ate up the first seven fat cows, but when they had eaten them no one would have known that they had eaten them, for they were still as gaunt as at the beginning. Then I awoke. I also saw in my dream seven ears growing in one stalk, full and good; and seven ears withered, thin and blighted by the east wind, sprouted after them, and the thin ears swallowed up the seven good ears. [5]

The court magicians had not been able to offer any explanation, but Joseph, bless his therapist's heart, read it like a letter, though he credited God with inspiring the interpretation. He told the confounded ruler:

The dream of Pharoah is one: God has revealed to Pharoah what he is about to do. The seven good cows are seven years, and the seven good ears are seven years; the dream is one. The seven lean and gaunt cows that came up after them are seven years, and the seven empty ears blighted by the east wind are also seven years of famine. It is as I told Pharoah, God has shown to Pharoah what he is about to do. There will come seven years of great plenty throughout all the land of Egypt, but after them there will arise seven years of famine, and all the plenty will be forgotten in the land of Egypt; the famine will consume the land, and the plenty will be unknown in the land by reason of that famine which will follow for it will be grievous. And the doubling of Pharoah's dream means that the thing is fixed by God, and God will shortly bring it to pass. [6]

And at this crucial point, at which his wisdom was most

impressive, and when the ruler felt most vulnerable, Joseph moved in to take over by offering the powerful but perplexed dreamer the following advice:

Now therefore *let Pharoah select a man discreet and wise, and set him over the land of Egypt.* Let Pharoah proceed to appoint overseers over the land, and take the fifth part of the produce of the land of Egypt during the plenteous years. And let them gather all the food of these good years that are coming, and lay up grain under the authority of Pharoah for food in the cities, and let them keep it. The food shall be a reserve for the land against the seven years of famine which are to befall the land of Egypt, so that the land may not perish through the famine.[7]

Guess who got the job! Right! Joseph's seemingly ruthless brothers turn out to have been wise in their uneasiness about his ambition to dominate. It can only be a matter of idle speculation as to whether the Pharoah's dream can represent an undeciphered message from that wiser, dreaming part of the ruler's unconscious that could have made a judgment about factors affecting the fertility of the land. At any rate, he took the dream to be prophetic and accepted Joseph's interpretation of its divine message. Dreams have power, and it is best that we each learn to read the meaning of our own nocturnal visions.

In cultures that do *not* value dreams highly, we may have to learn from special teachers, such as today's gurus, the psychotherapists. But the most instructive means of coming to know and trust oneself are determined to some extent by the culture in which we grow up. As for myself, the ways in which my life has not instructed me (or in which I would not listen and learn) have been compensated to some extent by the instruction of my therapists and my patients.

But some cultures are more supportive of trusting one's dreams than are others. We in the West, have long classified as "primitive" that silenced majority of peoples who live in non-industrial traditions where each man is more in touch with his unconscious than with progress, more taken with myth and dream than with history and science. Of course, some of our classifying of dark-skinned, tribal, non-Christian, non-capitalistic societies had the obvious imperialistic advantage of justification for economic exploitation, as we saved their heathen souls by sending in missionaries, defended by guns and bayonets, and followed by "trading companies."

Not only have we done many awful things to people who had the right to live as they pleased without our interference, but what is more, too often we have missed learning what they might have taught us, had we been open to their "primitive" tribal wisdom. Consider for example the Senoi Dream People.[8] In 1935 a Western scientific expedition first come across this preliterate society of some 12,000 people living in isolated communities in the central mountain range of the Malay Peninsula. The Senoi supported themselves in a mixed hunting-fishing and agricultural economy, lived in peace and harmony, and were very much in touch with their own primordial dream power.

The major authority of the Senoi community, once held by patrilineal elders, had now been passed on to *Halaks,* their primitive psychological healer/educators. But such men only guide and inspire, while the people rule themselves by democratic consensus, unsupported by any coercive structure such as a police force, army, jail or mental hospital. There appears to be no violent crime or seriously destructive conflict within the community. Physical and mental disease is minimal. And there is no war with the surrounding tribes. Extra-communal peace is maintained by encouraging neighbouring groups to believe that the Senoi practice black magic (thus scaring them off without having to fight them).

How is it then that the Senoi are able to maintain this harmony within their own community? Their power rests in their dream psychology which has a twofold emphasis: the interpretation of dreams, and the expression of dreams in voluntary trance states.

Though the Halaks are especially sensitive in such matters,

this dream power is common knowledge and everyday practice to all members of the Senoi community. Each small Senoi child learns dream interpretation at family breakfast time when the older family members analyze the dreams the child remembers and reports from the night before. Then the men and the older children gather to describe and explore the dreams which other members of the community share with the group.

The Senoi psychology of dream interpretation may be understood in this way:

> ... man creates features or images of the outside world in his own mind as part of the adaptive process. Some of these features are in conflict with him or with each other. Once internalized, these hostile images turn man against himself and against his fellows. In dreams man has the power to see these facts of his psyche, which have been disguised in external forms, associated with his own fearful emotions, and turned against him and the internal images of other people. If the individual does not receive social aid through education and therapy, these hostile images, built up by man's normal receptiveness to the outside world, get tied together and associated with one another in a way which makes him physically, socially, and psychologically abnormal. [9]

Without help, man does himself in, undone by his bewildering dream-beings. But when a Senoi is willing to turn to his brothers for aid, the tortuous dream-beings can be transformed into helpful allies. So it is that when a Senoi child has a nightmare of falling through space, his report is met with delight. He is told that this wonderful dream may lead to many good things if only he will explore the trip of where he would fall to, and what wonders he might discover there. All dream images have purpose and promise for the Senoi adult, so supported has he been as a child in learning to let his dream-creatures befriend him. A dream of falling is transfigured into one of being drawn to the land of falling-powers because they love the dreamer and would instruct him in pleasure and spiritual power. Eventually the very dream experience becomes joyful.

The young dreamer learns to thrust himself further and further into each dream. In dreams of danger, he gains the courage to fight on by learning that he can call on the potential ally of any other dream-image to come to his aid. Any foe subdued in the process will return as an ally or servant. Pleasurable dreams are always to be pursued to a point of resolution, which then gives something useful to bring to the other members of his community, while of course adding to his own pleasure as well. So it is that sexual dreams should always continue to orgasm. And from the dream-lover, it is possible to demand a poem, a song or a dance which can later be offered to the group.

There are no taboo images or actions in dreams. Not only is everything permitted, but each aspect can be a source of personal pleasure and communal usefulness. The Senoi know that we need everything we've got. Every aspect of an individual's unconscious is of value to him, if he can learn to enjoy it. Revealing himself to himself and to his brothers is supported in every Senoi from the time he is a small child. Those experiences which first make him anxious, are eventually understood to be sources of pleasure and of power. Social transparency minimizes distrust, and social conflicts revealed in dreams are resolved in the next day's communal exchanges. Nothing human is considered to be alien, and so all men are more aware of the brotherhood of every other man.

So it is that the Senoi show great intuitive psychological sophistication in their understanding and use of dream interpretation, just as have other so-called primitive groups, such as the Iroquois. [10] A search of the literature turns up a good deal of variation, admixture and alteration of psychological and non-psychological interpretation of dreams in different times and places. [11] In contemporary times, the psychological interpretation of dreams has been most influenced by Freud and Jung.

In Freud's masterpiece, *The Interpretation of Dreams*, [12] published in 1900, he has revealed to us the dream as a meaningful expression of the psyche, a symbolically disguised expression of repressed unconscious wishes. Freud's exploration of the dream restored in a new way the primitive's faith in such nocturnal visions. But Freud saw them only as expressions of conflict, of hidden psychological motives which could be of use only if we got beyond the anxiety which led us to repress that part of ourselves to begin with. In Freud's opinion, dreams were to be understood exclusively in terms of personal history (most often of early sexual development) serving the psychic economy by holding fast anxieties too overwhelming to be experienced consciously.

Jung, too, attributes great importance to dreams, not only as the royal road to the personal unconscious, but also as a way in which the unconscious compensates for the conscious imbalance. When we live out this imbalance in our waking life, dreams provide the regulative activity of the unconscious which helps the psyche toward individuation for the development of wholeness. Thus Jung accepts dreams as expressing anxieties and wishes but sees them as going beyond personal concerns of the individual dreamer. They also express fundamental human problems which occur again and again in the history of mankind.

The prophetic and compensatory character of dreams are as instructive about broad human concerns as their clinical aspects are about symptoms of personal conflict. Dreams provide a kind of wisdom of the heart, an echoing voice of a profound human sensitivity too often lost to us in the reasonable life of days. If we would but listen to the voice of our dreams we might be less alone, instructed by an often neglected power, echoes of our deepest human insights and visions of a world of experiences too overwhelming and too rapidly ongoing to yield to the scrutiny of intellectual analysis and scientific reason.

Jung tells us that: "Within each one of us there is another whom we do not know. He speaks to us in dreams and tells us how differently *he* sees us from how *we* see ourselves. When we find ourselves in an insolubly difficult situation, this stranger in us can sometimes show us a light which is more suited than anything else to change our attitude fundamentally, namely just that attitude which had led us into the difficult situation."13

Dreams are to our conscious waking experiences as the moon is to the sun, providing a special intensifying nocturnal light. It is no surprise that The Moon Tarot card foretells of the prevailing of imagination, intuition, and dreams. Turning up reversed it warns that practical considerations will prevail over imaginative urges, with peace gained at a cost.

Sometimes I forget that I have a secret friend, a wise but hidden counselor, whose voice I ought to listen to more often. This counselor is my dreaming self, that part of me who sees more clearly than my waking self, whose vision is less cluttered with reason, logic, and conventional wisdom. Sometimes when I feel stuck, even in my work, about how to deal with a situation that seems overwhelming, if I am open to listening my dreaming self will advise me well.

I remember some time ago I had been treating a man for several months, since shortly after the breakup of his marriage. His wife and children remained in the Middle West, he set up a new home here in Washington and tried to work out his confused and anguished feelings. At first he seemed terribly intellectual, abstracted, and detached. But soon, beneath this facade he revealed a good deal of sensitivity, tenderness, and pain. But he did come to realize that much of the marital disaster was a function of his own behavior and not just that of his crazy wife.

And he also came to see that he did indeed want to restore the marriage. He worked with his own feelings, returning to his original home some weekends attempting to work out a reconciliation with his wife. At first, she met his efforts with her bitterness and hopelessness. But eventually she, too, wanted to work things out.

One day she came with him to Washington and I met with the two of them and with another therapist who was visiting and operating as a consultant. This situation was messy--they were difficult to deal with as a couple, but I felt some promise. For this discussion the crucial aspect was that the wife came across as an emotionally unstable, terribly erratic, impulsive, aggressive, mercurial, seductive, but ultimately painful individual with whom to come to terms. One aspect of this was revealed in the fact that when she came in, she immediately sort of hopped up onto the couch in a pose that was gamin-like, innocent, and characterized by the unbridled, spontaneity of a nine-year-old girl. At the same time she was being actively and crudely seductive; drawing her legs up under her on the couch with her skirt riding up to her ass, and sitting in a naively seductive, self-exposing way.

There were many other problems: in dealing with her, everything was a dance. It was as though she invited some kind of co-operation, agreement, closeness, only to disappear when I or the other therapist or her husband moved forward in response. Actually, what disappeared was the sense of grace, warmth, or accommodation. What emerged in the face of anyone's extension was a very punitive, abrasive, painfully wilful set of retaliations. We ended the session all feeling that there was *some* hope, though certainly it would be difficult for us to work together. We'd all give it some time, think about it, come together again, and see where we'd go from there.

There were a number of false starts during which she and her husband made plans for her to come and live with him in Washington and for the treatment to continue and include her. None of these worked out. Finally, after three months she did move to Washington. They took a house and began plans for reconciliation of their marriage.

She called me, made an appointment and came in for an exploratory interview, during which time we were going to try and figure out how we might best proceed and whether indeed we would work together. I, for one, was uncertain and ambivalent. Of course my uncertainty made her absolutely sure that she must work with me, that nothing else would do.

When we finally made the appointment for her to come in I found that I was quite anxious. It had something to do with my uneasiness about her denied aggressiveness, her insistence on controlling the situation, and the ways in which she ignored what she was doing. The focus for me was vaguely in the sexual area.

That night I had a dream. I dreamed that she had come in alone to explore with me the possibility of setting up an ongoing therapy arrangement. She came into the room and as I closed the door, she threw off her coat, hopped up onto the couch in her cross-legged, crotch-spreading way, and sat there smiling. Her friendly readiness to talk ignored the seductively demanding posture which she had taken on. My thought in the dream (which I had not made clear to myself in my waking examination of the problem) was "How the hell am I going to work with this woman who is so sexually aggressive and so ignores it that I can't even deal with it with her? How can I get it out of the way and get to work on the problems of her feelings about her marriage, about our relationship, about who the hell she is and where she is going?" And then in the dream I knew what I had to do. I said to her, "Look, we will work together, but only on one condition. That condition is that when you come here you have to take your pants off." Her reaction was shock, but since she must have the treat- ment she agreed. I don't remember her taking her pants off in the dream but the next thing I knew it was clear that she did have her pants off. Only now she was wearing a long skirt pulled over her legs and down to her ankles, legs close together, sitting in a demure, prissy, prudish posture. It was clear that she was non- plussed by having the aggressive seductiveness of her posture robbed from her by my taking control and saying, "Okay, that's the way you want it, that's the way it'll be. But I'm in charge."

I woke realizing that somehow my dreaming self had made clear to me the nature of the problem, that is, that I was anxious about the aggressiveness which I was reacting to and she was denying. The metaphor for my dealing with this in the dream was to say, "You can be aggressive if you like, but I'm in charge, you'll have to deal with my instructions." It became very clear that at that point she was no longer aggressive. She returned to the scared little-girl self beneath her quaint posturing. The dream was a kind of self-supervision. I felt relieved knowing that now I could work with her without this being a problem. When she finally did come to see me I had no time free to work with her. I had committed my time elsewhere, since she had been playing fuck-around with the schedule and I wasn't going to keep my time open just waiting for her. And so I referred her to another therapist here in town who I thought would do a good job in helping her to work through her problems because he would not be intimidated by some of her aggressive defenses. She was disappointed and insisted that I should work with her. Finally she gave in and decided that her own well-being was more important than getting her way at that moment.

During the course of that interview, I told her of my dream. She laughed, with some embarrassment, but also with the understanding that she must be defeated in her efforts to keep people off balance if she is to get anything from them. I counseled her to tell my dream to the therapist to whom I was referring her, so that he might have the benefit of the supervision of my dreaming self until he got a chance to get his own dreaming self to work in supervising him with this difficult patient.

Again and again I find that my own inner counselor, my secret dreaming self, is not only wise and helpful but usually amusing as well. I consider it gratuitous good fortune that my secret self has so ironic a sense of humor. If I am to be possessed by this friendly *dybbuk* how lovely for me that *she* can help me to laugh at my plight as she instructs me. Sometimes I find it frightening to be possessed by the trickster within myself who gives me messages in a Cassandra-like fashion, dark tales of black humor for which I am often unprepared. I am always enlightened but I feel vulnerable and anxious in the hands of part of myself that I must trust, though I do not know her well or understand her.

She spoke to me clearly when first I considered private practice.

Many years ago when I was still spending most of my working time in a government mental hygiene clinic, I had testily begun to try my hand at private practice. The idea of working for myself on my own was very appealing. I had thought through some of the problems, had taken an office which I was sharing part time with someone else, and had a few patients. I was almost ready to give up complaining that the institutions and agencies for which I worked would not give me enough freedom. I felt ready to take on the responsibility that must underlie such freedom. I looked for a private office and let some other professionals know that I was ready to expand my tentative beginnings of private practice. I talked just a bit at the clinic about my plans to resign, had a tentative date in mind and was finalizing the decision for myself. That night I had a dream.

I dreamed that I was on an air field. My instructor was patting me on the shoulder telling me that I was to make my first solo flight. It was in an old World War I bi-plane. I wore the traditional leather jacket, leather cap tied under the chin, goggles and streaming white scarf. Though scared, I climbed into the plane and took off. In the dream I knew that up to that point I had never soloed before, only flown in the company of an instructor. I got the plane off the ground just fine. I took it up; began to try maneuvers. The sky was beautiful. I felt confident. The plane handled well.

But then suddenly it went out of control, hurtled downward with a screaming whine which World War I movies had told me preceded the flyer's catastrophe. In the dream, my own plane did crash but somehow I seemed to have been thrown clear and was unhurt. The plane itself was a burning mass of tangled metal, but I was uninjured.

A crowd gathered. They seemed delighted and amazed that I was all right. It was a miracle which they all accepted as they congratulated me on having been able to come through the crash uninjured. But I myself was upset. I explained to someone standing beside me "But you don't understand. I'm fine, but the plane was not insured, it cost me $13,000. I don't know how I'll pay it."

I awoke realizing that $13,000 was my yearly salary at the clinic. On the basis of the dream I decided that I was still too frightened to take on the solo flight of a full time private practice. I had not paid a hell of a lot of attention to my anxiety about money up to that point. Now it seemed to me too dangerous a hazard. As a result I put off going into full time practice for another six months.

Sometimes my dreaming self tugs at my sleeve, without my being in the midst of some particular struggle or problem that needs solving. Like a good parent or older sister, she merely offers me some bit of enlightenment about the nature of the universe because it happens to have occurred to her at that moment. Such was the case when I found myself in my dream in a large amphitheatre of a room in which there was hubbub and murmur, a sense that everyone was expectant, disturbed, upset. There were many, many people there costumed in different national garb. It was then in looking about that I realized that I was at the United Nations. It was a time of crisis. A nuclear war was only hours away, one that would destroy the entire planet. As representatives of our respective nations, we were gathered to try in those desperate eleventh hour moments to come up with some workable practical solution which might stem the holocaust.

The Secretary-General was speaking emotionally, trying to get each of us to bring whatever creative energy he had to finding some solution, any solution, so that the world might go on. I do not know what language he spoke. I saw him from far off, but each of us had a set of head phones and each of us received his frantic plea in his own language. He begged that we each do what we could to come up with some solution; that we put it in writing; that we submit it as soon as we possibly could; that no idea be deemed too outlandish; that no one hold back whatever he had to offer.

He had almost finished the speech when he paused significantly. Then he drew himself up and with great clarity he said: "You men who represent the peoples of the world, when you present these solutions there is one thing you must remember:

NEATNESS COUNTS!"

The dream had, of course, spotlighted my own repressively hidden concern for appearances and order. And so my dreaming self alerted me not only to that which I would criticise in our society, but to the compensating shadow-balance to my own obviously overstated life of the free spirit.

It was with bitter morning laughter that I responded to another such instructive joke about the state of our culture.

Several years ago when my children were quite young, visitors brought one of the boys a paint-by-numbers picture. It was one of those kits where the child need only check the number on a drawn pattern matched against the numbered jars of paints, paint the color in question and when he's finished a picture will emerge. I was a bit disturbed by this gift, feeling that it was the sort of present that limits a child's creative endeavors by giving him easy ways to know the sense that he has created something which does *not* really belong to him.

I did not at the time see that there was as well a broader response from me to similar elements in the entire culture. That night I dreamed that I myself received a *poetry kit* in the mail. It consisted of a large placard with numbers spaced out in lines across the face of it. In a separate compartment there were small strips of paper, with a number on the back and a word on the front of each strip. On the back of each of them there was a spot of dry paste. I was to take the strips of paper from the compartment, wet each one, and stick it in the appropriate spot on the placard. I did this in a random way, a piece here and a piece there and when I had finished, the placard was covered with lines of words. I discovered that I had "written" a poem. When I awoke I realized that this dream of the "write poetry by numbers kit" was a bitter commentary on our pre-packaged plastic culture.

This dream spoke as well of my own obscured proclivity in earlier writings to build a "creation" out of other men's writings, armed only with scissors and paste-pot.

Now that I get more and more beyond my apprehension to

take delight in listening to and responding to the voice of my dreaming self I find that I inspire like attention and responsiveness in those about me. In recent years a number of my patients have accomplished much of what they set out to do in therapy and found some new things for themselves. They are no longer anguished by the sense that their whole life is a problem. They are people who have worked through many of their struggles and who are much more competent, confident, free and expressive than they were when therapy began. Many of these patients have now come to ask if they can go on with treatment at a time when many other patients would terminate.

What they wish to do at that point is to spend some more time in treatment simply exploring their dreams. No longer do they see their dreams as symptoms which need to be analyzed away in order to solve problems. Rather now they come to see their dreams as sources of strength and spiritual guidance. They wish to be more in touch with their unconscious. They love dreaming. They ask to come to therapy even more often. Together we exchange dreams and find new ways of being together and new ways of being ourselves.

One such young woman had a dream which again and again has since served as a guide to the exciting personal adventures upon which she has embarked. My playfully kidding her about what she might expect from me in my role as companion on her trip made her surer of herself and less subject to my interference. The laughter between us has always helped both of us.

This, then, is her dream:

I've arrived at a beautiful harbor where I stand on a pier looking over the sun-shiney blue sky and the wide curve of the shore line. A fine, full-feathered bird has come there, too. It's a magnificent, giant bird; it's pleasant to regard its patience and grace, its strength and vision. I've been told that the sails of the boats that use this harbor have been fashioned after the wings of this bird, and the large boat that appears, its frame shaped like a fresh Santa Maria, its large white sail taut for a voyage, confirms this knowledge. The bird hovers abreast of the sails, each a motionlessly posed source of energy, perfectly complementing the other. As the bird vanishes, I sense that I am to board this boat.

We are beyond the harbor, on the open sea. The wind is great, but I, a novice at the sails, must learn to use it to advantage. My teacher holds the rudder steady, while a shadow woman, who had unsuccessfully tried her turn before me, sits silently near at the bow. I ease into handling the large, heavy sails, discovering confidence in motion as I intently maneuver the sails with deftness I didn't know I had. Just as I realize the pleasure of this accomplishment, my teacher says: "Now I'm going to make it harder for you!" He suggests I double up a crumpled canvas and try it as an additional sail. A seemingly absurd and impossible task. I give him a quizzical, mildly hostile look, and notice that he's paused in thought. I suppose that he's wondering if, indeed, it is a fair task. I decide that as a challenge to adventure, it is. When I wake up, we are still sailing.

Her growing familiarity with a trust in her dreaming self gives her courage when she falters, inspires hope that she may go places she has not yet dreamed of, and lets her dare to find the rest of herself. She had never written a poem before the night that her dreaming self nudged her awake from time to time between fragments of dreams and fantasies. Her dreaming self whispered in her ear, lines that she could not quite understand but willingly wrote down. By morning on the pad beside her bed, she found that she had written:

At night the creature stalks
me,
lying in wait;
sound signals
his nearness.

The creature is a headless bust

No head
No room
Arms folded
in solemn repose.

Something to leave
To get
to know
In later years
to maybe tame

Into aloneness
again;
The universal mist
takes fear aside;
replenishing comfort.

O

THE FOOL.

Chapter Eleven

BECOMING WHO YOU ARE

The differences between the Western Judeo-Christian traditions and their Oriental Hindu-Buddhist counterparts can be partially understood as a contrast between a *straight line* and a *circle.* In the West, the secular ideals of hard work, achievement, and progress fit well within the religious burden of avoiding temptation, living the good life, pursuing the straight and narrow course, and striving to imitate the never-to-be-achieved perfect nature of Christ. The straight line that we must follow if we are to be saved is that awesome distance between the badness of who we are and the goodness that is sweet Jesus.

In the circular way of the Orient, we need only recognize that *each of us is already the Buddha.* We need only surrender to our true nature. The guiding principle of the Western cosmos is the higher intelligence called the *Logos,* toward whose perfection we may ascend along that long straight line. In the East, in place of Logos, the Sanscrit word *Lila* is the term for the Lord's cosmic playfulness through which He creates the illusion of the world by casting all of us (and indeed all that is) in varying modes of His Divine Energy. All that separates anyone from the bliss of *Nirvana* is the *maya* of illusion. Our true nature is at the center of the circle of ourselves (called *Atman,* the Universal Self). As we find ways to give up the struggle to change our ways, we may let go of our passionate attachments to the bondage of trying to be what we are not.

What is often taken to be the fatalism and pessimism of the Orient is a sense that life is a wheel of sorrows, a continuing cycle of birth, suffering, and death into which people are again and again reborn through the ignorance of thinking they can change their true natures. Each person's *karma* is just that life into which he is born (sometimes defined as the rewards and punishments inherited from previous incarnations). The karma of this life is both the effect of previously led lives and the cause of what is to be endured or enjoyed in future lives.

I do *not* believe in reincarnation. I believe we are not punished *for* our sins, but *by* them. Yet the metaphor of karma is both compelling and enlightening. It seems to me that we are born and develop to become who and what we are, largely beyond the power of our will. We may explain our development psychoanalytically in terms of early family experiences, but even so, the issues of ensuing personal unhappiness can be attributed to little more than having been born into the wrong house. Had I grown up in the house next door, perhaps I would have been more fully loved, more tenderly accepted, and better appreciated. Who knows?

As is, family and culture encourage us to "improve" upon ourselves, to develop "good character." Too often the distinction between *character* and *personality* is really the *doctrine of the mask*. At best it covers the differences between the way other people conceive of my personality and the way I myself know it to be. At worst, the defensive armor of the mask goes even deeper, obscuring the differences between my own noble idealized conception of myself and the angel-beast of a double soul I truly am at heart.

I believe that biological inheritance and later arbitrary circumstance provide both opportunities for joy and necessities for suffering. But just how happy or unhappy I am to be with this personality which is mine and this life which I have been handed is largely a matter of how well I can accept my fate rather than one which demands a reshuffling of the cards, a new deal, a better hand. I may not always win, but I must continue to play. After all, it's the only game in town. Fighting fate, trying to will that which cannot be willed, demanding that I be someone else living some other sort of life, all of this is an absurd demand to get my own way which can only invite needless suffering. It's enough to experience the suffering that is absolutely required without whining away what pleasures I may yet have with cries of "Why me? Why did this have to happen to me?"

The building of character is the denial of the true nature of the self, a search for an improved model. I no longer hope to achieve good character, so long as that implies that my Buddhahood is not already at hand. My aim is not to improve my Self but only to know it all more clearly and to learn to celebrate all that I am. I need no more change my personality by building my character, than change my fate by trying to be so good that someone will save me. Remember how many times you said, "Please God, if only this one time You will let me get a passing grade (or a sought-after promotion, or a longed-for sweetheart), then I promise that from now on I'll never lie again (or masturbate, or talk back to my parents)."

This distinction between character and personality is akin to the distinction between *fate* and *destiny*. If I am not willing to know what I feel, to say what I mean, and to do what I say, then my life is that of a passive object of fate. However, to the extent that I am willing to fully accept, to own, to treasure that fortune (or misfortune) which is my own personality, which is myself, to that extent am I able to turn my fate into my destiny. Only then can I become who I am by willingly surrendering to living my life as it is given to me instead of trying to be someone or something other than myself.

In order to transform my fate into my destiny, I must give up the romantic habit of telling a bit more than the truth. I must be willing to present myself first to my own eyes just as I am, and then when it is safe, to the eyes of others. There is no need to hide my strength, my virtue, my special beauty. Yet all of these must be presented within the context of the ordinariness of my weaknesses, my wrinkles, and my warts. William Butler Yeats counsels us well when he tells that "soul must become its own betrayer, its own deliverer, the one activity, the mirror turn lamp."[1]

A life without pain is not possible. Often patients come to

therapy hoping that if they can improve their personalities sufficiently, if they can achieve "maturity" or "mental health," then they can live a problem-free life. It takes a long while to learn that:

"In all the world
There is no way whatever.
The stag cries even
In the most remote mountains."[2]

They need not try to become someone else for their hopeless seeking of the ouroboric peace and perfection of reunion with the Great Mother will never be. There is no peace till death, and perhaps not even then. And, ironically, whatever peace there might be for any of us comes from accepting the good/bad nature of who we are, as well as the lucky/unlucky quality of our lives.

It matters less that one man is an extrovert engaging in the outer world, while another is an introvert who finds more meaning within himself, than that each become who he is rather than try to be the other. For after all, long before Christ (or Jung), Lao Tzu told us:

"A man with outward courage dares to die,
A man with inward courage dares to live;
But either of these men
Has a better and a worse side than the other."[3]

Perhaps neurosis is no more than the struggle to get our own way, to change others, to correct fate, or failing that, the refusal to give in to our own deepest wishes and sense of self, so that if we cannot get *our* own way at least we can keep someone else from getting *his* own way.

I am reminded of a patient with whom I have worked for a number of years who has gotten well-beyond much of her depression, is far more expressive, assertive, and creative, and has (in conjunction with her husband's therapy) much improved her once unhappy marriage. She finds it difficult to conclude her work in therapy because of one remaining seemingly insoluble problem.

At first she began by describing the problem as her marriage not being solid and satisfying enough to dissuade her husband from being interested in pornography. Only gradually did she come to see that the problem was really not *his* behavior but *her response* to it. When he reveals his interest in pornographic books and movies, she reacts with anxiety and resentment as though he were betraying her.

With my help, she was able to relate these reactions to her distress as a young teenager when her father deserted the family and his own unhappy marriage to give himself over to an affair with a young serving girl. At that time the patient protected herself from the panic of recognizing her total helplessness over these losses by rejecting any further efforts by her father to have anything to do with her at all. As she connected the two events the patient's response shifted from diffuse anxiety and resentment to a bitter, stubborn insistence that she certainly was *not* willing to give in, that is, not willing to settle for accepting what she could get from either her husband or her father, by tolerating her losses and her dissatisfactions, whatever they might be.

I met the somber telling of her tale with the old Hungarian scissors story. It is told that in Hungary some years ago there was a couple who met, fell in love, and married. At first they seemed very happy together until a seemingly trivial argument arose. They were co-operating in the wrapping of a package and when it was done there was a bit of extra string to be cut off. The husband said, "I'll get a knife and get rid of the bit of string." But the wife insisted that when she was growing up and packages were to be wrapped, the final bit of string was always cut off not with a knife, but with a scissors. And so the argument began. And for years their marriage was plagued by discomfort and irritability as they argued chronically again and again the dilemma of the knife and the scissors. After a while, of course, the issues were so clear that they needed only to challenge one another by the husband saying "knife!" and the wife answering angrily "scissors!"

Finally the husband felt that he could stand it no longer. He decided that such a stubborn wife must be gotten rid of. Deviously, he invited her to come down to the lake for a boat ride one sunny summer afternoon. He rowed her out to the middle of the lake which was quite wide and deep and there he said to her, "We're going to settle this once and for all. You must either surrender to me and admit that the knife is the proper instrument for cutting the bit of string or I will take this oar and knock you into the water, and since you cannot swim you will surely drown." Her answer was a defiant "scissors!" With that, the husband took an oar and lustily swung it, knocking his wife from the boat. Indeed she could *not* swim and floundered helplessly for a moment as her husband demanded "knife?" She sputtered "scissors" in response, and down she went for the first time. Moments later she fought her way to the surface again and once more her husband demanded "knife?" Spitting water from mouth and nostrils she gurgled "scissors!" and went under for the second time. When after a bit, exhausted and bedraggled, she reached the surface once more and was about to go down for the third and last time, he said, "Okay, this is my last offer, it's a matter of life or death. Knife, I tell you!" And as she sunk beneath the surface of the waves all that could be seen was her slowly sinking raised right hand, index and middle finger separating and coming together in the mimed gesture of a cutting scissors.

Although this tale helped the patient to laugh at herself as she recognized her own stubbornly spiteful, self-destructive insistence on not giving in, she could not shake free of the problem. I offered the analogy of my own struggle with the pain and imminent death with which I am faced daily by my inoperable brain tumor, "What am I to do then?" I asked her. "It is the only life that has been given me. Should I waste it insisting that this cannot happen to me? That it's not fair, that it's too upsetting, that I cannot enjoy the rest of my life because there are parts to it that I find unacceptable? My only hope lies in finding the calm of self-surrender. If I surrender to that which I cannot change, do what I can without attachment to the results, then I will have what I might." Her love for me helped bridge our common human dilemma and she could experience both the absurdity and the profundity of each of our situations. But before she was able finally to be free, she had to journey in fantasy into the experience of forgiving her father (and her husband), of no longer trying to change what she could not change, and of living in the grief over her helplessness. It is enough that we all must suffer losses, disappointments, and betrayals. We need not add to the unhappiness and misfortune which life puts upon us by struggling against our karma, that which is our lot in this our one and only life.

And if the therapist is to help another to find his way, to accept his karma, what manner of man must he be? Again, Lao Tzu is instructive in saying:

"One who knows his lot to be the lot of all other men

Is the safe man to guide them...[4] (for)...

A good man, before he can help a bad man,

Finds in himself the matter with the bad man."[5]

It is the same for the therapist as it is for the patient. If a man is to live fully he must look unblinkingly at all that emerges from his unconscious. If he is to be more than a cardboard figure he must peer into the shadow. All that his conscience tells him that he is *not,* secretly he *is.* The aspirations of his idealized social philosophy are no more than denials of the dark underside of what it is to be truly human. A man cannot flee from evil without unwittingly yielding to it. Evil must not be avoided but rather transformed. Should a man try to be generous without acknowledging to himself his own self-interest he will surely turn out to be a prideful despot, giving only when it suits his aspiration to appear benevolent. If charity were anonymous, God pity the poor. Our only hope lies in turning the life of consciousness toward those dark aspects of ourselves which we are taught we should not even think about.

Yet even our seeking to know that which is unconscious in our hidden selves can turn out to be merely another form of seeking after an unobtainable perfection of the self. Though each man must commit himself to plumbing the depths of his own dark soul, no man can know it all. The exploration can never be completed. It is the very nature of the beast to be ever partly hidden.

By now, should you feel committed to this exploration of the darkness of the heart, you may be tempted to feel that surely if you try hard enough and long enough, all will be known. The inevitable human pursuit of the illusion of control, of having it in hand once and for all, of no longer having to face helplessness and the loneliness of the solitary pilgrimage through the disturbingly powerful morass of the forces of darkness will surely tempt you all the rest of your days.

It is instructive to see the limits of the light of consciousness and of the powers of reason in their encounter with the forces of darkness. A story is told of William James, a psychologist who sought to discover and understand all of the varieties of religious experience, and of the success of his failure. In his travels, Dr. James encountered an Indian sage from whom he hoped to get some final answers. Possessing more knowledge than understanding of oriental philosophy James had learned that it is written that:

Brahma, the creator, conjured forth eight celestial elephants, which then were assigned to the four corners of the world and the four points between, to stand as support for the upper firmament.[6]

And so he enquired of the Mahatma, "I understand that your people believe that the universe is supported on the backs of great white elephants, right?"

"Indeed, it is so," replied the Mahatma.

"Good, good," Dr. James went on. "Now tell me, just what is it that stands beneath the great white elephants?"

"In each case," the sage replied at once, "there stands another great white elephant."

"And what is beneath that great white elephant?"

"Why only another great white elephant."

Hurrying on with his enquiry, Dr. James began again, "And beneath that great..."

But at this point the Mahatma interrupted. "Dr. James, Dr.

James," he responded gently, "before you go any further, I must tell you. It is great white elephants, *all the way down.*"

And so, committed though we must be to peering into the shadows, to facing the dark primordial images, to revealing the rest of ourselves to our consciousness, we must remember that it is great white elephants *all the way down.* Yet we must come to know what we can of what we are, or suffer the illusions we create by projecting onto others what we cannot accept of ourselves, seeing the enemy as outside of ourselves, living a life of degrading dogmatic defining of others and dehumanizing isolation of ourselves. Because the unconscious provides a compensatory force to one-sided conscious attitudes, the spontaneous self-revelation of our dreams will teach us what we need to know about the parts of ourselves which are usually hidden in the shadows. In this sense, dreams can be prophetic, revealing the tryptic of past, present, and future, of where we have come from, where we are along the way, and where we are headed.[7]

Here are three dreams all dreamed in one night and presented in one therapy session by a young woman several months into treatment who was experiencing a strange combination of panic at what she is getting into and excitement about where she might be headed.

Dream one: *I am at a cocktail party chatting with some people, I don't know about what. Again and again I see my husband going off into another room with one or another of the women guests at the party. I am surprised to find that instead of feeling jealous, I merely begin to feel curious about what is going on.*

Dream two: *I enter a lavishly decorated powder room. I am appalled to see that the beautifully decorative wallpaper is peeling in many places. I just stand and look at it peeling off the walls without knowing what to do.*

Dream three: *I am in an exciting place. I believe it is a carnival. I am on a platform at the center of things, in charge of some dancing bears. I am having a wonderful time. A man comes by and asks me what I am doing. I am surprised to find that I can answer his question easily. I say to him, "I am the Bear Lady* (she laughs) *I can see now that that was a pun, meaning I was a lady with no clothes on."*

After exploring the dreams with her at the level of her own personal associations I suggested an overview of the dreams as representing past, present, and future. The first dream represents the past, that is the situation that brought her to therapy. Chatting at the cocktail party represents a superficial, ego-oriented, empty social life. In the dream her husband represents her father on a personal association level and his spending time with her younger sisters. However, he also represents her *animus* as characterized by her own husband's actual adventuring out into a more complex and demanding world than the one in which she lived. By becoming free of her commitment to simple jealousy, that is a threat to her ego, she has become curious enough to wonder what it would be like for her to get out of that cocktail-party-life and off into another room. And so it is, in part, that she is coming to therapy.

The second dream represents her present ambivalence and dilemma as she finds that after several months of therapy she is beginning to uncover the shadow side of herself, what she refers to as "primitive" things in her. At a later session, she admitted that she had not been standing in this dream, but sitting on the john, her metaphor for unearthing unconscious material. This is distressing for a woman raised in a family of upper class standards, people who feel that they are above the experience of ordinary people. Thus it is that she euphemistically refers to the shit-house in which she finds herself as a powder room. She would deny that she functions as everyone else but as Montaigne tells us "Kings and philosophers defecate, and ladies too."[8] And so despite the lavish decoration of her powder room she finds the wallpaper peeling away to reveal the underlying structure. Her commitment to therapy, to look and see what lies beneath, is experienced now as a kind of helplessness as her *persona* peels away and she is more and more fearful of what she might find beneath it.

The third dream represents her hopefulness and excitement about the future. The atmosphere is that of carnival, a time when all things will be allowable. The dancing bears are her delight and enjoyment of her own instinctual drives, once the dangerously aggressive aspect of them is under control. She knows who she is and she knows what she is doing, and so she can easily answer the question "Who are you?" asked by her animus. She is the Bear Lady. She has resolved her negative mother complex by taking over the mother aspect of herself. She is the instinctual lady, the powerful woman. And too, she is the *bare* lady which makes her laugh with delight, that she is the naked, transparent, open sensual creature who can be what she is for all to see.

Her dreams led me to further exploration of my own wolf dream. Now I could interpret the wolf as my own predatory destructive nature, which I live out as a therapist by committing myself to its other face. That aspect of the wolf is the Romulus-and-Remus Mother-of-Outcasts, nurturer of those faced with destruction. I must yet become the nursed waif who can learn to live with the tamed brutality as well.

Further help came that same week, this time from an old friend who had read a journal account of my wolf dream.[9] You don't always get what you want, but you get what you need. He sent me a reprint of a piece of his own [10] in which he described the work of a German psychiatrist named Levner who has developed a technique known as Guided Affective Imagery. Frank's article stresses using this technique around a theme of feeding-the-beast. The patient is asked to imagine that he stands on the outskirts of a forest and told that if he looks carefully a beast will emerge from amidst the trees. As the animal reveals itself in fantasy, he experiences negative feelings such as fear, rage or disgust. He is encouraged to fantasize approaching, petting, and feeding the animal. If he is willing to do so, a transformation occurs in which the dangerous adversary becomes an ally or a playmate. My old friend goes on to explain:

The feeding technique invokes imaginary behavior of a nurturant, supportive, and kindly sort in the face of fearful feelings that have been aroused by a sense of threat. To the extent that the threat and fear are projected and are not appropriate to the situation, the co-operative patient stands a good chance of overcoming them and of freeing himself from their influence over his behavior. [11]

Both the patient's third dream and my friend's paper were of help to me in reclaiming my own dark brother. My characteristic counter-phobic overcoming of anxiety lead me more easily (both as therapist and as patient) to favor changing places with the beast, to see what it feels like to become the dangerous spider when I feel helplessly trapped in the terror of feeling like the fly caught in its web.

I have cautioned that in seeking to accept ourselves, we must first pay attention to that which is hidden. It is obvious enough that to some extent we each hide our *unsocialized attitudes* behind our *persona*. This mask of the social self tells more about the cultural demands that shape our interactions than about those disruptive instinctual impulses which culture seeks to tame. And psychoanalysis has for many years made us aware of the need to try to understand the *repressed contents of the personal unconscious* which underly the more rational, reality-oriented aspects of the *ego*. Jung has added to our understanding of what is hidden through his concept of the *shadow,* that disowned or not-yet-revealed aspect of the self which includes not only the personal unconscious, but also the *archetypal motifs of collective unconscious* and the *inferior functions of a particular individual's psychological type.*

Out of my own struggle, I emphasize being in touch with the freedom to be powerful in a tough world. But you are right to be wary in following any of my advice because "for men with different types of psychological makeup, different types of ethics are appropriate." [12] Even so, hear what I have to say, let it be your option if you want it, and set it aside if you do not. What I wish to tell you is that it is crucial that we not fool ourselves. When we can, we must act lovingly, but when anger, aggression or even violence is called for we must learn to strike out expediently, effectively, and with gusto. I try to act honestly, openly and with compassion and tenderness toward those I love and even toward other human beings who pass my way in whom I have little stake but who are merely doing their own thing without jeopardizing my well-being. However, in the presence of my enemies I must be able to fight like an alley rat. Margaret Mead once said that manners are useful in dealing with people with whom we don't get along. Honesty is for dealing with friends. Diplomacy and aggression I save for my enemies.

All of this would seem clearly destructive and cynical if men were indeed simply good or at least respectable, but as Machiavelli points out, as men are not good, it is sometimes necessary to invoke the force of a lion or the cunning of a fox. If that fine Italian hand is too cynically manipulative for your humanistic sensibilities, then look instead to the great and ancient sub-continent of India, that traditional seat of reverence and peace. Modern Western humanists have looked to the Orient in recent years for a model of spiritual freedom, inner peace, and non-violent means of attaining social accord. But this idealized social model has an often unexamined underside. "The blank pessimism of the Indian philosophy of politics (is) untouched...by any hope or ideal of progress and improvement."[13] And so it is that in the *Mahabharata,* a traditional Indian work of practical guidance, four chief means of approach to an enemy are outlined. They include *Saman,* the way of conciliation or negotiation; *Danda,* the rod of punishment or retaliatory aggression; *Dana* or bribery; and *Bheta* or splitting and sowing dissension as a means of dividing and conquering. And finally, ironically, to these four chief means of meeting an enemy is added *Maya.* While Maya is usually defined as the illusory nature of everyday life which must be seen through, transformed, and given up in order that a man may reach the level of spiritual awakening and freedom, in this context Maya is defined as a trick, a deceit or the display of an illusion with which one might snare an enemy. Other minor devices are suggested such as *Upeksa* which means overlooking, pretending not to be concerned because one is not ready to make a decision about whether or not to become involved in any particular affair, *Indrajala* which translates to mean the net of the god Indra (India's Zeus), which involves all the varieties of stratagem and tricks of war. These suggestions constitute "the seven ways to approach a neighbor in this unsentimental ocean of the fish,"[14] under the doctrine of *Matsya-nyaya,* the Law of the Fishes: *The big ones eat the little ones.*

We must not mistake manners for morals. Life can be merciless and pain a necessity. Steinbeck somewhere once pointed out that we need only look in a tidal pool to see life in the raw. There we may observe the predatory Law of the Fishes in action. The big ones eating the little ones is part of *man's* animal nature as well. We may build temples, offer charity for our fellow man, make paintings and play music. But *first* we must survive! And at times that means that if one of us is going to get hurt, and it's either got to be you or me, if it's up to me, I promise that it will be you.

So it is that what is hidden must be revealed before what appears to be can assume its true shape and substance. Yet I would caution against the *psychoanalytic fallacy* that only what is hidden is really true. A man who acts and speaks lovingly of his woman, may sometime reveal in a fantasy, in a dream or through a slip of the tongue, some underlying hitherto unconscious hatred of that same woman. This certainly does not mean that he *really* hates her. It need only suggest that in addition to all that one-sided positive feeling, there is of course a shadow, an ambiguity, a basic human polarity. *Impurity is the only reliable criterion for the reality of any feeling.* For me, his love would be more believable when I see it maintained in the face of the hatred which must accompany it. If truly "pure," it would seem too-good-to-be-true. So far as I know, I have never in my life had a pure motive.

This need to accept the other side, the shadow side, is one of the bases for the Trickster-Healer's *Be Where They Ain't* approach. One patient's response to my shadow-revealing trickery, was to experience her struggle with me (really with the underside of herself) as "Fighting the Windmill." She described it this way:

I know I'm better because I feel worse.
The nicer you are, the harder it gets.
The stronger I grow, the weaker I feel.
You can't give it to me because I already have it.
I can't be littler because you're not bigger (damn it!).
The more lost I become, the clearer it gets.
I'm feeling confused, I must be in the right place.
I move the furthest when I'm stuck.
The worst part is knowing that I can make it.
The safest places are the most dangerous.
The more I cry, the harder I laugh.
The more I try, the harder you laugh.
The more I love, the more I hate.
The more I fight, the more friends I have.
I can't make you love me, you already do.
I can't be special, everyone/no one is.
Given permission to rest, I work harder.
When I rest you call it work; When I play you call it
work; When I work you call it work. I can't mess
up (damn it!).
Since I can't please or displease you, guess I'll just
have to do what I want.
I don't get to win, but I don't have to lose.
There is no winning or losing, but I get to keep what
I have.[15]

It is not possible to appreciate the light without knowing the darkness, the heavens without the earth, the dry lands without the sea, warmth in the absence of cold. *Human* lacks meaning if *animal* is unknown, just as being a man takes its shape most fully in the presence of woman. Angel and devil are Janus faces. Cain cannot be understood without knowing his brother, Abel, and much of Jesus is incomplete without Judas.

The transformation brought about by the recognition and acceptance of the hidden shadow-identity does not make the person into someone else so much as it completes him. So it is that I would amend the traditional Hindu Story of the King's Son:

There was a king's son, once upon a time, who, having been born under an unlucky star, was removed from the capital while still a babe, and reared by a primitive tribesman, a mountaineer, outside the pale of the Brahman civilization (i.e., as an outcast, uneducated, ritually unclean). He therefore lived for many years under the false notion: "I am a mountaineer." In due time, however, the old king died. And since there was nobody eligible to assume the throne, a certain minister of state, ascertaining that the boy had been cast away into the wilderness some years before was still alive, went out, searched the wilderness, traced the youth, and, having found him, instructed him: "Thou art not a mountaineer; thou art the King's Son." Immediately, the youth abandoned the notion that he was an outcast and took to himself his royal nature. He said to himself: "I am a king."[16]

I believe that nothing had changed in the sphere of facts, only his awareness was transformed. Is he now a Prince who believed he was a mountaineer, or a mountaineer who only now realizes that he is also the King's son? Perhaps it is only that "he is united, at last, with the hidden fullness of his own true nature."[17]

I do not argue for an oriental reconciliation by the ultimate harmony of opposites so much as for the need to recognize and cherish the existence of the other side. My goal is not some idealized perennial peace and absence of conflict, but rather a vital and viable state of dynamic tension. I seek not agreement but rather a balance of forces, both of which are needed. Politically, for example, I know that when the Left is victorious, the liberators soon become the new oppressors who must be acted against so that the fluid flow of human process can go on. My commitment is to the ebb and flow, the rhythmic ever-changing, never-changing state of flux, of life on the move.

Having emphasized at some length the need for making more vivid that which can be seen by exposing what is hidden, I would like to turn now to how we are to *become what we are* once all of it has surfaced. The fullness of my vision will once again be brought forth by turning my gaze Eastward, this time toward the twenty-five century old Hindu singing of *The Song of God: Bhagavad-Gita.* [18]

The Bhagavad-Gita is a powerfully poetic battlefield dialogue which takes place before an epic encounter of a long-ago civil war among royal Indian kinsmen, a dialogue between one of the commanders, Arjuna, and Sri Krishna, an incarnation of the Supreme Godhead who has taken it upon Himself to appear in the form of Arjuna's charioteer. A family power struggle has arisen among the offspring of the sons of King Vichitravirya. The King's eldest son was born blind, and so his younger son, Pandu, took the throne when their father died. The elder brother bitterly raised his sons with stubborn determination that someday they should reclaim his lost seat of power. And so these young men have come to challenge Pandu's sons in battle. The sons of Pandu, Arjuna and his brothers, had been willing to work out some sharing of the power, but their bitter and dispossessed cousins have forced a battlefield confrontation instead.

Our Lord Krishna has offered to mediate between the warring cousins but only in accordance with the wishes of the antagonists. He has offered to either of the opposing sides the forces of His army, and to the other Krishna Himself as counsel and advisor. So it was that He became the driver of Arjuna's chariot. On the eve of battle, Krishna drives the chariot into the open space between the two armies so that Arjuna may view the enemy hordes. Recognizing so many of his kinsmen, Arjuna is appalled at what he must do and exclaims in despair: "I will not fight!"

Krishna instructs Arjuna on his alternatives and helps him to see what he must do. Though the commander is enlightened by his

charioteer to the effect that he *must* fight, Krishna's teachings are
by no means war-like. To appreciate what He has to offer us even
today, we must understand the battlefield as a metaphor for one
aspect of life, and Arjuna's caste as a symbol of his identity. At that
time in India men found themselves divided into four categories:

Seer and leader,

Provider and server.[19]

These categories reflect the four Hindu castes: the *Brahmins* who
were priests, the *Kshatryas* who were warrior-politicians like
Arjuna, the *Vaishyas* who were merchants, and the *Sudras* who
were constituted the servant class.

Krishna tells Arjuna that there is more than one solution to
his problem just as there are many paths to fulfillment, alternate
ways to find release from spiritual bondage, and more than one
way to seek enlightenment. *Yoga* is the term for such personal
oriental disciplines, for the ways in which one may seek release
from the trap of life's endless sorrows. Krishna describes to him the
Yoga of Renunciation (the ascetic way), the Yoga of Meditation
(the inner seeking), the Yoga of Mysticism (through faithful
surrender to the Divine), and the Yoga of Devotion (through
worshipful love). But it is toward *Karma Yoga* that Krishna turns
His disciple, and toward which I would turn your gaze.

Karma Yoga is the doctrine of salvation *in* the world, in life *as
it is*, by *becoming who you are*. It is not possible, of course, *not* to
act, *not* to live your life, *not* to be yourself. "All are helplessly
forced to act."[20] But the way to salvation is to act by giving
yourself over fully to the moment by *renouncing the fruits of your
activity*. All activities must be performed, not in terms of what you
seek to be or how well you hope to do, but in accordance with who
you are and what you feel here and now.

In the Bhagavad-Gita, the nature of your particular life is
defined in terms of your *dharma* or duty which you find in the
karma of the life into which you are born, the karma of the
personality that is the *you* of this your one and only life. And so it is
that Krishna instructs Arjuna:

Do your duty, always; but without attachment. That is how a man reaches the ultimate Truth; by working without anxiety about the results. [21]

You need only discover who you are, and act according to the tendencies of your own nature. The most important aspect of your life and your personality is simply that it is *yours* and none other's. As Krishna tells us:

It is better to do your own duty, however imperfectly, than to assume the duties of another person, however successfully. Prefer to die doing your own duty; the duty of another will bring you into great spiritual danger. [22]

Better your own life, imperfectly performed, than the life of another, well performed. In every life, in each particular human being, *Brahman,* the Holy Power is present and each person can perform his or her own particular Act of Truth:

The story is told, for example, of a time when the righteous king Asoka, greatest of the great North Indian dynasty of the Mauryas, "stood in the city of Pataliputra, surrounded by city folk and country folk, by his ministers and his army and his councillors, with the Ganges flowing by, filled up by freshets, level with the banks, full to the brim, five hundred leagues in length, a league in breadth. Beholding the river, he said to his ministers, 'Is there anyone who can make this mighty Ganges flow back upstream?' To which the ministers replied, 'That is a hard matter, your Majesty.

"Now there stood on that very river bank an old courtesan named Bindumati, and when she heard the king's question she said, 'As for me, I am a courtesan in the city of Pataliputra, I live by my beauty; my means of sustenance is the lowest. Let the king but behold my Act of Truth.' And she performed an Act of Truth. The instant she performed her Act of Truth that mighty Ganges flowed back upstream with a roar, in the sight of all that mighty throng.

"When the king heard the roar caused by the movement of the whirlpools and the waves of the mighty Ganges, he was astonished, and filled with wonder and amazement. Said he to his ministers, 'How comes it that this mighty Ganges is flowing back upstream?' 'Your Majesty, the courtesan Bindumati heard your words, and performed an Act of Truth. It is because of her Act of Truth that the mighty Ganges is flowing backwards.'

"His heart palpitating with excitement, the king himself went posthaste and asked the courtesan, 'Is it true, as they say, that you, by an Act of Truth, have made this river Ganges flow back upstream?' Said the courtesan, 'By the Power of Truth, your Majesty, have I caused this mighty Ganges to flow back upstream.'

"Said the king, 'You possess the Power of Truth! You, a thief, a cheat, corrupt, cleft in twain, vicious, a wicked old sinner who have broken the bounds of morality and live on the plunder of fools!' 'It is true, your Majesty; I am what you say. But even I, wicked woman that I am, possess an Act of Truth by means of which, should I so desire, I could turn the world of men and the worlds of the gods upside down.' Said the king, 'But what is this Act of Truth? Pray enlighten me.'

" 'Your Majesty, whosoever gives me money, be he a Ksatrya or a Brahman or a Vaisya or a Sudra or of any other caste whatsoever, I treat them all exactly alike. If he be a Ksatriya, I make no distinction in his favor. If he be a Sudra, I despise him not. Free alike from fawning and contempt, I serve the owner of the money. This, your Majesty, is the Act of Truth by which I caused the mighty Ganges to flow back upstream.' " 23

We make a mistake if we ask ourselves, "Am I good enough?" or "Is it worthwhile to be me?" Whoever or whatever we are or do is who and what we are supposed to be. It is our Act of Truth. Psychologically, many of our problems began when as children someone led us to question the worth of our particular existence or performance. Whoever heard of a baby who was inadequate, or a child who did not know just exactly how to be a child? How could it *not* be all right for me to be me? How could it *not* be just right for you to be you? The Divine Spark of every single person is just that he is that particular person whether we define being human in the Western Judeo-Christian tradition of the Messiah:

How should a messiah behave? Now tell me. Do you know? You know only one thing: that he relieves your pain, your precise pain. He is messiah to your particularity.[24] ...a particular man saves...(one other) particular man.[25]

or in the Oriental Hindu-Buddhist tradition of the universality of the Supreme Being who Himself says:

Whatsoever is the seed of all creatures, that am I. There is no creature, whether moving or unmoving that can exist without Me. I am the gambling of the fraudulent, I am the power of the powerful. I am victory; I am ethic. I am the purity of the pure.[26]

It is the joker of the Tarot deck, The Fool who is wise enough to ask, "Who am I?" Innocently and openly, he steps forward into the unknown so that he may become who he is. Upright, he makes the right choice. Reversed, he will mistake his identity and live some other's life.

Our only hope is to learn to yield to each moment as it is as best we can, to live life as a work done as much as possible without anxiety about results "in the calm of self-surrender."[27] Only then can we fully live our own lives and be our own person by being engaged in just what we are doing at the moment, by doing it our way, by being able to declare *not* that my life is perfect, but that imperfect as it is, surely it is *mine alone* and nobody else's. For Krishna tells us:

When a man acts according to the law of his nature, he cannot be sinning. Therefore, no one should give up his natural work, even though he does it imperfectly. For all action is involved in imperfection, like fire in smoke.[28]

And in response, we can then rejoice in the surrender of becoming who we are, as does Arjuna when he answers:

By your grace, O Lord, my delusions have been dispelled. My

mind stands firm. Its doubts are ended. I will do your bidding.

...OM. Peace. Peace. Peace.[29]

CHAPTER NOTES

Chapter One — THE MYTH IS EVERYONE'S STORY

1. Elie Wiesel. *One Generation After,* Translated by Lily Edelman and the author, Bard Books/Published by Avon, New York, 1972, pp. 94ff.
2. C.C. Jung, Review of G.R. Heyer, *Praktische Seelenheil-kunde. Zentralblatt fur Psychotherapie,* IX (1936, 3: 184 - 187. *Coll. Works,* final vol. Quoted in *Psychological Reflections; An Anthology of the Writings of C.G. Jung,* selected and edited by Jolande Jacobi, Harper & Row, Publishers, New York, 1961, p. 68.
3. Ralph Metzner, *Maps of Consciousness,* Collier Books, New York, 1971, p. 55 (no Italics in original.)
4. *The I Ching or Book of Changes,* the Baynes translation, Bollingen Series XIX, Princeton University Press, Princeton, New Jersey, 1950. From C.G. Jung's Introduction p. xxxv.
5. Richard Cavendish. *The Black Arts* Capricorn Books, New York, 1967, p. 1.
6. Genesis 3: 4 - 5 (no italics in original.)
7. Archibald MacLeish, "Hypocrite Auteur," *Collected Poems 1917 - 1952,* Houghton Mifflin Co., Boston 1952, p. 173
8. Alan Watts."Western Mythology: Its Dissolution and Trans-formation", in *Myths, Dreams, and Religion,* Edited by Joseph Campbell, A Dutton Paperback, E.P. Dutton & Co., Inc., New York, 1970, p. 14
9. Joseph Campbell. "Mythological Themes in Creative Literature and Art", in *Myths, Dreams, and Religion,* (1970), pp. 138 - 175.
10. James Joyce. *Ulysses,* Random House, New York, 1934, p. 574.
11. C.G. Jung. *The Archetypes and the Collective Unconscious,*

from the Collected Works of C.G. Jung, Volume 9, Part 1, Bollingen Series XX, Princeton University Press, Princeton, New Jersey, Second Edition, 1968.

12. Ibid. p. 183

13. C.G. Jung. "Wotan," *Neue Schweizer Rundschau* (N.S.), III, 11, (mar., 1936: 657 - 69. In *Coll. Works,* Vol. 10, p. 12). Quoted in Jacobi, p. 36.

14. Martin Buber. *Moses: The Revelation and the Covenant,* Harper Torchbooks, Harper & Row, Publishers New York, 1958, p. 17.

Chapter Two

LET ME TELL YOU A TALE TO EASE YOUR TASK

1. *Black Elk Speaks: Being the Life Story of a Holy Man of the Oglala Sious,* as told through John G. Neihardt (Flaming Rainbow), Pocket Books, New York, 1972, p. 2

2. C.G. Jung, "Psychological Aspects of the Mother Archetype", *Collected Works,* Volume 9, Princeton University Press, Princeton, New Jersey, 1969, p. ?.

3. Heinrich Zimmer. *The King and the Corpse: Tale of the soul's Conquest of Evil,* Edited by Joseph Campbell, Princeton University Press, Princeton, New Jersey, 1957.

4. Ibid. p. 207.

5. Ibid. p. 213ff.

6. William V. Schutz. *Joy: Expanding Human Awareness,* Grove Press Inc., New York, 1967, pp. 90 - 115.

7. Eugene D. Alexander. "In-the-Body Trips: A New Therapeutic Technique: 'Preconscious Sharing ' ", *Psychotherapy,* Excerpted and reprinted in *The Intellectual Digest,* Vol. 11, No. 10, June 1972, pp. 78 - 79.

Chapter Three

THE UNCEREMONIAL NATURE OF PSYCHOTHERAPY

1. Lewis Carroll. *Alice's Adventures in Wonderland and*

Through the Looking-Glass, with all the original illustrations by Sir John Tenniel, Macmillan, London, Melbourne, Toronto, St. Martin's Press, New York, 1968, p. 48.

2. Erving Goffman. *Relations in Public: Microstudies of the Public Order.* Basic Books, Inc., New York, 1971.

3. a. Robert Ardrey. *The Territorial Imperative: A Personal Inquiry into the Animal Origins of Property and Nations,* a Laurel Edition, Dell Publishing Co. Inc., New York, 1971.
    b. Goffman (1971)
    c. Edward Hall. *The Hidden Dimension.*, Double Day, New York, 1966.
    d. Konrad Lorenz. *On Aggression,* Bantam Books, Inc., New York, 1967.
    e. Lionel Tiger and Robin Fox. *The Imperial Animal.* Holt, Rinehart and Winston, New York, 1971.

4. William Golding. *Lord of the Flies.* Capricorn Books, G.P. Putnam's Sons, New York, 1959.

5. Anna Freud and Dorothy T. Burlingham. *Infants Without Families.* Medical War Books, International University Press, New York, 1944.

6. Colin Turnbull. *The Mountain People.* Simon and Schuster, New York, 1972.

7. Philip G. Zimbardo. "The Psychological Power and Pathology of Imprisonment," *Selected Documents in Psychology,* MS. NO. 347, American Psychological Association Journal Supplement Abstract Service, Washington, D. C., 1973.

Chapter Four

BEING WHERE THEY AIN'T

1. Adolf Guggenbuhl-Craig. *Power in the Helping Professions,* Spring Publications, New York, 1971, pp. 38 - 40.

2. Sheldon B. Kopp. Guru: *Metaphors from a Psychotherapist,* Science and Behavior Books, Palo Alto, California, 1971.

3. Joseph Campbell. *The Flight of the Wild Gander, Explorations in the Mythological Dimension,* A Gateway

Edition, Henry Regnery Company, Chicago, 1972, p. 162.

4. C.G. Jung. "On the Psychology of the Trickster-Figure," in *The Archetypes and the Collective Unconscious,* Second Edition, Volume 9, 1, of the Collected Works of C.G. Jung, Translated by R.F.C. Hull, Bollinger Series XX, Princeton University Press, Princeton, New Jersey, 1959, pp. 255 - 272.

5. Paul Radin. *The Trickster: A Study in American Indian Mythology,* with Commentaries by Karl Kerenyi and C.G. Jung, Introductory Essay by Stanley Diamond, Schocken Books, New York, 1972, pp. 25 - 27.

6. *Shaking the Pumpkin: Traditional Poetry of the Indians of North America,* Edited with Commentaries by Jerome Rothenberg, a Doubleday Anchor Book, Doubleday & Co. Inc., Garden City, New York, 1972, English version of this poem by Carl Cary, p. 271.

7. Sheldon B. Kopp. "Easy Choice," *American Academy of Psychotherapists Newsletter,* April 1972.

8. Donald D. Lathrop. "Shelly," *American Academy of Psychotherapists Newsletter,* June 1972.

9. Joseph Campbell, *The Masks of God: Primitive Mythology,* Viking Press, New York.

10. Arthur Waley. *The Way and Its Power: A Study of the Tzo Te Ching and Its Place in Chinese Thought,* Evergreen Edition, Grove Press, Inc., New York, 1958, p. 187.

11. Wilhelm Reich. *Character Analysis,* Orgone Institute Press, New York, 1949.

12. Kopp. Guru (1971), p. 96ff.

13. Guggenbuhl-Craig. (1971), p. 91.

14. D.T. Suzuki. *Zen Buddhism: Selected Writings of D.T. Suzuki,* edited by William Barrett, a Doubleday Anchor Book, Doubleday & Company, Inc., Garden City, New York, 1956.

15. Suzuki, p. 207.

16. Suzuki, p. 210.

17. Suzuki, p. 225.

18. Suzuki, p. 208 & 223.
19. Waley, p. 238.
20. Jung (1959), p. 270.
21. *Shaking the Pumpkin,* etc. (1972), from Rothenberg's commentaries, p. 422.
22. Radin, pp. 25 - 27.
23. Campbell (1959) p. 274.
24. Guggenbuhl-Craig (1971) p. 29.
25. Donald D. Lathrop. Excerpt from unpublished personal correspondence.

Chapter Five

COMMUNITY OF SINNERS

1. Martin Buber. Quoted in *Martin Buber: An Intimate Portrait* by Aubrey Hodes, The Viking Press, New Yor, 1971, p. 21

Chapter Six

THE TUNNEL AT THE END OF THE LIGHT

1. Sheldon B. Kopp. *Guru: Metaphors from a Psychotherapist,* Science and Behavior Books, Inc., Palo Alto, California, 1971.
2. Sheldon B. Kopp. "The Whimperings of a Wounded Lion," *American Academy of Psychotherapists Newsletter,* April 1973.
3. Dylan Thomas. "And Death Shall Have No Dominion," *The Collected Poems of Dylan Thomas,* New Directions, New York, 1946, p. 77.
4. Isaac Loeb Peretz. "Bontche Shweig," in *The Jewish Caravan: Great Stories of Twenty-five Centuries,* Selected and Edited by Leo W. Schwartz (Revised and Enlarged), Holt, Rinehart and Winston, New York, Chicago, San Francisco, 1965, pp. 342 - 348.
5. Heinrich Zimmer. *Philosophies of India,* Edited by Joseph Campbell, Bollingen Series XXVI, Princeton University Press, Princeton, New Jersey, 1951, p. 22f.

6. Edmond Rostand. *Cyrano de Bergerac,* Translated by Brian Hooker, Act V, p. 195.

Chapter Seven

THE KARMA OF PERSONALITY

1. *Encyclopaedia Brittanica,* 1950 Edition, Volume 21, p. 917d.
2. C.G. Jung. "Psychological Types," in *The Collected Works of C.G. Jung, Volume 6,* A revision by R.F.C. Hull of the Translation by H.G. Baynes, Bollingen Series II, Princeton University Press, Princeton, New Jersey, 1971.
3. C.G. Jung. "Approaching the Unconscious," in *Man and His Symbols,* by Jung, von Franz, et al., a Laurel Edition, Dell Publishing Co., New York, 1972, p. 47.
4. Arthur A. Cohen. *In the Days of Simon Stern,* Random House, New York, 1972, p. 197.
5. Jung. *Collected Works,* Volume 6, p. 518.
6. Marie-Louise von Franz. "The Inferior Function," in *Lectures on Jung's Typology,* Spring Publications, New York, 1971, pp. 1 - 72.
7. Sheldon B. Kopp. *Guru: Metaphors from a Psychotherapist,* Science and Behavior Books, Inc., Palo Alto, California, 1971, pp. 123 - 130.
8. Edward C. Whitmont. *The Symbolic Quest: Basic Concepts of Analytical Psychology,* Published by G.P. Putnam's Sons, New York, for the C.G. Jung Foundation for Analytical Psychology, 1969, p. 154.
9. Quoted in von Franz, p. 39.
10. Example suggested in von Franz, p. 43.
11. Jung, *Collected Works, Volume 6,* p. 392.

Chapter Eight

WHAT EVIL LURKS IN THE HEARTS OF MEN

1. George Seferis. "Argonauts" from *Mythical Story in Four Greek Poets: C.P. Cavafy, George Seferis, Odysseus Elytic,*

Nikos Gatsos. Poems chosen and translated from the Greek by Edmund Keeley and Phillip Sherrard, Penguin Books, Harmondsworth, Middlesex, England, 1966, p. 45.

2. Madame de Villeneuve. "Beauty and the Beast," in *The Arthur Rackham Fairy Book*. J.B. Lippincott Co., Philadelphia and New York (no date), pp. 49 - 65.

3. C.G. Jung. From "Psychology and Religion" in *Collected Works, Volume 11*, quoted in *C.G. Jung: Psychological Reflections*. Selections Edited by Jolande Jocoby, Harper Torchbooks, The Bollingen Library, Harper & Row, Publishers, New York, 1961, p. 214

4. C.G. Jung. From "The Psychology of the Unconscious" in *Collected Works, Volume 7*, quoted in *Psychological Reflections* (1961) pp. 214ff.

5. C.G. Jung. From "Aion," in *Collected Works, Volume 9, Part II*, quoted in *Psyche & Symbol: A Selection from the Writings of C.G. Jung*. Edited by Violet S. de Laszlo, Doubleday Anchor Books, Doubleday & Company, Inc., Garden City, New York, 1958, p. 9.

6. C.G. Jung. From "Psychology and Religion," in *Collected Works, Volume 11*, quoted in *Psychological Reflections* (1961), p. 216.

7. C.P. Cavafy. "Ithaka" in *Four Greek Poets* (1966), pp. 15 - 16.

8. Dietrich Bonhoeffer. *Letters and Papers from Prison*. Revised Edition, Edited by Eberhard Bethge, The Macmillan Company, New York, 1967, pp. 7ff.

9. Bonhoeffer, p. 8.

10. C.G. Jung. From "Psychological Types" in *Collected Works, Volume 6*, quoted in *Psychological Reflections* (1961), p. 208.

11. Mark Zborowski and Elizabeth Herzon. *Life Is With People: The Culture of the Shtetl*, Foreword by Margaret Mead, Schocken Books, New York, 1962, p. 149.

13. Martin Buber. *Tales of Hasidim: The Early Masters*,

Edited The Curatorium of the C.G. Jung Institute, Zurich, Northwestern University Press, Evanson, Illinois, 1967, p. 157.

13. Nietzche. From *Thus Spoke Zarathustra,* quoted in *Evil,* Schocken Books, New York, 1961, p. 315.
14. Martin Buber. pp. 109ff.

Chapter Nine

WOMAN BLUES

1. Quoted in *Alpha: The Myths of Creation* by Charles H. Long, Collier Books, New York, 1969, p. 38.
2. Sheldon B. Kopp. *If You Meet the Buddha on the Road, Kill Him: The Pilgrimage of Psychotherapy Patients,* Science and Behavior Books, Inc., Palo Alto, California, 1972, p. 76.
3. Mark Zborowski and Elizabeth Herzog. *Life is With People: The Culture of the Shtetl,* Foreword by Margaret Mead, Schocken Books, New York, 1962.
4. Erich Neumann. *The Great Mother: An Analysis of the Archetype,* Translated from the German by Ralph Manheim, Bollingen Series XLVII, Princeton University Press, Princeton, New Jersey, 1972.
5. Toby Tate. "Mother of Sorrows," an unpublished poem.
6. Robert Graves. *ADAM'S RIB and other anomalous elements in the Hebrew Creation Myth,* with wood engravings by James Metcalf, Thomas Yoseloff, Inc., New York, 1958, p. 38.
7. Joseph Campbell. *The Hero with a Thousand Faces,* Meridian Books, The World Publishing Company, Cleveland and New York, 1949.
8. Erich Neumann. *Amor and Psyche: The Psychic Development of the Feminine, A Commentary on the Tale by Apuleius,* Translated from the German by Ralph Manheim, Bollingen Series LIV, Princeton University Press, Princeton, New Jersey, 1971.
9. Neumann. *Amor and Psyche,* pp. 4ff.
10. *Ibid.,* p. 26.

11. *Ibid.,* p. 85.
12. *The Thirteen Principal Upanishads,* Translated from the Sanskrit, with an outline of the Philosophy of the Upanishads and an Annotated Bibliography by Robert Ernest Hume, with a list of recurrent and parallel passages by George C. O. Haas, Humphrey Milford, Oxford University Press, London, Edinburgh, Glasgow, New York, Toronto, Melbourne, Capetown, Bombay, 1934, p. 81.
13. Arthur Waley. *Three Ways of Thought in Ancient China,* A Doubleday Anchor Book, Doubleday and Co., Inc., Garden City, New York 1939, p. 16.
14. Elizabeth Gould Davis. *The First Sex,* Penguin Books Inc., Baltimore, Maryland, 1972.
15. Hellmut Wilhelm. *Change: Eight Lectures on the I Ching,* Translated from the German by Cary F. Baynes, Bollingen Series LXII, Princeton University Press, Princeton, New Jersey, 1973, p. 27.
16. *I Ching: The Chinese Book of Changes,* Arranged from the work of James Legge by Clae Waltham, An Ace Book, Ace Publishing Corporation, New York, 1969, p. 43.
17. *I Ching,* Legge & Waltham (1969), p. 44.
18. C.G. Jung. Quoted in *I Ching,* Legge & Waltham (1969) p. 14.
19. Alfred Douglas. *How to Consult the I Ching: The Oracle of Change,* G.P. Putnam's Sons, New York, 1971, pp. 25ff.
20. Kurt Vonnegut, Jr. *Breakfast of Champions: or Goodbye Blue Monday,* Delacorte Press/Seymour Lawrence, 1973, p. 209.
21. William McNaughton. *The Taoist Vision,* Ann Arbor Paperbacks, The University of Michigan Press, Ann Arbor, Michigan, 1971, p. 30.
22. Irene Claremont DeCastillejo. *Knowing Women: A Feminine Psychology,* published by G.P. Putnam's Sons for the C.G. Jung Foundation for Analytical Psychology, New York, 1973, p. 77.
23. Ernest Nagel. *The Structure of Science: Problems in the*

Logic of Scientific Explanation, Harcourt, Brace, and World, Inc., New York and Burlingame, 1961, p. 547.

24. *Ibid.,* p. 548.
25. *Ibid.,* p. 548.
26. Eleanor Bertine. *Jung's Contribution to Our Time: The Collected Papers of Eleanor Bertine,* edited by Elizabeth rohrbach, published by G.P. Putnam's Sons for the C.G. Jung Foundation for Analytical Psychology, New York, 1967, p. 103.
27. Jill Johnston. *Lesbian Nation: The Feminist Solution,* Simon and Schuster, New York, 1973, quote from book jacket.
28. Donald Lathrop. Excerpt from unpublished personal correspondence, May 1973.
29. Olive Schreiner. *Dreams,* Little, Brown and Co., 1922. Quoted in Bertine, p. 143.

Chapter Ten

LET OUR DREAMS INSTRUCT US

1. Ann Faraday. *Dream Power,* Coward, McCann & Geoghegan, Inc., New York, 1972, p. 37.
2. Joseph Campbell. *The Flight of the Wild Gander: Explorations in the Mythological Dimension,* A Gateway Edition, Henry Regnery Company, Chicago, 1972, p. 75.
3. Black Elk. *Black Elk Speaks: Being the Life Story of a Holy Man of the Oglala Sioux,* as told through John G. Neihardt (Flaming Rainbow), University of Nebraska Press, Lincoln, Nebraska, 1961, p. 254.
4. Genesis 37:5, *Revised Standard Version of the Old Testament,* Volume I.
5. Genesis 41:14, *R.S.V.*
6. Genesis 41:25, *R.S.V.*
7. Genesis 41:25, *R.S.V.* (No italics in original).
8. Kilton Stewart. "Dream Theory in Malaya," in *Altered States of Consciousness,* edited by Charles T. Tart, Anchor Books, Doubleday & Company, Inc., Garden City, New York, 1972,

pp. 161 - 170.

9. Stewart, p. 163.

10. Anthony F.C. Wallace. "Dreams and the Wishes of the Soul: A Type of Psychoanalytic Theory Among the Seventeenth Century Iroquois," in *Magic, Witchcraft and Curing,* Edited by John Middleton, The Natural History Press, Garden City, New York, 1967, pp. 171 - 190.

11. Erich Fromm. *The Forgotten Language,* Rinehart & Company, Inc., New York, 1951.

12. Sigmund Freud. *The Interpretation of Dreams,* translated by James Strachey, Basic Books, New York, 1956.

13. C.G. Jung. Review of G.R. Heyer, *Prakstische Seelenheilkunde Zentralblatt for Psychotherapie,* IX (1936), 3:184 - 187. (Quoted in *Psychological Reflections: An Anthology of the Writings of C.G. Jung.* Selected and edited by Yolande Jacobi, Harper & Row, Publishers, New York, 1961, p. 67).

Chapter Eleven

BECOMING WHO YOU ARE

1. William Butler Yeats. Quoted in *Yeats: The Man and the Masks,* by Richard Ellmann, A Dutton Paperback, E.P. Dutton & Co., Ind., New York, 1948, p. 280.

2. Fujiwara No Toshinari. Untitled Poem, in *One Hundred Poems from the Japanese,* Translated by Kenneth Rexroth, A New Directions Book, New York, 1964, p. 81.

3, Lao Tzu. *The Way of Life According to Lao Tzu: An American Version,* Translated by Witter Bynner, Capricorn Books, New York, 1962, p. 71.

4. Lao Tzu. p. 31.

5. Lao Tzu. p. 41f.

6. Heinrich Zimmer. *Philosophies of India,* edited by Joseph Campbell, Bollingen Series XXVI, Princeton University Press, Princeton, New Jersey, 1951, p. 120f.

7. Gerhard Adler. *Studies in Analytical Psychology,* Capricorn Books, New York, 1969, pp. 92 - 119. The "three-fold

chronological pattern" is explored at length in his chapter, "Study of a Dream."

8. Michel de Montaigne. *Selected Essays,* Translated by Charles Cotton and W. Hazlitt, Edited by Blanchard Bates, Modern Library, New York, 1949, p. 563.

9. Sheldon B. Kopp, "My Own Dark Brother," *Voices,* Vol. 9, Number 2, pp. 60 - 61, Summer 1973.

10. Frank Haronian. "The Ethical Relevence of a Psychotherapeutic Technique," *Journal of Religion and Health,* Volume 6, Number 2, April 1967, pp. 148 - 154.

11. Haronian. p. 152.

12. Erich Neumann. *Depth Psychology and a New Ethic,* English Translation by Eugene Rolfe, Harper Torch Books, Harper and Row, New York, Evanston, San Francisco, London, 1973, p. 21. (From the Preface to the Spanish edition, 1959).

13. Zimmer, p. 127.

14. Zimmer, p. 127.

15. Marcia Deinelt. "Fighting the Windmill," Unpublished, 1973.

16. Zimmer. P. 308, Quoted from the Sankhya Sutras, 4. 1.

17. Zimmer. p. 310.

18. *The Song of God: Bhagavad-Gita.* Translated by Swami Prabhabananda and Christopher Isherwood, with an Introduction by Aldous Huxley, a Mentor Religious Classic, published by the New American Library, New York, 1956.

19. *The Song of God.* p. 125.

20. *The Song of God.* p. 44.

21. *The Song of God.* p. 46f.

22. *The Song of God.* p. 48.

23. Zimmer. pp. 160 - 162.

24. Arthur A. Cohen, *In the Days of Simon Stern,* Random House, New York, 1972, p. 346.

25. Cohen. p. 347.

26. Zimmer. p. 398, Quoted from the Swami Nikhilananda translation of *The Bhagavad-Gita,* New York, 1944.

27. *The Song of God.* p. 41.

28. *The Song of God.* p. 127.
29. *The Song of God.* p. 130.

SUGGESTED READINGS

Joseph Campbell. *The Hero with a Thousand Faces,* Meridian Books, The World Publishing Company, Cleveland and New York, 1949.

Joseph Campbell. *Myths to Live By,* The Viking Press, New York, 1972.

Irene Claremont DeCastillejo. *Knowing Women: A Feminine Psychology,* published by G.P. Putnam's Sons for the C.G. Jung Foundation for Analytical Psychology, New York, 1973.

Erich Fromm. *The Forgotten Language, An Introduction to the Understanding of Dreams, Fairy Tales and Myths,* Rinehart & Co., New York, 1951.

Erving Goffman. *Relations in Public: Microstudies of the Public Order,* Basic Books, Inc., New York, 1971.

Eden Gray. *The Tarot Revealed: A Modern Guide to Reading the Tarot Cards,* A Signet Mystic Book from New American Library, New York, 1960. (The Albano-Waite Tarot Deck is also available from the New American Library, Inc., at $5.00--Dept. M/Box 120, Bergenfield, New Jersey 07621).

C.G. Jung. *The Archetypes and the Collective Unconscious,* from *The Collected Works of C.G. Jung, Volume 9, Part 1,* Bollingen Series XX, Princeton University Press, Princeton, New Jersey, Second Edition, 1968.

C.G. Jung. *Memories, Dreams, Reflections,* Recorded and Edited by Aniela Jaffe, Translated from the German by Richard and Clara Winston, Vintage Books, A Division of Random House, New York, 1961.

C.G. Jung, *Psychological Types,* from *The Collected Works of C.G. Jung, Volume 6,* A Revision by R.F. C. Hull of the Translation by H.G. Baynes, Bollingen Series II, Princeton University Press, Princeton, New Jersey, 1971.

Sheldon B. Kopp. *If You Meet the Buddha on the Road, Kill Him! The Pilgrimage of Psychotherapy Patients,* Science and Behavior Books, Inc. Palo Alto, California, 1972.

Ralph Metzner. *Maps of Consciousness,* Collier Books, New York,

Erich Neumann. *Depth Psychology and a New Ethic,* English Translation by Eugene Rolfe, Harper Torch Books, Harper and Row, New York, Evanston, San Francisco, London, 1973.

The Song of God: Bhagavad-Gita. Translated by Swami Prabhabananda and Christoper Isherwood, with an Introduction by Aldous Huxley, a Mentor Religious Classic, published by the new American Library, New York, 1956.

Heinrich Zimmer. *The King and the Corpse: Tales of the Soul's Conquest of Evil,* Edited by Joseph Campbell, Princeton University Press, Princeton, New Jersey, 1957.

Additional copies of *The Hanged Man*
can be purchased through
writing to this address:
Science and Behavior Books, Inc.
P.O. Box 11457
Palo Alto, California 94306

Book and cover design: Kenneth Kinzie
Book set in 11 point Baskerville.
Typography by Nanaimo Printers (1969) Ltd.,
Nanaimo, Vancouver Island, B.C.